MW00358760

Talking About A REVO— LUTION

Also by Yassmin Abdel-Magied

Yassmin's Story

For younger readers

You Must Be Layla

Listen, Layla

Talking About A REVO— LUTION

YASSMIN ABDEL-MAGIED

VINTAGE BOOKS

Australia

VINTAGE

UK I USA I Canada I Ireland I Australia
India I New Zealand I South Africa I China

Vintage is part of the Penguin Random House group of companies
whose addresses can be found at global.penguinrandomhouse.com

 Penguin
Random House
Australia

First published by Vintage in 2022

Copyright © Yassmin Abdel-Magied 2022

The moral right of the author has been asserted.

All rights reserved. No part of this publication may be reproduced, published, performed in
public or communicated to the public in any form or by any means without prior written
permission from Penguin Random House Australia Pty Ltd or its authorised licensees.

Cover design by James Rendall © Penguin Random House Australia Pty Ltd
Typeset in Granjon by Midland Typesetters, Australia

 A catalogue record for this
book is available from the
National Library of Australia

ISBN 978 1 76104 459 5

penguin.com.au

We at Penguin Random House Australia acknowledge that Aboriginal and Torres Strait Islander
peoples are the Traditional Custodians and the first storytellers of the lands on which we live
and work. We honour Aboriginal and Torres Strait Islander peoples' continuous connection to
Country, waters, skies and communities. We celebrate Aboriginal and Torres Strait Islander stories,
traditions and living cultures; and we pay our respects to Elders past and present.

. . . to the revolutionaries, living hidden lives,
or resting in unvisited tombs . . .

Contents

Introduction

For my thirtieth birthday, my father dusted off and digitised our old family VCR tapes. My favourite of the surviving clips is one from 1991, the year of my birth. I had just learnt to walk, the excitement at newfound freedom visible in my gappy grin as I doddered around the beige living room in our flat in Khartoum, Sudan. Despite baba's cooing calls, my attention throughout is focused on one thing only: the tape deck sitting at eye level, playing the first song of the self-titled album that has scored my life: 'Talkin' Bout A Revolution', by Tracy Chapman.

It has never felt more prescient to talk about revolution. Whether ideological or emancipatory, industrial, technological or simply within us, revolution, resistance, transformation and change are the currents charging every aspect of twenty-first century life. This moment, then, is a period of transition, a liminal space offering incredible opportunity, but there are no guarantees for how things will turn out. So the moment is now, there is no time to waste. We must act.

But wait!

Action alone is not enough. We must also *think*, deeply. Consider, carefully, with intention and nuance, the world we live in. Diagnose the challenges, ensuring our assumptions are accurate and our energies are strategically targeted. Commit to creating, in language and in deed, a *collectively* liberated future. We must act, yes, but with intention; with grace, care and justice.

This collection is one of my many attempts to contribute to such a project. For if we cannot even properly talk about revolution, how are we meant to achieve it?

First, we create the world we want with language, then the language builds the world.

I have wanted to pull together a book of essays the moment I knew such a thing was possible: I find the form compelling, suited to thoughtfully drawing together a diverse array of topics connected by a broad, rich theme. Individually, single essays offer deep dives into, or meditations on, a particular issue. A collection allows the pieces to be in dialogue with one another, to arrive at a sum greater than its parts. So, as the third decade of the twenty-first century began while mine was just ending, it seemed the perfect time to reflect on my writing and thinking thus far; select, revise, and republish some of the work that I am most proud of from the last nine years, while also taking the time to craft a number of new pieces, capturing the questions, reflections and conclusions I have arrived at, at the end of my tumultuous twenties. Together, the collection strips back the layers of story, myth and obfuscation obscuring so much contemporary discourse today, revealing the underlying dynamics and asking the questions: What is really going on here? Are we satisfied? Is this the best we can do? How do we build a better world?

I approach these questions with a philosophy deeply influenced by Islamic liberationary theology, Black feminist civil rights activists and the legacy of anti-imperialism, critiques of our current neoliberal world order naturally folded into the approach. I offer alternative ways of thinking about the world from the perspective of a diaspora African Muslim woman deeply committed to the concept of *justice for all,* regardless of who it means I must stand against. I make space to eulogise and lament for bygone eras, but do not let my nostalgia hold me back from facing forward, into our future, and marching determinedly into it.

While eight new pieces are the throbbing heart of this collection, together, the old and new all speak to some idea of change, transformation, resistance, revolution. Split equally between the two sections, 'The Public and Private Self', as well as 'Systems and Society', the most recent pieces were written while on my writer's residency at the Cité Internationale des Arts in Paris. They encapsulate my current thinking on several disparate, yet connected, contemporary issues: Islam and social justice, power, language, relationships and change. Sitting alongside some of my earliest pieces exploring life on the rigs, the 2019 Sudanese uprisings, an engineer's explanation of the South Australian blackouts and a vignette of my first trip to the famed (or infamous) Summernats car festival, I hope not only to reflect on collective revolutions, but my own personal one. From a twenty-year-old rig worker with engineering training that led me to believe I had all life's answers, to a peripatetic life in the heart of the old Empire, I talk of revolution because that is all I know now, it is all I can think of. It is what we have left.

I hope you will consider my offerings deeply; that you will think them through and discuss them with those around you, that they challenge and affirm you and inspire you to continue believing

xii TALKING ABOUT A REVOLUTION

a better way is possible and help in some way to imagine how you can be a part of it. *Inshallah.* I trust that you will receive my vulnerability with grace, because there are parts of me I have left on these pages, in the hopes that you, dear reader, will recognise something of yourself in the grief I express. *Inshallah.* These are lofty aspirations, to be sure – but fortunately, hope is free, and a renewable resource! Read the pieces at your leisure, take them slowly or all in one go, find what works for you and run with it. If anything, may this collection convince you that it is no longer the time for just *talking* about a revolution. Perhaps it's time for us to do something about it. Yallah! *On y va!*

PART ONE
The Private and Public Self

Words mean things

I'm not a huge one for reading thick philosophical texts. I'm a lass who needs plot and action, and let me tell you, Heidegger is just not that. But, for better or for worse, a few of these twentieth-century European philosophers did produce some useful ideas for making sense of the world. Against my better judgement, I have occasionally fallen into a Wikipedia-induced whirlpool, swimming in hyperlinks, exploring the web's depths for ever-elusive illumination. So it came to pass one balmy afternoon, with my guy, Ludwig Wittgenstein.

Wittgenstein did a lot during his sixty-two years on this planet (including receiving a diploma of mechanical engineering, good man), but it was his work on philosophy of language I found most enthralling.

See, I had become increasingly frustrated by contemporary cultural conversations that seemed to go . . . nowhere. Discourses online, on mainstream media, even those hosted by prestigious cultural institutions, felt stale, circular and rarely enlightening. These fruitless arguments wormed their way into my personal life, consuming valuable oxygen at dinner parties, casual coffees, Facetimes with family. Half-baked anecdotes thrown around like confetti, substitutes for critical thought. 'You can't say anything anymore,' an Oxford-educated banker tells me at a party, sand-wiching trite complaints between boasts of his cryptocurrency investments. I smile and excuse myself, reluctant to endure another 'hot take' that is neither as controversial nor original as the speaker would like to believe. 'Just to play devil's advocate . . .' is another canary in the conversation coalmine. I wasn't aware of Satan's need for a defence team.

I began avoiding these 'debates', which frequently appeared in national broadsheets, in part because I was never quite sure what exactly was being examined; indeed, their set-up was rarely in good faith. Whether on 'cancel culture', 'wokeness', or the evergreen 'free speech', little interest existed in defining terms, grounding them in reality, making them make sense. Winning, not understanding, was evidently the primary objective, as if we were trapped in meaningless student debates à la Sally Rooney. Any hopes of improved circumstances were summarily dashed when a British cultural institution invited me to speak on yet *another* grab-bag panel of international guests, discussing whether cultural appropriation had 'gone too far'. It all made me want to tear my hijab off.

Words mean things! I would scream into the ether, and that is where Wittgenstein stepped in.

Well, Yassmin, his ghost's aristocratic Austrian-British accent intoned. *Yes and no . . .*

Bloody philosophers, eh.

In his *Philosophical Investigations*, Wittgenstein suggests that the 'meaning of a word is its use in the language'.[1] In essence, words gain their meaning from their context. Wittgenstein refuted the idea that any word has a universal truth (or, the fancier term, 'epistemic objectivity'). He didn't even totally buy that a word needed 'clarity' for meaning. It was all about *how* it was used, and critical to that operation was that all those using the words were playing the same 'language game'.

I know it is getting a bit abstract, but stay with me for a second.

The rules of a language, Wittgenstein would say, are similar to the rules of any game. Saying something in a language is like playing a move. The meaning of the move, word or sentence comes from the rules of the game.

For example, kicking a soccer ball to a stranger in a park might indicate the beginning of a casual kickabout. The exact same action, if on a field during an actual match, might indicate to a striker it is time to attack, and they should run towards the ball to complete the cross. Similarly, the word 'water' could be an order, the answer to a question, or a simple description, depending on the context. This context is not only grammatical but also socio-cultural: 'Thank you so much for your contribution' may be a warm demonstration of how valued you are, or, if spoken by a tight-lipped English woman at the end of your worst ever pitch meeting, might mean your idea will forever remain in purgatory, never to be spoken of again (not that I am speaking from experience).

Wittgenstein's interpretation leaves unanswered one vital question. If the rules of the language game give words meaning, who decides the rules? What happens when someone decides to change said rules (halfway through the game) *in their favour* without consultation? Forgive me the pun, but whose rules Trump?

This is the tension persistently playing out in how words or phrases operate in mainstream and social media, as well as everyday conversation today. Pundits and politicians are constantly changing the rules of the language game, tilting the board, moving the goalposts; whatever works in their favour. And, as is so often the case, he with most power wins.

'Woke' started out as a word within the Black American community as a warning to each other to stay 'awake', to be on the lookout for the violence of the state. It has ended up as a bizarre pejorative, a term co-opted by conservative pundits who use it to delegitimise anyone and anything they disagree with. Almost anything they oppose is derided as 'woke', from decolonising the curriculum to gender-neutral traffic lights to non-dairy milk (regardless of the health implications!). This is also how, for example, 'leftie' has become 'a slur' in working-class British towns,[2] an unfathomable development in what used to be staunchly Labour-held territory. From spoken language to body language, this process has happened time and time again, words and symbols completely recast, unrecognisable from where they began.

In a preseason National Football League game in 2016, San Francisco 49ers quarterback Colin Kaepernick and his teammate Eric Reid knelt on one knee during the national anthem, a silent demonstration against police brutality and racial injustice in the United States. In the years since, 'taking the knee' became a popularised method of peaceful protest, with football players in the English Premier League, Formula 1 drivers and a range of Olympians at the Tokyo 2020 Olympics (in 2021) demonstrating solidarity by kneeling during their national anthems. Despite the benign nature of the action, echoing Martin Luther King Jr's solemn kneel[3] in prayer during the 1965 voting rights campaigns, remonstrations from the powerful have been endless and extirpating. Former President Donald Trump stated that NFL owners should fire players who kneel.[4] Let go at the end of the 2016 season, Kaepernick remains unsigned.* When the English football team announced their decision to take the knee during the Euro 2020 Championship, the reaction in the United Kingdom was stark. *The Times* columnist Melanie Phillips said it was in fact a 'racist gesture'; Education Minister Gillian Keegan said players were 'creating division'; and Conservative MP Lee Anderson boycotted them completely for their choice to support 'a political movement whose core principles aim to undermine our very way of life'.[5] The then Foreign Secretary Dominic Raab even described taking the knee as 'a symbol of subjugation and subordination'.[6] Not to be outdone, Australian broadcaster Rowan Dean stated the entire Australian men's cricket team 'disgraced themselves' when they took the knee on a 2021 tour in the West Indies, describing Black Lives Matter as a 'sinister cult'.[7] Protest against injustice has been slyly reframed as the problem, distracting from the issue it was designed to highlight. Such recriminations have real world impacts, not easily undone.

None of this is new, but it has taken on urgency in a world where the myth of a 'culture war' takes up an inordinate amount of column inches and airtime. It is unclear if anyone knows what the culture war actually is (in a 2021 British radio poll, 76 per cent of respondents said they didn't[8]), although pundits insist it is alive and kicking. The British historian Dominic Sandbrook suggests it is more 'a dispute between two sides of an educated

---

* As of March 2022, he has not been.

elite'.[9] Indeed, 'culture war' exchanges dominate the preserves of small, politically motivated groups, active consumers of mainstream and social media,[10] universities, literary festivals. Are they worth paying attention to? I find myself avoiding the question, instead choosing to focus on who propagates and benefits from this landscape.

That brings to mind the work of another twentieth century philosopher, German Jewish thinker Walter Benjamin. In his essay 'The Work of Art in the Age of Mechanical Reproduction', Benjamin argues fascistic governments maintain power and control by allowing the public to express themselves aesthetically, keeping them far from the work of material reform. Similarly, today's 'culture war' binds us to the realm of words and symbols *alone*, rather than using them as leverage to push for sustainable structural and material change. Decrying athletes who take the knee keeps the focus on 'gestures', rather than on the reality of expanded police powers, immigration detention, voter suppression legislation. Not only does this approach distract, but it creates new realities. As *Guardian* columnist Nesrine Malik writes, 'culture war is an aggressive political act ... aim[ing] to create its own truth', a battle between manufactured narratives that seeks to mould a nation.[11]

If the 'culture war' is a battle of narrative, then language itself is the frontline. Control of the language game rules becomes a war-time strategy.

Today's weaponisation of 'context', 'narrative', and, ultimately, 'language rules' is all about *power*. It's winning votes, advancing agendas, gaining electoral majorities – it is *politics*. But though the personal may always be political, the opposite isn't necessarily true. We can argue about what 'freedom of speech' means until the cows come home, but though it acts as a proxy, it is not *intrinsically* personal. It does not replace a sense of self. It is a concept or an ideal, rather than an *identity*.

What, then, of the words we use to define *ourselves*?

In his 1996 text 'Citizenship, Identity and Social History', Charles Tilly states that 'language provides a medium for the establishment and renegotiation of identities'. But what do we do if, reflecting on Wittgenstein, language itself is unstable, because the language rules are changing? What do we do when the language used means something different in every context? Selfishly, what does it mean for someone like me – born in Sudan, bred in Australia, living in the United Kingdom and working across the United States and Europe – to talk about who I am, if in every context the words I use mean something slightly different?

That is to say, what does it mean for me to say I am 'Black'?

—

Race, British cultural theorist Stuart Hall tells us, is a 'floating signifier'. In another Wikipedia-induced whirlpool, I discover Hall's 1996 lecture at Goldsmiths College London, where he notes that signifiers of racial identity change with time and place. In Hall's reading, what defines race 'floats' freely of anything which may 'stabilise' its meaning. Race is 'more like a language than it is like the way in which we are biologically constituted',[12] Hall argues, bringing him closer to Wittgenstein than I ever thought possible.

Indeed, Eurocentric understandings of race come not from biology, but from the desire for power. As academic and author

Emma Dabiri writes, our current understanding of 'white' and 'Black' as separate and distinct 'races' finds its earliest expression in the introduction of the 1661 Barbados Slave Code.[13] This was the first legal system in which race and racism were codified into law. Those classified 'Negro' slaves were now chattel (property), denied the basic rights of human beings under English common law, while 'Christian Servants' ('whites') worked under a contract.[14] This was explicitly about subjugation and control of the enslaved Africans, but also had the secondary benefit of decimating any solidarity between oppressed peoples of different ancestries and ethnicities (including the indentured Irish[15]). Classic divide and conquer. As Black American author and journalist Ta-Nehisi Coates so poignantly reminds us in his award-winning book *Between the World and Me*, race is the child of racism, not the father.

There are a multitude of differences in the world, but it is only when those differences have been 'organised within language, within discourse ... that [they] can be said to acquire meaning'.[16] In the late eighteenth century, German anatomist Johann Blumenbach visited the Caucasus Mountains and declared the people living between the Black and Caspian seas the most beautiful in the world. This was where the human race had begun, he decided, and therefore all light-skinned people from this region, including Europeans, must belong to the same race. He named that race 'Caucasian',[17] synonymous with 'white'. The term was swiftly adopted by the United States, and soon scientists were working backwards, creating meaning that suited their interests. It was one thing to claim 'Negroes' and 'Caucasians' have different-sized skulls, but concluding somehow

Caucasians have 'superior intellectual capacity', as American craniologist Samuel George Morton did in the nineteenth century, was another.[18] The expression of power through language categories has been deadly.

Understanding this begs the question: if the original 'rules' of the language game are born of injustice, is it ever possible to truly change them, to undo the horror unleashed by their creation? Or is it like entropy, an irreversible process once begun? What happens when a word is taken out of a specific context, when it migrates, when it ages, when it is moulded by the passing of time or the interests of the powerful? Who decides the rules? Who decides what it means to be 'Black', today?

—

My family arrived in sunny Queensland five years after the end of the premiership of the 'Hillbilly dictator', Joh Bjelke-Petersen. It was 1992, and my father claims we were only the second Sudanese family in Brisbane, the next arriving almost a decade later. That is to say, I did not grow up with any other Sudanese people. In fact, I knew hardly anyone from 'the continent'. The community we were absorbed into was faith-based, and any Africans I did know – Egyptians, Algerians and the occasional South African or Zimbabwean – defined themselves by their language group (Arabic), faith (Islam) or ethnicity (Maghrebi, Habashi) rather than by 'race'. We were mostly first-generation migrants, our politics defined by anti-colonial independence movements, not by a European/Anglo-American conception of race. 'Black' was only really ever used in the context of African Americans. For as long as I can remember, my parents identified as Sudanese, and not much else. Me? Well, it depended on who was asking, really. But I went to the local Islamic school; there was no nearby Sudanese one. Being Muslim was something that was all mine, between me and Allah, that nobody else could touch.

Bureaucracy forced our hand, sort of. Our family was classified by the state as 'CALD': 'Culturally and Linguistically Diverse', a term introduced in 1996 to replace the even-more-jaunty 'NESB' ('Non-English-Speaking Background'). My parents embraced the stilted acronym referring to anyone not descendent from British or Irish migrants; Italians, Greeks, Poles, Vietnamese, Lebanese, Sudanese.* CALD recognised our place outside the dominant culture, and for my parents, fostered a cobbled sense of solidarity. But like the British 'Black, Asian and Minority Ethnic' (BAME), the phrase is othering, unspecific, not quite fit for purpose. Or perhaps it is, just not *our* purpose. These were not the rules of our language game, but as new Queenslanders, we had little choice but to play.

Either way, being 'culturally diverse' was not my main source of strife. Strangers were not hurling invectives and abuse at me in the street because I blew in from the Sahara. They hated me because I was *Muslim*. After the attacks on the Twin Towers half a world away in 2001, being (or even being seen as)[19] Muslim acquired the texture of a racial 'floating signifier', now signifying 'enemy'. The mechanism does not operate identically due to the differing historical contexts, but the outcome was analogous. Animosity sent our way had little to do with our actual beliefs, with our relationship to our God, or our character or behaviour.

---

* That is, conditional Australians, although the borders of what that includes are forever shifting.

It was all to do with the meaning being read as 'Muslim' took in the western world. Snarling adults pulled my hijab off when I walked past in shopping centres, jerking my little skull back. Teenagers pelted my Islamic school's bus with jagged rocks, smashing it with green beer bottles until we became accustomed to showers of glass. Someone torched our local mosque, scorching the earth, and we drove past the blackened husk for years as the community quietly rebuilt it, brick by brick. I was a 'terrorist', a 'sand n*gger', a 'towel-head' more often than 'monkey', 'darkie' and plain old 'n*gger'. As a child I knew what it was to be discriminated against, but the language of race, the complication of my ancestry, was still far from my consciousness.

I did, however, understand colourism, a disease born of colonialism, rife in both Muslim and Sudanese communities. I understood darker-skinned Sudanese folks were treated unjustly, considered 'Black', both in Sudan and in Australia. My skin is light- to medium-toned, 'red' within the Sudanese context. Not dark enough to feel the brunt of colourist discrimination, not light enough for it to be considered a boon. I spoke of myself as 'brown' by way of compromise. A nod to my light-skinned privilege, while acknowledging my 'otherness' in Australia. Fitting, I thought. Appropriate.

Others disagreed.

An Australian friend I made in my twenties, also of the African diaspora, diagnosed me with a terminal case of internalised anti-Blackness. In their view, not referring to myself as Black meant I hated myself and my ancestry. *You are Black, and if you can't see that, there is something wrong with you*, I was told, sans explanation. The charge felt removed from my own experience. I felt proud of being Sudanese and African. Why did calling myself 'brown' mean I was filled with self-loathing? And how could I call myself Black when my lived experience was totally different to those with darker skin? When I knew that my cousin in Sudan was barred from marrying her love for almost a decade because he was considered 'too dark'? My experiences were not as bad as others, especially compared to folks in the United States. Wouldn't I just be taking up valuable space?

I didn't feel like I had the right to call myself Black. Stuart Hall calls this the 'search for a guarantee'.[20] We are addicted to the preservation of race as a biological trait because we want some sort of *proof* that we are authentically 'Black', he observed. 'We don't know what it is like to conduct the politics [of anti-racism] without a guarantee.' Hall was right. I ached for legitimacy, and not finding a clear answer in biology, I turned elsewhere.

Are we Black? I asked my parents. *We're Sudanese*, my mother said, skirting the question. *Black is used by the Indigenous people here*, my father replied. I nodded, thinking I understood, but we were all playing different language games.

I decided to try again, in a changed context, referring to myself as 'Black' at a conference. The moment was painfully short-lived. 'You're not Black.' The correction came immediately, from a First Nations person. *Black means Indigenous in this country, and you're not Indigenous.* They scolded me publicly, in front of a large group of our peers. I nodded, swallowing my shame and accepting my place. *Baba did warn you*, I thought to myself. First Nations trumps African Diaspora. Brown would have to do.

But being Muslim felt easy, comfortable. The language rules – for me – were clear and straightforward. Indeed, *being* Muslim is itself a matter of language: state the shahada, the profession of faith with belief,[*] and you are Muslim. 'I bear witness that there is no god but God and that Muhammad is the messenger of God.' An act of speech guarantees your Muslim identity, one that no human has the right to deny or question. But race, in Queensland, when I was growing up? It felt like I couldn't get it right.

A generous reading might say I lived through a transitionary period, a time when language rules were shifting and trans-forming in response to changing demographics, politics, political consciousnesses. Certainly, African diaspora kids today seem comfortable claiming their Blackness in ways I would never have conceived of twenty years ago. Access to knowledge online has turbocharged their political and racial consciousness, intro-ducing them to concepts it took me years to understand. Although there is an ever-present risk local nuances and contexts are lost in the globalised melee, I cannot help but be impressed by the comfort and fluency this younger generation has in the language of race. They seem to wait for guarantees from no one.

I described myself as 'brown' in my memoir, *Yassmin's Story*, first published in 2016. Six years later, I describe myself as Black and have done so since moving to London in 2017.

The shift occurred early on. A Nigerian British friend asked why I referred to myself as 'brown'. 'You're born in Sudan, right?' she asked. Her next words delivered my craving for permis-sion. 'Well then, here, you're Black.' It didn't matter that I was light-skinned? 'Well, you're light-skinned Black, but you're still Black.' She explained in the United Kingdom, the African and

---

[*]   In front of witnesses, so there is a socially constructed element – but they are observers rather than adjudicators of your 'Muslimness'.

Afro-Caribbean diaspora were all referred to as Black. I nodded and made the mental adjustment. After all this time, it was surprisingly easy.

Does my change of heart or perspective mean that my previous position was a lie, that I had a false sense of self? Why was I so happy to accept being 'Black' in the United Kingdom, when I found it such contested territory in Australia? Did I have some internal self-loathing that I was unaware of, perhaps inherited from my light-skinned African parents? Or was it simply because I had not yet learnt the rules of the language game it was assumed I understood?

I would later learn that even in the United Kingdom, 'Blackness' has a contested history. In the seventies and eighties, one could be 'politically Black', a coalition-focused term arising from trade union movements describing *all* who experience racial discrimination. The notion has fallen out of favour, not because of any culture war, but because of shifts within communities, changes in organising. It goes to show that our own language rules are always being written and rewritten, but as long as we are on the same page, as long as we are playing the same game, we can continue to move forward. The work towards that agreement repeats, recurs, reprises, without guarantee.

—

When in France, I am constantly asked where I am from. I am not offended by the question, because it's clear I am not a native French speaker (though I do try). But what do I tell them? *'Je suis née au Soudan, j'ai grandi en Australie, j'habite normalement à Londres ...*' (I was born in Sudan, grew up in Australia and usually live in London). It's a bit longwinded, even for me.

Even then, the questions grow stranger.

So you're Sudanese? Are both your parents from Sudan?

Uh, yes?

Your mum, and your dad, Sudanese?

Bah oui!

People with your skin complexion, I am told, are *métisses* – 'mixed'. They have one Black parent and one white parent.

Well, both my parents are the same complexion as me.

But aren't Sudanese people dark? Darker than you?

My mum's brother is as dark as Omar Sy, and my mum's sister is as light as Edith Piaf. Same for my father. It's really a luck of the draw.

Hmm ...

I don't quite fit in France, it seems. Not quite Arab, not quite Black; again I find myself simply and broadly 'other'.

One thing *is* clear. I am Muslim. I believe that there is no God but God, and Prophet Mohammed (SAW*) is his Messenger. As part of my faith, I wear the hijab, and no matter which way I dice it, in France, that is the basis on which my otherness hinges. I have come full circle.

Being Muslim is the one identity which the language rules of others cannot touch, where there is no search for guarantee. Regardless of the politicising of the 'identity' of being Muslim, the 'floating signifier' elements that have evolved over time, my faith is not solely a socially constructed entity, but a relationship

---

*   SAW is 'sallallahu alayhi wa salaam'. It is the Arabic abbreviation of PBuH – 'Peace and Blessings be Upon Him'; what Muslims say after the name of the Prophet Mohammed (SAW).

between myself and my God. A 'Muslim' is 'one who submits', and that *means* something. No matter what game is being played, and who is in power, this is the self I can always claim, the self over which I have complete control.

Perhaps that is what frightens them so . . .

In defence of hobbies

It happened, like so many other things didn't, during the first year of the COVID-19 pandemic.

I had meandered through now-familiar lockdown phases: Instagramming attempts to recreate the fluffy wonder of Italian focaccia via an ailing oven and yeast long expired, purchasing a drill too powerful for my needs and installing shelves on every empty section of exposed brick wall space, binge-watching British TV shows, and wondering if I had a future as a barrister (I'd be quite good at getting paid to argue with strangers, I thought, and the wig is quite hijabi friendly . . .). As I settled into the isolation-induced stupor that may better be characterised as 'low level depression', I cast around for a distraction, an anchor. My eyes eventually lit on leftover yarn stuffed in a back corner of the TV cabinet, cheap lilac strands long forgotten. The fine pastime of knitting, the oldest artifacts of which date back to eleventh-century Egypt, called my name, and not for the first time.

At nine years of age, my best friend Hafsa and I whittled our lunchtimes away, utterly consumed by what we thought were quite cool crafts. Our backs pasted against the broiling corrugated walls of the grade five demountable building at the Islamic School of Brisbane, she embroidered, I knitted. That Brisbane enjoys a humid, subtropical climate rarely calling for anything heavier than a light jumper was no deterrent. With sweat running down my back, darkening the trouser waistband of my primary school uniform, I dreamt of the retail store I would launch, a cosy space bursting with niche, handmade woollens. Alas, as is the case with childhood obsessions, the phase ended before my vision was realised. I managed only to fashion a twenty centimetre by twenty centimetre blue woollen square, and swiftly endowed it with more utility than deserved by referring to it as a 'dining table trivet'. Before the term was out, the whole exercise was duly abandoned for the next grand adventure: jewellery making. My brief childhood knitting phase was relegated to a funny anecdote at staid networking events for 'young entrepreneurs'.

It would be two decades before yarn came into my life again. This time it found me dispirited, crashing in a friend's spare room in Melbourne, nervously awaiting the approval of my long-term United Kingdom visa. I had flown for a night and day back across the seas to submit my paperwork, the application costing me all my savings in lawyer fees with no guarantee I would be permitted to remain in Britain, the country I now called home. The abject uncertainty and stark lack of control over my future rendered me self-conscious, insecure. I spent days wandering around the suburban neighbourhood, craving a distraction; something to take me out of my head, something to do with my hands. A yarn shop, with bright beanies and pastel pullovers in the window, whispered sweet nothings as I walked past. The needles had no demands, the wool no questions about my future. Soothed by a sense of purpose, I picked up the needles once again.

Finally, I had something to do, knitting's arbitrary goals the Ariadne's thread through the darkness. My fingers, like a tongue retuning to a language it once knew, started clumsily, slow. I began humbly, returning to form with a simple square. Joined together along one edge with a hole for your thumb, the square transformed into a fingerless glove. It took three separate attempts for me to get the ribbing right and another before the colour blocking matched the online pattern, but soon, I was proud enough to show my creations off to the friend I was staying with. She was impressed. I pretended I cared less than I actually did.

A week later, I attempted a beanie; this time with thicker needles and heavier yarn, the chunkiness of the knit obscuring the glaring errors in my craft. Coarse creations evolved into finer, more refined hats for babies, a design perfected by watching and re-watching YouTube videos. My fingers loosened, quickening with each day's work.

I knitted constantly, at the café, watching Netflix, waiting in queues. I reached for the needles like a child for their favourite soft toy: for comfort and safety. They were protection anytime tendrils of dread slithered their way into my thoughts. If I focused on what my hands were doing, I wouldn't dwell on the uncontrollable. I knitted to save myself.

By the end of my third week, I had progressed to a single wobbly, yet rather wearable, adult-sized hat. It was the sort of thing that looked trendy if you were wealthy and concerning on me. When I dropped a photo of the beanie in the family WhatsApp group, my mother sweetly asked if I had enough money to get by. When my visa was approved just before the month's end, it was to everyone's relief. I couldn't get on the plane back to London fast enough.

2020 marked the beginning of my 'talent' visa period, the year I was to hit my stride, the year to bear the fruits of all the seeds I had diligently planted. Life blushed with promise, and a smidgen more certainty than I had become accustomed to.

Then, a global pandemic. COVID-19 made a farce out of all our plans.

Events, book tours, the first theatre show I co-wrote: cancelled. The TV show I had been developing with a good friend: shelved. Collaboration and rehearsal spaces: shuttered. I was embarking on a career path in the arts just as the sector was facing an existential threat, and as my work evaporated, so did my appetite, motivation, creativity. The hours and days between government press conferences stretched, yawning precipitously. All of a sudden, there was t i m e. So much *time*.

I reached towards the familiar, the woolly thread that had kept me safe before. I found the needles and yarn brought back from Melbourne, tucked away untouched for months, and settled back into the security of the knit and purl. The click-clack of bamboo gently welcomed RSI back into my joints, and the hobby, quietly dormant at my side since I was a child, again offered me refuge.

And so, when I sent a photo of my latest knobbly creation to a friend – a beanie of teal mohair looped in a simple cable knit – their reaction felt borderline repulsive.

'Oh wow! Amazing. Have you thought about selling them?'

Have I thought about *what*? I recoiled, nauseated, my lip quivering. Why would I want to sell these? I'm giving them away to my friends for free! My reaction came as a surprise even to myself. My friend was, arguably, complimenting me. They noted that my craft had progressed, and the final 'product' had reached a high enough level that it would be commercially viable. Yet here I was feeling resentful? It was a downright un-millennial response.

Turning your side hustle into your main hustle is the hustler's dream, and we twenty-first-century millennials without an inheritance, well, we're the hustling generation. Grind and shine, baby! 'The age of the side hustle is upon us,' proclaimed a Henley Business School white paper, reporting that small businesses and secondary jobs generate '£72 billion for the UK, or about 3.6 per cent of UK GDP'.[1] In Australia, research has shown almost half (48 per cent) of the working population either have a side hustle or are planning to start one.[2] Erin Griffith's piece in the *New York Times*, 'Why are young people pretending to love work?', comments on the ubiquity of this culture, where ambition is glorified 'not as a means to an end, but a lifestyle'.[3] '"Rise and Grind" is both the theme of a Nike ad campaign and the title of a book by a "Shark Tank" shark,' she writes. 'Techies here [in San Francisco] have internalized the idea . . . that work is not something you do to get what you want; the work itself is all.'

It's not just a millennial vice, either. The Open University found in 2017 that 95 per cent of Gen Z-ers wanted to start their own business, and reportedly 72 per cent of Gen Z-ers wanted to pursue a side hustle.[4] In the words of Kennedy Hill, writing in *Business Insider*, her cohort are 'overly attached to the idea that if there's money to be made, it's foolish to not make it'.[5]

The irony, of course, is that those selling 'hustle culture' are often not the ones actually hustling. 'The vast majority of people beating the drums of hustle-mania are not the people doing the actual work. They're the managers, financiers and owners,' says Basecamp co-founder David Heinemeier Hansson.[6] As Alissa

Quart reminds us, far from being the 'moral good' it is advertised as, 'more often, people take on second or third side hustles because of wage stagnation or low pay at their full-time jobs'.[7] Even the Henley Business School white paper acknowledges this bind. 'Those who are underwhelmed and under-financed by their work, but have the appetite, if not the confidence, to go it all alone as an entrepreneur, will not let the chance slip,' said Professor Bernd Vogel, the founding director of the Henley Centre for Leadership.

Here, Vogel is more on point than he realises. For we are not hustling because we necessarily *want* to, regardless of what the motivational posters might shout. Instead, these side hustles are 'a way to make some desperately needed money because your current job isn't paying enough to make ends meet', as Alex Collinson writes.[8]

It follows, then, in a culture accustomed to the making of money where possible in an effort to survive, my friend would suggest selling off my little creations. A creature of my environment, I had in fact caught myself suggesting the exact same to another mate who had recently gifted me a gorgeous handmade birthday card. I was not at all immune from the overworking, grab-every-opportunity, burn-out culture of my generation. By this point, I had made so many bloody beanies, in so many odd shapes and sizes, that I was starting to donate them to charity. Selling them wasn't so audacious an idea. Why then, was my reaction so piqued?

I stewed, casting on a new ball of yarn with my needles, playing absent-mindedly with the loose end. Images flashed before my eyes as I hallucinated my potential future: fingers callused by needles, wrists aching from repetition, hair moulting from the stress of trying to fulfil orders fast enough. I saw myself spending endless hours attempting to market my small business on the Zuckerberg Trifecta (Facebook, Instagram and WhatsApp) wondering if I was ever going to break even, worried about whether I would have enough time for my writing ('If I knit that much, will I be able to type?'). Was there no place for the committed amateur, no recognition that perhaps something might *not* be for the money? Neoliberalism got our hobbies, too?!

It felt as if there were no template for enjoying something purely for its own sake. Like we didn't even know *how* to.

Author Wendy Brown explains how this is the result of the normalisation of neoliberal values that has been at work over the past forty years. 'If you understand yourself as a bit of human capital, in a fully economic way,' she says on the US National Public Radio podcast *Throughline*, 'it means you might approach your dating life or your educational life or your leisure time not so much as a profit-making undertaking but still as one to manage in economic terms and think about in economic metrics.

'This is basic Wall Street . . . that has gone into all of our souls.'

Her reflections cut close to the bone. I would be lying if I didn't admit that I had thought about 'what success looks like' in knitting, or mulled on whether I was wasting my time perfecting a new row of cables. Perhaps this was why I only knitted when I could do nothing else, for it seemed too superfluous to spend time on when my head was clear, and I was fighting fit. To my horror, I realised I *do* quite often think of myself as a bit of human capital, to be maximised and optimised. I had put it down to being the child of migrants, brought up in a culture where we needed to make the most of the opportunities a new land offered. But though my parents taught me to make the most out of life, they have also often said I work too hard, frequently asking me to take a break, to rest, to spend time with family. I was, and perhaps still am, the only constant optimiser in the Abdel-Magied household, a thought that is mildly terrifying.

I am not sure when I opted in to being a 'bit of human capital'. I am not sure when my social media platforms went from being a fun place to hang out to a place where brands contact me for 'collabs' and random people send haranguing direct messages demanding I share a GoFundMe page. I cannot remember when my follower count grew to the point that I began to feel a mild expectation to 'stay up to date', 'report back', 'keep people posted'. The entire ecosystem is set up for humans to be little bits of capital, and although we might make *some* money from it, the Zuckerbergs of the world make exponentially more.

To be fair, I do not have an overly tortured relationship with social media: the majority of my work is unconnected to these platforms, and I have, by necessity, developed pretty solid boundaries. Being buried alive by social media hatred will force you to either construct impenetrable walls around your soul or quit completely. I did the former. It also helps that there is nothing I dislike more than being 'expected' to do something or be a certain way, my obstinacy an unexpected advantage in this respect.

But if I can admit that I, too, am affected by the murky neo-liberal sewage we find ourselves swimming in, why does any hint of monetising my hobby annoy me so much?

Maybe the resentment springs from the vestiges of my non-corrupted self, fighting back. It may be a sliver of my soul screeching, *Yassmin, no, save yourself! You found a hobby, protect it!* For there is so little left in my life that isn't work! Almost every inch of my life has been excavated for content, for story, for 'value'. *Oh, but you should have better boundaries, Yassmin*, I hear you say. May I remind you of why most people take up a side hustle? Because our work *doesn't pay us enough*.

Wages growth for Australian workers is among the worst in the industrialised world, as per David Peetz, writing for the *Conversation*.[9] The United Kingdom's Trades Union Congress reported in 2018 that real wages had been 'in decline for seventeen years', the worst period in modern British history.[10] While wage growth has been complicated by COVID-19, it seems real wages are unlikely to rise.[11] The only time in my life I had a clear demarcation between work and 'life' was when my actual job paid me enough, and that was on the *oil rigs*. I might be more 'morally pure' now, but I cannot pay the bills with my ethical righteousness. In the United Kingdom, inheritance, not work, is the main route to home ownership. Australia isn't much better.

So, when folks speak of 'choice', of choosing *not* to be on social media platforms, *not* to be on the lookout for side hustles, *not* to be always working, there is a denial of our lived reality. For many, like myself, it is simply unaffordable. Add the precariousness of living on temporary visas, of being self-employed, of not having a safety net, and it is no wonder that I feel to stop swimming is to die. Indeed, one must recognise this has been the lived reality of many of the working class and working poor for a long time. One could argue critiques of hustle culture are only heightened today as levels of inequality have begun to creep into the lives of university-educated middle classes.

Some of you might be reading this and thinking, *Well, I don't see what the problem is, Yassmin. Is this not the life you chose?* Maybe. I did choose – or more accurately, fall into – a life outside the traditional realms of work, as many women (especially of the global majority) do. However, even in the face of unaffordability, neoliberalism and the like, I remain certain that not everything should be monetised. I am, after all, *not* a bit of human capital. I am not a brand, not an enterprise with shareholders, not a factory that needs to be running at 99 per cent uptime. I am a regular ol' human who does love her work, but who, truthfully, adores doing other things too.

The fact of the matter is, I bloody love learning! I adore it, always have. Why else would a nine-year-old start knitting in grade five? Trust me, it had nothing to do with my level of social capital in the playground. In adulthood, learning has often been related to something which has ended up being commercialised, whether upskilling as an engineer, or learning to write. Thus, in a minute act of resistance, I have arrived at a new approach. Choosing to learn things for the *hell of it*.

My new hobbies are foolishly and thoroughly uncommercial. Learning how to wood-turn. Flower arranging. Bladesmithing. Equestrian. Some are more immediately useful, others so unconnected to what I do on a daily basis, I can't imagine I will be utilising them in a work context anytime soon. Whether it's sewing, water colouring, squash, I am going back to the dictionary definition of 'hobby': a 'spare-time activity or pastime, etc., pursued for pleasure or recreation'. It means ensuring I have some spare time, as a start, but demands that I prioritise the pleasure, the recreation.

Sometimes, I share my progress on my social media platforms, bringing people along the step-by-step process of beating a piece of carbon steel into a blade, heat treating, quenching, sharpening. It's not part of my 'brand', whatever my brand is by now (#middlegradeauthor #muslimactivist #ilooklikeanengineer). But I do share, and when I do, folks tell me they have been inspired to sign up for a similar class or have decided to return to that hobby they loved as a child. To inspire others to do fun things for the sake of it – what a treat! Not to be the best, nor to sacrifice themselves on the altar of the free market, but to take up a new skill or have a little adventure on the weekend because we can, because we're human.

There are some activities that I may never be able to treat as a hobby. Writing, for example, has long become something that is 'work' rather than 'recreation'. The thought of writing a book without an eye to publishing feels rather incomprehensible to me. Perhaps the pleasure of writing a book is in the sharing of the story, more connected to the oral tradition of storytelling than the solitary activity of putting sentences together. Or perhaps such a noble explanation cloaks a more capitalist reality: why write a book for free if I can find someone to pay me for the job? A hobby, thus, must be enjoyable and interesting, but in no way tied to my (potential) income. It is to allow me to revel in the pleasure of remaining an amateur, perhaps even scandalously mediocre.*

I don't want to jealously guard everything I own, squeezing dollars out of every inch of my life. I want to give things away, share the love. I want to make enough money to not be worried,

---

* That being said, I reserve the right to strive for low-stakes excellence!

but not too much that it becomes a source of worry in itself. (The woes of owning a castle are truly uninteresting.) I want skills that will never find their way onto my LinkedIn profile but make the best dinner table conversations. I want to relearn the idea of a self de-coupled from my value as a piece of human capital. I want to focus on my hobbies as activities that bring joy – not money – to my life, in a world that expects me to monetise everything I do. My defence of hobbies is a desire for self-worth outside the neoliberal framework. Indeed, it is a small, quiet, personal revolution.

So. Let's knit, shall we?

Islam and social justice

The consensus, agreed upon by people who I have yet had the fortune to meet, is that a single Facebook post heralded my demise. But like any grand political saga, a clean, neat narrative rarely reveals the whole truth.

One could plausibly venture, as I have occasionally done myself, it was my departure from the opening address at the Brisbane Writers Festival eight months earlier that fatally loosened the guillotine's blade. The article I wrote afterwards* was certainly the first time I went viral for all the wrong reasons, causing consternation in literary circles around the world. Even Roxane Gay, one of my literary heroes, remarked, 'Oh, you're *that* writer,' when I met her almost a year later. While I gained a modicum of international infamy, however, the catastrophe was contained, the blast radius reaching no further than the edges of publishing's rarefied milieu.

But neither a single online status update nor blog post entirely explains why a woman like myself, one who had 'done all the right things' as per the good-migrant handbook, fell so foul of, well, everything.

---

* See 'As Lionel Shriver made light of identity, I had no choice but to walk out on her', on p. 74.

To understand what truly transpired, we must look to February, 2017.

—

I had been a guest on the ABC show *Q+A* numerous times prior to the ill-fated evening, so there was no reason to believe this night would be any different. I was accustomed to the mild nerves accompanying debates on live television, the prior week's rush to stay abreast of the news (panellists were not provided audience questions beforehand), the unbelieving giddiness at appearing on one of the nation's most prestigious current affairs shows.

My legs carried me through the well-worn corridors with earned familiarity. Here was my favourite make-up artist who knew how to correctly match my foundation; there were producers whispering wordlessly on beeping walkie talkies; moving somewhere unseen was a soundie, wrapped by a swinging belt of tape, wires, batteries. The orchestral movement of live television. A producer assured me, in the green room that was not quite green, that a certain elected representative's comments on Muslims were not going to be the central theme of the show. Nodding, largely unworried, I turned to my real concern; whether my patterned black and white top brought out the best in the blue and yellow scarves I had donned hastily in my hotel room that afternoon. The combination of colours was unusual, a risk I was not completely confident in taking. I chewed on my lower lip as I eyed my reflection, the bright lightbulbs bordering the mirror turning me from a twenty-five-year-old with a youth organisation into a prepping prima donna. *It'll just be the show and then it will be over*, I thought to myself. *No big deal.*

Never wear an outfit out of the house you don't want to go viral in.

Like any ambush worth its salt, I didn't see it coming. Pass, set, spike. Following a question from the audience about migration, the establishment host turned to one of the panel's politicians to reference a statement they made in the press.

'Did you say to the *Advocate* in Tasmania that we should follow Donald Trump's example by deporting all Muslims who support sharia law?' he asked, the familiar steel gleam of a dog whistle glinting under the studio lights.

'Yes, I did,' the elected representative coolly confirmed. 'Anyone who supports sharia law in this country should be deported.' They brandished their ignorance like a semi-automatic rifle.

'Do you know what sharia law is?' I retorted, with the deadened irritation of a scientist discussing vaccine microchips over Christmas lunch.

'Yes—' They shot back, careless and trigger happy.

I interrupted. 'But do you know what it [sharia] is?!'

Thinking back to this moment years later fills me with lead-bone exhaustion. Do you know what it is to have to *constantly* defend yourself, your faith, your right to exist? Never mind the playing field isn't fair, never mind the history, never mind the hypocrisy, or your denied humanity. To be Muslim in Australia in the twenty-first century is to be the enemy, forever under suspicion, guilty until proven innocent. The game was rigged, nary a shred of good faith in sight. I knew this, but I was twenty-five, filled with fighting words, convinced of my ability to change the world on a panel.

I doubt any of the panellists would have confidently known 'sharia' literally means 'street', or 'way', or that describing sharia as 'law' betrays a fundamental fault, not least for assuming an English word can accurately represent a canon, history and conception produced through strikingly different languages. Sharia's fundamental objective is to guide us on living an ethical life, with a focus on protecting 'life, intellect, family, property and the honour of human beings'.[1] It is almost like a bill of rights, but you couldn't guess that from its reputation. Arguably, writes Islamic scholar Wael B. Hallaq, the 'cultural and conceptual ambiguities' related to the term 'law' are responsible for 'a thorough and systematic misunderstanding of the most significant features of the so-called Islamic law'.[2] The outcome of such conflation superimposes the 'conceptual specificity of nation-state law' on the legal culture of Islam, the moral imperative of which equipped it with 'efficient, communally based, socially embedded, bottom–top methods of control that rendered it remarkably efficient in commanding willing obedience'. To top it all off, its implementation was 'less coercive than any imperial law Europe had known since the fall of the Roman Empire'.[3]

But without time to go into such detail on Q+A, I scoured my mind for a way to articulate the chasm between representation and reality. The crowd waited with bated breath and made-up minds. Voice steady, my right-hand thumb and index finger in an 'O' shape, holding the delicate thread of the moment up high, I began. 'Islam, to me, is one of the most' – I shifted, clarifying my position – 'is *the* most feminist religion.'

Groans of disbelief rose up from the audience, bubbles of bigotry floating into the air, popping with prejudice. I pressed on, words pouring from my mouth, years of pent-up fear and frustration released from the depths. I listed rights radically afforded to women over 1300 years before they appeared in Europe: the right to own property, inherit, choose our husbands. We kept our last names, I pointed out, just as my impassioned monologue was interrupted. 'There is one law in this country, and it is the Australian law, it is not sharia law,' the politician pronounced, jabbing at the table. But I was not yet done. I raised my voice, then repeated myself, emphatic in my desire to be heard. 'In Islam, it says you follow the law of the land on which you are on!'* I felt a primal need to correct the record, make clear any talk of a 'dual legal system' was a red herring, a non-starter. Their framework was all wrong, couldn't they see?

My statements were disregarded. 'Do you accept that some of the things you say can come across as quite hateful?' the host asked the representative. 'To a minority,' they admitted. 'But this is what the majority want. The majority want to be safe.' They defended Donald Trump's Muslim ban,[4] invoked the coded spectre of 'national security' and pointed a finger in my direction, yelling that I should 'stop playing the victim'. Adrenaline pumping, I felt both sorry for and enraged by the populist Tasmanian senator. Here was a person who clearly cared about their constituents, rare and honourable in an elected representative. But the commitment to aiding *some* vulnerable people

---

* From the Quran (4:59), 'O ye who believe! Obey Allah, and obey His Messenger and those who are in authority among you', interpreted to mean Muslims are to obey the laws of the land. Further, a hadith states: 'It is necessary upon a Muslim to listen to and obey the ruler, as long as one is not ordered to carry out a sin. If commanded to commit a sin, then there is no adherence and obedience.' Sahih al-Bukhari, no. 2955.

over others, letting the ends justify the means, was dangerous. 'O Liberty, how many crimes are committed in thy name!'*

The exchange was soon brought to an end by the host, our heated altercation over after a few short minutes. We moved on to another question from the audience, with someone asking whether the current shift in politics betrayed the majority of Australians who did not vote for the hard-right.

Afterwards, I felt satisfied with my performance. I felt I had found a way to reframe the conversation, have the discussion mostly on my terms. *You did good, Yassmina*, I thought to myself as I shook hands with the panellist I had so vehemently dressed down, wishing them luck with all their future endeavours. It would not be until two nights later, scrolling on Twitter, my eyes would catch an image that ran my blood cold. The bloodhounds had caught my scent, dark shadows began circling in.

It was the front page of the national broadsheet, an enormous above-the-fold story in response to my statements on *Q+A*. The attack piece was reinforced with a gigantic photo taken from my Instagram, topped with an incendiary headline. Somehow, I had become the story. I zoomed in on the picture, unbelieving. *This has got to be some Photoshopped joke*, I thought. But no. It was the beginning of the end.

—

Much of the US–European imperial justification and self-styled supremacy has used the pretence of 'saving women' from the

---

* Quote by French Revolutionary Marie-Jeanne Roland de la Platière (Madame Roland) as she was led to her execution.

'barbaric talons' of their faith. It is 'white men saving brown women from brown men', wrote Gayatri Spivak, introducing a phrase encapsulating much of the colonial approach. Spivak was referring to the British abolition of *sati*,[5] a tradition compelling Hindu widows in India to climb atop their husbands' funeral pyres. The ritual horrified Victorian sensibilities, and soon 'saving brown women' became part of the raison d'être for European 'civilising' missions in South Asia[6] and across the globe.

Scholar miriam cooke breaks the imperial logic down further. If women have rights in 'our'* universal civilisation, says the gendered logic of empire, 'civilised' men recognise these rights. 'Other' men, those outside said civilisation, *must* therefore be denying women rights. Defending universal civilisation means separating colonial subjects along gender lines: men as 'Other', to be fought and dominated, and women as 'civilisable', to be rescued and saved. 'Saving the women' becomes part of the imperial project not because the women *want* to be saved, but because it feeds the myth of the coloniser's self-declared 'civility'.[7]

'Even as the Victorian male establishment devised theories to contest the claims of feminism, and derided and rejected the ideas of feminism and the notion of men's oppressing women with respect to itself, it captured the language of feminism and redirected it, in the service of colonialism, toward Other men and the cultures of Other men,'[8] writes scholar Leila Ahmed in her pioneering book *Women and Gender in Islam*. Colonial feminism was the use of 'feminism' as a tool in the colonial mission, tailored to fit the culture it was working to dominate. The hijab, or the

---

* Read: the Empire's.

veil, was the most obvious symbol of 'differentness' in western eyes, and an immediate target.

Lord Cromer, the British consul general in Egypt from 1883 to 1907, was a classic example of the 'civilising coloniser'. Convinced of Islamic inferiority,* he stated he had many reasons to believe 'Islam as a social system has been a complete failure', but 'first and foremost' in his view, was its apparent treatment of women. Cromer claimed that practices like wearing the veil constituted the '"fatal obstacle" to the Egyptians' "attainment of that elevation of thought and character which should accompany the introduction of Western civilisation"'.[9] He made these claims while pursuing policies detrimental to women: discouraging the training of female doctors, raising school fees and placing restrictions on government schools, and back home, founding the Men's League for Opposing Women's Suffrage in Britain. A man of integrity, clearly.

The 'liberating women from their faith' rhetoric broiling in France today offers another pungent example of imperial machinations, in their case stretching back to the invasion of Algeria almost two centuries earlier. Colonising Algeria in 1830, the French viewed the control of Algerian women as indispensable to their 'civilising mission'. 'In the colonialist fantasy, to possess Algeria's women is to possess Algeria,'[10] writes academic Winifred Woodhull. Veiling, or hijab, would become a key battlefield. In 1958, during the War of Independence, mass 'unveiling' ceremonies were staged across Algeria,[11] public demonstrations where

---

* Stating 'The European is a close reasoner; his statements of fact are devoid of ambiguity; he is a natural logician ... he loves symmetry in all things. The mind of the Oriental on the other hand, like his picturesque streets, is eminently wanting in symmetry. His reasoning is of the most slipshod description.' Earl of Cromer, *Modern Egypt*, 2 vols, Macmillan, New York, 1908, vol. 2, p. 146.

women unveiled to show they were siding with their 'French sisters'. Although presented at the time to the French government as spontaneous, it would later be revealed some women were pressured into participating by the army,[12] while others had never worn the veil at all.[13]

In his 1959 essay *'L'Algérie se dévoile'* ('Algeria Unveiled'), psychiatrist and political philosopher Frantz Fanon underscores how the veil was 'the bone of contention in a grandiose battle, on account of which the occupation forces were to mobilize their most powerful and most varied resources'. Fanon writes about the hijab from a political perspective, seeing its importance primarily through the lens of the colonial struggle. Fanon's reading of the coloniser's approach to the veil was thus: the French believed if they gained control of the women's thinking about the veil, they would control their bodies, and if they controlled their bodies, in a sense they would control the Algerian men. France would win, and Algeria would be lost.[14] In essence, the French believed by 'unveiling' women, they would create agents of assimilation in colonised families and societies.[15] This attitude runs parallel to contemporary French attitudes and policies, with the French Senate attempting to ban girls under the age of eighteen from wearing a hijab in public in March 2021.[16]

At the dawn of the twenty-first century, the administration of George W. Bush would also use the pretence of women's rights to bolster his case for the invasion of Afghanistan in 2001. On Saturday, 17 November 2001, more than a month after the United States had begun bombing Afghanistan, First Lady Laura Bush delivered a national radio address in her husband's place. The announcement was to launch a 'worldwide campaign to focus on the brutality against women and children by the al-Qaeda terrorist network and the regime it supports in Afghanistan, the Taliban'. The 'fight against terrorism is also a fight for the rights and dignity of women,' the First Lady declared, intimating that only military action by 'civilized' powers like the United States can ensure the 'rights and dignity' of the women (and children) of Afghanistan.[17] Conveniently absent from the record is a meeting only ten days earlier, of the Afghan Women's Network, calling for an end to military action, and for Afghan women's participation in the peace process.

Twenty years later, the United States clumsily withdrew from Afghanistan, leaving the Taliban in control and a death toll in the hundred thousands, including over 47,000 civilians.[18] During the United States's military departure, Mahbooba Seraj, the founder of the Afghan Women's Network, gave the US National Public Radio (NPR) station a message to all Americans on the nature of the 'civilising' mission: 'Your government has been lying to you from day one about this. All the way. They've been lying to you so much that they don't even know what is the truth anymore.'[19]

———

By making a clear, unequivocal statement on national television directly contravening a foundational myth of modern western imperialism, that civilising nations must 'rescue women' from 'uncivilised men', I had fashioned a bright, gleaming target on the back of my headscarf. Claiming agency as a proud, strident, *Muslim* woman, unapologetic in her faith, genuinely believing in its liberationary ethic, in its *civilising force*, I became a danger to the accepted status quo, threatening to expose the lie that had justified centuries of violence. As academic and journalist Susan Carland wrote in the *Saturday Paper* two weeks after the episode aired, 'it doesn't matter how moderate or modern or feminist or liberal or patriotic one is – if they are also proudly Muslim, they are a problem'.[20] My only crime was to claim my (women's) rights as my own, in a form that wasn't 'western, liberal and secular'. And for this audacity, I was made an example of.

Admittedly, I could have chosen slightly different terminology. 'Islam is the most gender-just religion' would have been *plus precise*, as many Muslims do not identify with the term 'feminist', including some of the most prominent gender-egalitarian scholars, non-binary African American theologian amina wadud and Pakistani American writer and academic Asma Barlas. The resistance towards 'feminism' as a term arises from the 'universalising' nature of traditional feminism, where religion, and Islam in particular, is only seen as 'an impediment to women's ambitions'.[21] Although in recent decades modern feminism has attempted to cast its elitist net a little wider, the movement still suffers from being unable to look beyond its own conception of 'equality'.

Either way, a soundbite on a panel show will never do a world view, and the fastest growing faith on the planet, justice. And it is this concept that lies at the core of my faith. Two syllables, a radical theology of liberation, and something oppressors have made a Houdini-like art out of escaping: *Justice*.

> Allah created the heavens and the earth for just ends, and in order that each soul may find the recompense of what it has earned, and none of them be wronged. (Quran, 45:22).

What does it mean to believe God is justice?

As South African scholar Farid Esack explains, verses such as these suggest *justice* is one of the reasons God created the universe. Justice, therefore, has a divine quality, calling humans to 'establish an enduring, ethically based order on Earth'.[22] This includes radical commitments to justice across *all* experiences of oppression: economic, gender, racial, and beyond. As author Shadaab Rahemtulla explains in *Qur'an of the Oppressed*, this commitment goes back to the very beginning.

'Intrinsic to the Islamic call,' he writes, 'was a comprehensive reconfiguration of the existing order, and it was because of the profound socioeconomic implications of Muhammed's monotheism that the Meccan elite rejected his prophecy.'[23] Asma Barlas's exegesis also demonstrates the Quran's commitment to justice, locating it as an *anti-patriarchal* text. Using the vital concept of tawhid, the oneness of God, she argues that any human attempts to partake in this sovereignty undermine the core concept of Islamic monotheism.* Therefore, any system that gives 'men sovereignty over women is at odds with divine sovereignty and thus must be dismantled on Quranic grounds'.[24]

Of course, not everyone subscribes to liberatory readings of the texts;** I am reminded of this every time I speak on Islam in any public context, as if all the oppression in the world meted

---

* To break this down: As Islam is a monotheistic religion, there is only one God, and therefore no one else can participate in God's divinity. (This is also part of the shahada, the oath required to become Muslim). An aspect of this divinity is sovereignty, i.e. the ability to rule over people, but as God's divinity is not shared, neither is God's sovereignty. Thus, the patriarchy, where men claim sovereignty over women, would necessarily be counter to Islam, as it would place men at the same level as God – the biggest sin in Islam, shirk.

** The Quran and hadith, specifically.

out by Muslims has somehow slipped my notice. Indeed, much injustice is done in the name of Islam, a saddening, sullying truth that I do not deny. But the desire to essentialise Islam, into either good or bad, patriarchal or not, is a trap. I myself have tripped into it before. Who has the right to tell anyone how to practise their religion, what it even is to be a believer? There is no 'one true Islam', just as much as there is no 'one true democracy' nor 'one true Christianity'. These are all sites of contestation. As the saying goes, you don't read the Quran, the Quran reads you. Interpretations of faith oft reflect the desires and values of the individual. If you seek mercy, you will find it. If you seek an excuse for your vengeance . . .

In scholar Farid Esack's Quranic hermeneutic of liberation, pluralism and universal salvation are vital. Genuine pluralism, he observes, must entail 'not the mere toleration of other religious communities but the humble acknowledgment that there exist multiple pathways to salvation'.[25] In Esack's view, Muslims of today do not have the monopoly on salvation, or on justice. Even in the Quran, 'Muslim', or the 'submitter', does not refer solely to those who take their shahada, the testimony or oath required to become Muslim.* Allah refers to 'those who believe', and only Allah can judge who meets this requirement.

Esack's view is emancipatory, for it presents a faith system that is open, non-restrictive and mutually inclusive. If Islam does not have the monopoly on justice, then liberation theology is not the *only* school of thought that understands the importance

---

* 'I bear witness that there is no god but God and that Muhammad is the messenger of God.' A single honest recitation of the testimony is all one needs to become Muslim.

of the divine ideal. But ideals aside and looking around our globe, I wonder where this justice is to be found.

—

I consider the lived experience of being a believer in the countries I have resided in: Sudan, Australia, England, France. Two former colonies, two colonisers.

In bitter irony, my family left one former colony for another, sneaking out of Sudan to Australia after a bloodless coup in 1989 brought Omar al-Bashir to power. Bashir, a military dictator, implemented a particularly *unjust* legal system that codified Islamic principles inappropriately and in bad faith, one more concerned with control and oppression rather than accountability and justice. Despite – or perhaps because of – Bashir's repression, women were at the forefront of protests which ousted the dictator from power in 2019, reportedly making up to 70 per cent of the protestors.[26] At the time of writing, Bashir is being handed to the International Criminal Court, facing charges of genocide, war crimes and crimes against humanity. The Sudanese people are putting their faith in western international law; only time will tell whether 'justice' will be served. And although there is a sense of satisfaction among some of my Sudanese peers that Bashir will face *some* accountability for his actions, the conversation often turns back to who will *never* be held to account: leaders of the imperial nations like former US President Bill Clinton.

On 20 August 1998, out of the blue, the Clinton administration bombed the Al-Shifa pharmaceutical factory, the largest manufacturer of medicines in all of Sudan. In action supported then by current US President Joe Biden,[27] fourteen cruise missiles wiped out the production of approximately *half* of all the drugs in the nation, including vital anti-malarial products. Clinton's spokespeople said it was 'a disguised chemical weapons factory', but reports show the intelligence was completely faulty. The United States Ambassador to Sudan would later concede '[t]he evidence was not conclusive and was not enough to justify an act of war'.[28] Germany's Ambassador to Sudan Werner Daum wrote in 2001, 'tens of thousands of deaths' of Sudanese civilians were likely caused by the medicine shortage. Sanctions against the country made it incredibly difficult to import enough medicine to cover the serious gap left by the attack.

The factory has never been rebuilt. Sudan has not dealt with its people justly, but neither has the world dealt justly with Sudan. I wonder what that means.

Fast forward to 2021; I find myself wandering the fabled cobbled streets of Paris, ambling through the Haussmann-conceived city fresh from a French visa rejection after I refused to remove my headscarf for the ID photo. I recall the story of George Orwell as told by British academic Paul Gilroy in a 2021 *Guardian* long read.[29] Orwell sported 'the symbolic form of a series of circles tattooed onto the backs of his hands' while he served as a colonial police officer in Burma in the 1920s,[30] and though he never wrote of why he chose to mark himself in this manner, it has been posited they were 'probably a sign to members of the British establishment in Burma that he was not "one of them"'.[31] Gilroy references this as he speaks of his dreadlocks,[32] and I wonder how much my desire to wear the hijab is undergirded by the same sentiment. As amina wadud explains in a 2020 interview, the hijab 'is one of the clearest, symbolic representations of

Islam'. In some ways, it becomes 'a public performance', a sign to the establishment of my choice to stand apart.[33]

When the French state dangled the tantalising prospect of a licence to stay in the city to develop my craft, only with the *small* price of becoming a 'little more like them' by taking my hijab off, my recoil was visceral. Many friends and observers struggled with my choice. It was just an ID photo, everyone else does it, why was I so pressed? No big deal, right?

It was, of course, a 'big deal'. If it weren't, the state wouldn't have made it a requirement. The hijab does not cover the face, does not change the shape of your visage, does not hinder identification in any way. Taking my hijab off for a photo would practically make it *less* useful for identification, as I haven't been out in public sans head covering since 2001. But as should now be evident, this requirement was bound up in French ideas of 'universalism', in their so-called 'civilising' mission. If you want to stay, you will have to be more like us, said the state whose motto is *'liberté, égalité, fraternité'* (liberty, equality, fraternity). The hypocrisy burnt, as did the rejection. I could not accept conditional equality.

—

Justice may not be reliably found in other people, institutions or nation-states, but for me, it is reliably found in a life guided by values, lived with integrity. For me, that is in liberation theology. It is in the words of the Quran; it is in the praxis of my Islam. The Arabic word for faith, iman, means not just believing in God, but *acting in a just manner*. This is not to say that one's belief is uncritical. In fact, critical engagement with the text is vital: it is through 'the process of praxis truth manifests itself, in complex and manifold ways'.[34] Liberation theologists such as Esack emphasise action as much as belief, going so far as to say one's fitra (humanity) is compromised if one does not *act* in the face of oppression.[35] As Pakistani Islamic intellectual Khurram Murad writes, 'the real key to understanding the Quran is the practical application of its meaning'.[36]

And so again, I turn to the verse of the Quran cryptically referenced in my Twitter bio, 4:135:

> O you who believe, be upholders of justice – witnesses for Allah, even though against (the interest of) your selves or your parents, or your kin. One may be rich or poor, Allah is a better caretaker of both. So do not follow desires, lest you should swerve. If you twist or avoid (the evidence), then, Allah is all-aware of what you do.

Life, age and study have named what I already knew. My allegiance is to justice, to no one but the divine. It is no wonder then, when I sat up in my chair on *Q+A* and firmly made this known, my very essence was metaphorically lynched. For what is more terrifying than a Muslim woman who states her liberation is in virtue of, not despite, her Islamic faith, who refuses to be 'saved', who stands only for justice?

—

After finishing this essay, I held off sharing it with my publisher for a few days, remaining unsatisfied with the above conclusion. The piece's weight languished on my chest, a sign there was something lingering in my system, a truth not fully told. I could feel it, a slight hollowness in the walls of the argument I'd constructed, as if termites had found their way into the innards, ceaselessly chewing through wood and ply, blood and bone. What was I missing?

My conclusion, strong and forthright, earnest and hopeful, attempts to make meaning out of an experience I have spent more time forgetting than understanding. I state my case with the confidence of an Eton boy claiming epistemic authority, when the truth is I may never be able to supply the full and true account of what happened to Yassmin Abdel-Magied in 2017, not least because the trauma has corrupted my mind, leaving me unable to remember most of that year, most of my youth. Islam was my lifeline, the framework I gripped on to with desperation as I was hurled into the maelstrom, choking on my own spit, drowning in darkness.

What does it mean when we carve noble sentiments from the lumber of our trauma? How do I avoid the danger of a single story, even one written by me?

—

After some time, the pressure on my chest eased. I stopped fighting so hard to control 'the story', and drew my focus in, closer to home. Indeed, there may never be a full and true account of what happened to Yassmin Abdel-Magied in 2017. Perhaps expecting order from such chaos is in itself folly. But it doesn't matter to me so much, anymore. For if the events of that year brought me closer to my faith, to an understanding of the Islamic ideal of justice, rooted in praxis . . . well, that is a story I can get behind, one full and true enough for me.

To all the cars
I've loved before

It was fourth generation, Japanese. Eggplant violet, glinting in the Brisbane summer heat, searing to the touch. Six cylinders of combustion, twinned turbos pushing hot compressed air into tight chambers of power, sultry rumbles rising into roars. Shivers, shooting down my spine. My first love, the Toyota Supra.

The Supra had slipped into my life via the same medium initially igniting my passion for petrol: film. After discovering the world of motorsport racing in the B-grade teenage-kid version of *The Italian Job* – *Catch That Kid* – I inhaled every car-related movie I could find. The *Fast and Furious* movie franchise, interminable today, had begun just in time. In 2001's *The Fast and the Furious*, veritable heartthrob Paul Walker (RIP) rescues a tangerine-coloured 1994 Supra (complete with a factory-installed 2JZ engine) and brings it back to eye- and ear-throbbing life, skyrocketing the already-popular drifter to cult-like status (in my adolescent eyes, at least). A Los Angeles cop, Walker is tasked with stopping a heist crew led by Dom Toretto, played by the indomitable Vin Diesel, but soon finds himself forced to choose between his duty as a police officer and the blossoming friendship of the Toretto family. The films were entry-level streetcar racing, but at their beating, four-stroke heart was, undeniably, love. 'I don't have friends, I got family,' Dom says in *Furious 7*. Love of the machine, love of family.

My childhood neighbourhood on the southside of Brisbane was Queensland's answer to the fuel-filled movie franchise. Various versions of the gun-grey R34 Nissan Skyline GT-R street-racing in the opening scenes of *2 Fast 2 Furious* cruised around Sunnybank Shopping Town on a regular school night. The burnt orange Mazda RX-7 from *Tokyo Drift* had identical twins up and down Mains Road, and every third kid had a Honda, either the S2000, Civic, or all-aluminium NSX. (With VTEC, of course.) I spent my high school years envious of the 'olders' drifting in empty car parks, practising and perfecting the art of steering with one hand; flawless control as they flicked handbrakes up at just the right moment, loosening the rear wheels of traction, their steeds sailing impossibly gracefully around bends, gliding as if enchanted. I would lie in the inky darkness of my childhood bedroom, strain-ing to hear the not-so-far-off sounds of neighbourhood scraping: rising acceleration; downshifts towards corners; the whip-crack ricochet of unburnt droplets of fuel expiring in the header, unused yet still part of the show. Wafts of burnt rubber, ethanol, benzene, aphrodisiac. Dark tyre marks beginning and ending haphazardly on the asphalt were the only clue left the next morning of all the fun that was had.

I did everything I could to be around the objects of my desire. I took buses to the Moorooka Mile – a stretch of industrial road crammed with car dealerships, panelbeaters, import–exporters, mechanics – knocking on garage doors and asking if I could volunteer, get my hands dirty, fill the underbelly of my fingernails with grease. *This is no place for a young girl like you*, I would be told; turned away, turned away, turned away. *It's for your own good*, they would say to my face, young like their daughters'; their instinct one of protection. But shelter was not what I sought. Each time I walked down a cracked concrete path of a cavernous warehouse, caught the scent of WD-40, heard snatches of engine-related chatter, my chest would tighten, heart quickening, an illicit grin sneaking onto my face. *Why do you love cars so much?* people would ask, confusion colouring their features. They saw in me potential for 'worthier' desires. I had no real answer. Why does anyone love anything? I just did.

As soon as I could, I got my licence and joined the fray. It was everything I dreamt of. Late-night speeding down the highway, midday dashes drifting around roundabouts, impromptu trips through the dark of the mountains. I had found peers at university, age-mates who would never dare turn me away. We would be five or six cars in train, rowdy, petrol-head engineers, flush with adrenaline, dopamine and underdeveloped lateral prefrontal cortexes. Me in my first car, the 156 Alfa Romeo, bought with holiday-job savings. The memory is a sensual thrill: senses sharp, ears tuned to the pitch of the engine, palm cupped around smooth pleather ball of gearstick, chest slightly forward, eyes straining to see beyond the yellow beams ahead. Two distant red lights ahead the only indication that you were not completely alone. But in my car – heavy on the road, seats the colour of unripe mango, cocooned in hundreds of kilos of metal, plastic and glass – I was never alone.

Loving cars brought with it family. I was fluent in the argot of petrol-head, could talk suspension set-ups, best block for the chassis, camber, castor, toe. Two minutes in a garage and I would forget who I was, forget the wars fought against people who looked like me, prayed like me, spoke in my tongue. Two minutes under a car bonnet and all my problems slid away like water over grease; the only thing that mattered was getting her started again, tuning her up, helping her sing. These machines were portals, gateways to community the world over. Trading jokes with unsubtly armed southerners at swap meets in West Texas, snatching up my first set of imperial Snap-On wrenches for a steal. Ogling my latest obsession, the 1969 Corvette Stingray C3, with curves to make the Mississippi River blush, as she purred down Canberra streets. Hugging hairpins on Italian roads, revs in red on the German autobahn, crunching icy terrain under my tread in the Alps, Rockies, Pyrenees. Freedom.

During the worst week of my life, I hired a car with an engine I knew how to coax and drove for eight hours straight, stopping only once to see twelve apostles hidden in the fog of the Victorian coastline. Months later, my mother received the three speeding tickets I had acquired that day. I thanked Allah I had enough money to pay them off. The combustion engine was my vice. I was uninterested in rehab.

On 4 September 2021, Australia's weekly progressive paper published a piece titled 'Why your current car may be the last fossil-fuel vehicle you own'.[1] The era of the electric car is all here, author Mike Seccombe wrote. I know he is speaking true, and I know the shift away from fossil fuels is vital, necessary, humanity saving. There is no part of me that denies this reality. There is no part of me that fights it! I understand it, rationally, with every one of my little grey cells.

But there is no part of me that isn't heartbroken.

My love is old-fashioned.

My love is seen as dirty, filthy, unimportant, unworthy.

My love is, ultimately, replaceable.

What do you do with a love that is no longer viable? Not because either of you has changed, but because the world around you has.

I'm a horseshoe maker in the time of Henry Ford, I've often joked. The reality is more that I'm a builder who loves asbestos, for all its supple strength, sly resistance to water and electricity, its wondrous sound and heat insulation. It is such a shame it is also a hidden killer. What do you do with such love?

Electric cars have great acceleration, say people to me, assuming the love is one-dimensional, a simple exchange policy. They are better for the environment, they cajole, as if I don't know that, as if I want the Earth to overheat, as if I love cars *because* of their contribution to the climate crisis. You don't fall in love with something just because it's *good*.

There will be no love story between me and the electric vehicle that will rival what came before. There are no electric-motor-heads; it was not called *The Fast and the Gearless*. Where is the fury in an electric motor? I did not become an electrical engineer, though my father was one. I was uninterested in the power of the invisible, currents which could kill but I wouldn't see coming. I chose mechanical. I wanted more from what I worked with;

wanted to see it, smell it, bathe in it, be afraid of it, and keep coming back. It blows my mind that I may be of the last generation this applies to.

There will come the day where young people will have never been in a petrol-fuelled vehicle. Indeed, such a day is already on its way, arriving soon, Lady Earth crying out for it. I welcome it, with open arms and tears running down my face. My fingernails will stay clean; my heart, unstirred.

My love is old-fashioned, deadly, lifesaving, defunct. The revolution has arrived.

Here's to all the cars I've loved before.

On the rigs

Released as part of the 40th edition of Griffith Review *in April 2013, this was my first long-form piece of writing. I wrote it at the urging of the incredible Julianne Schultz, editor of the* Review *at the time, with whom I served on the Queensland Design Council. She saw in my twenty-one-year-old self a storyteller, the potential for a writer, possibilities of a future inconceivable to me at the time. This essay came together in the mornings after twelve-plus-hour night shifts, lying cross-legged on the rough pale blue sheets of my single bed in an ice-cold donga, somewhere in outback Australia. 'Show, don't tell,' Julianne said to me at the time, and through draft after draft, I worked to try to show the world what it was to be a young, Sudanese engineer on rigs around Australia. Who knew it would be the beginning of an entirely new career?*

'You're working on the rigs?' one of the drillers from my camp asked, his voice heavy with surprise. 'We assumed you were just with the camp. Respect hey, that's awesome, we love having chicks actually on the rigs.'

Another chimed in. 'Yeah, that's great. What do you do?'

'I'm a contract service hand, a "measurement while drilling" specialist. You really think we're welcome here?' I asked.

'Yeah! We need more of it.'

Later that day, I had another conversation that challenged this view. Clearly women in the oil and gas industry were not universally welcomed. The rig manager was quite clear about his views: 'I said nope, no, absolutely not. There was no way I was going to let a female be on my crew. Everyone agreed. Sean [the manager on the other shift] even said to me that if she was hired, he would quit.'

The rig manager shrugged as he explained the reaction to a 'lady' applying to be a leasehand on the rig – the lowest level job, responsible for cleaning and errands.

'I just didn't want to deal with the extra hassle that it would bring,' he said.

I am the only woman on the twenty-five-person rig in Central West Queensland.

Later that evening as I begin my regular twelve-hour night shift, I touch my iPod screen and select my current favourite anthem. In a flash Seal's velvet voice reverberates through the white earbuds: 'It's A Man's Man's Man's World'.

Accepting that your twenty-one-year-old Muslim daughter is going to work on remote oil and gas rigs is not easy. I am fortunate to have parents who understand (although perhaps not always share) my interest in adventure and not being ordinary. Their view is simple: as long as the rules of Islam are followed and there is a coherent and beneficial reason for me doing the things I choose, they will support me.

My parents say they weren't sure what to expect when they immigrated to Australia almost twenty years ago, fleeing the oppressive political regime of Omar al-Bashir in Sudan. They may not have had a concrete idea of where it would lead, but I certainly inherited from them a willingness to seize opportunity and embark on adventures. That may explain how they found themselves with a daughter who boxes, designs racing cars, and while visiting family in Sudan in 2012, got wrapped up in an attempt to overthrow the same oppressive government that forced them to leave.

They came to Australia looking for a new beginning; now they are parents of a female, Muslim rig hand.

As part of my faith, I wear the hijab, and have been doing so since I was ten, as a personal choice. It is truly something that has become a part of my identity, and I like to be flamboyant and creative with colours and styles. My head covering on the rig is a little less obvious and obtrusive, the turban and bandana combination conveniently paired with the hardhat and a little cooler. In true Australian fashion, however, religion is one topic that is fastidiously avoided on the rig, and people don't always realise the significance of my head covering. It makes for some interesting conversations.

'So when's that tea cosy come off?'

I turned around to my colleague and chuckled to myself.

'Nah, it doesn't come off, I was born with it, eh!'

His jaw dropped slightly and he looked at me in confusion. 'Wha-a-?'

I laughed out loud. 'Nah mate! It's a religious thing. We call it a hijab, I guess this is the abbreviated hardhat friendly version . . .'

'Oh yeah, righto . . .'

He nodded, uncertain, then shrugged and went back to his meal.

When I told my family at home, my father couldn't get enough of it.

'Let's call you Tea Cosy now!'

———

The oil and gas industry in and around Australia has existed for decades. The onshore coal seam gas industry has, however, only begun to boom since the mid-2000s,[1] and became a subject of vocal controversy. Companies like Santos, Arrow Energy, Queensland Gas Company and Origin battled it out throughout the Bowen and Surat Basins, drilling as fast as they can to have enough gas to fulfil the contracts they have signed. The numbers advertised by the companies are incredible, going from just ten wells in the early 1990s to more than 600 in 2010–11 and peaking at 1634 wells drilled in 2013–14.[2]

This means that there are many job opportunities in the gas industry for new mechanical engineers, like me. Many opt for graduate positions in one of the large client companies that produce liquefied natural gas from the coal seam gas that has been extracted. There they work on the design, procurement or project management aspects of drilling and production.

Others want to get their hands dirty, to see what is happening in the field, and they take another route. This suited my sense of adventure and I opted for field experience. As a field engineer, I live, eat and work on remote oil and gas drilling rigs throughout the country and the world.

It is unusual and full of challenging learning experiences. It is also an extremely humbling opportunity to be part of a world that is unknown to many. What has been most surprising about the experience, however, is not the physical aspect or the male-dominated environment – studying engineering will accustom any woman to this; only five women graduated in my year (2011) in a class of 200 – but the constant reminder of gender. What I considered an innocuous detail looms as the most important for many others.

———

Drilling rigs drill holes – wells – in the ground in order to reach a 'payzone'; usually either oil or gas. Onshore and offshore drilling rigs look similar, despite the obvious difference in location. Australia has both onshore and offshore operations, but the onshore rigs are typically smaller. I work mostly on these onshore outfits, often in remote locations anywhere from thirty minutes' drive to a few hours' flight away from the nearest town. They operate twenty-four hours a day, seven days a week, every day of the year. I spent Eid celebrations, Christmas and New Year at work. This is common, the drilling and pumping never stops.

In a typical operation, a rig will be set up on a cleared piece of land – a pad – and the operating crew will live in a camp up to (and sometimes over) twenty minutes' drive away.

The rig is basically made up of a rig floor (where the main rig operations occur, usually at least four metres above the wellbore ground level), the derrick (the tall mast that holds the pipe as well as the drive system, and ranges from ten to thirty metres high), the dog-house (a small room on the rig floor for the driller), and varied tank systems on the ground nearby, housing the fluid (usually mud) that is pumped down the drill string (as it is called when the drill pipe is joined together). The 'catwalk' attached to the rig raises the pipe to the rig floor while drilling. There are also various water tanks, other equipment (generators, pumps) and shacks for the personnel. All up, this can all be housed on a piece of land that is less than a hundred metres square.

The quality of the camp depends on the company; generally there are between five and twenty 'dongas' (converted shipping containers) with three to five rooms each. Each room houses two people, on opposite shifts – one person sleeps while the other works – and depending on the camp, there are either camp-wide communal bathrooms, shared bathrooms or individual ensuites.

It is not luxurious, but crew are compensated for the lifestyle. Most rig workers, like mining workers, work a rotational fly-in, fly-out shift – two weeks on, two weeks off. The contractors who provide supplementary services to the rig tend to have on-call arrangements with no formal rotation: you work when you are needed. I have been fortunate and have not had to work extremely long 'hitches' yet. To my parents' relief, my longest attachment was twenty days in Central Queensland. The longest hitch I've heard about is eighty-four days straight, with not a single day off. Such is the life of a service hand.

—

The environment is unapologetically male. It is also isolated and basic: all everyone does is sleep–eat–work. I found it relatively easy to acclimatise, given my studies and interests, but I underestimated the impact that being the only woman for most of my time, in a group of between twenty and sixty men, would have on me. I found it more challenging than I expected to navigate work–life nuances on the rigs.

There are few workplaces where a woman is made more aware of her gender: where you must learn to find the balance as a woman in such an overwhelmingly male world. Many – most – of the men who work in oil and gas still consider the industry to be a 'man's domain', and even those who welcome women have particular expectations of how a woman should act to be fully accepted.

'This is a man's world,' I was told once by an older male colleague, 'so as a woman you have to learn the rules and fit in. You can't change the men.'

Most surprisingly for a Muslim woman focused on academic and formal equality, 'learning to fit in' has included navigating the sexual double standard that is ever present in the field.

I became wary of being seen as a woman who would come in to 'change the ways of the men'. Such a reputation would make life very difficult for me. So when I was on a rig I would make a point of joking with the crew and let their comments roll. It was a way of showing that I could 'take it'. I had four years of mechanical engineering under my belt, after all, where females made up less than 5 per cent of the class, so I thought it was something I was used to. I soon discovered that I was not.

Things were turned on their head, and I had to rethink the best way of coping, one afternoon when a rig worker made an announcement over the two-way radio.

'Yassmin, I'll give you $100 to wrestle in the mud with Bazza!' the voice cackled over the speaker.

I scoffed to myself; who did he think he was?

'You wish – I wouldn't even dream about it for less than half a million,' I shot back, secretly proud of myself for fobbing him off in what I thought was quite an effective manner.

'Half a million! Do you know what I could get with half a million?' the voice came back, incredulous.

Not me rolling around in the mud on a rig for you, I thought.

Later that night, an older colleague took me aside.

'You gotta put a stop to that kind of talk, you know,' he said. I looked at him, puzzled.

'It diminishes you. People will start thinking you're a slut.'

I was shocked – how did they interpret my comment like that? The double standard of sexual promiscuity for men and women took me by surprise. How could I, as a young, practising Muslim woman on a rig, standing up for myself, possibly be considered promiscuous?

The same banter that makes 'men, men' on the rig is not open to women. Too much backchat and your value is 'diminished'; too little, and you're perceived as uptight and hard to work with. A fine line and not one that I ever expected to walk.

Drilling rigs are places where large groups of men are isolated for at least two weeks at a time and left to their own devices, an environment where base instincts take hold. Humiliating hazing that should be illegal, like tying people up and urinating on them, is, according to stories I have heard from other rigs, surprisingly commonplace. In this environment women are seen as fair game. Adolescent-like practical jokes are common and almost everyone talks openly about viewing pornography. On my second job in the field, a colleague offered me free access to his one-and-a-half-terabyte pornography collection. 'Take what you want!' he said. 'I've got stuff from almost any country, and there is exotic stuff in that folder,' he indicated. 'I collect it!'

I politely but firmly declined.

I had thought pornography was something people grew out of in high school. Not so, I was assured by a motorman on my first job.

'If the dongas aren't perfectly level, you might feel the room rocking when you're trying to get to sleep. That usually means someone in one of the rooms is having a ...' I interrupted at that point, not wanting to hear the details. The image stayed in my mind, though, and I involuntarily cringe every time my donga moves now, even though usually it's someone walking up the stairs.

—

It is not all rough, and the industry has changed significantly since the turn of the century.[3] Despite the traditional male dominance, there are strong factors forcing welcome change. Two catalysts for change are the increasingly strict Occupational Health and Safety regulations and the presence of women on rigs.

While there are relatively few women in the physically demanding rig environment, there are increasing numbers of women working as geologists, engineers, and in wireline and drilling and measurement services.

The transition has not been easy and as my experiences show, reactions vary from acceptance and encouragement to fear of the change that the presence of women might bring. 'It makes it feel more like the real world,' several rig hands have told me. 'When there is a woman around, people argue less, talk about different things and it doesn't feel like such a strange place to come to.'

This perspective was slightly surprising and equally encouraging. The more common opinion, however, is shaped by fear. Although some men enjoy having women as part of their workforce, they still believe it is their domain and women are 'more trouble than they are worth'. I have heard this many times. In part this stems from the fear of sexual harassment claims, which are not uncommon in the industry in both the field and office environment. Numbers are difficult to come by, but anecdotally, it seems that two-thirds of the rigs in Queensland have had some sort of sexual harassment complaint from a woman in the recent past.[4]

I have found it takes an average of three shifts (tours – three consecutive twelve-hour days or nights), before the crew begin to interact with me, even after I've made an extensive effort to get to know the individuals. By the third tour, crews may start having conversations in my presence. It usually takes a week or two on the same job before I can walk into a room and the conversation doesn't completely stop. It is rarely an aggressively threatening environment, although it can be extremely intimidating. It is more that the crew don't know how to behave with a woman in their midst. Do they act normally? Should they be on their best behaviour? They wait for cues.

'We gotta suss the chicks out,' an assistant driller commented. 'You don't know if she's going to just report you on a joke you didn't even realise you made. I don't want to lose my job, so I just stay quiet.'

This view is not uncommon; a lot of people have said the same thing in different ways. On one hand, it is heartening to see the system working, to see that women's rights in the field are taken seriously. On the other, it instantly causes an 'us and them' rift. The men band together; their view is that 'the women are the same and out to get them' or that they are 'too sensitive' and won't be privy to the men's banter. Unfortunately, on most sites there are not enough women to form their own gangs.

The men are right to be uncertain about how their banter will be received. It is usually extremely racist, sexist and offensive. It can't be just excused as 'rig talk'.

Charlie is a sixty-eight-year-old directional driller. He grinned at me when he decided he could talk to me and said with a smirk, 'Oh yes, I have some blacks in my family tree!' I was naively impressed (and surprised) that we might have some shared heritage, as Charlie looked like an average 'Aussie battler'.

'Oh yes, yes I do. I think they're still hanging there out the front of the house!'

His wizened face creased into a smile as he began to chortle. I began to laugh as well, mostly in shock. 'Charlie, you're a terrible man!' I replied, shaking my head.

'I know! It's great isn't it!'

—

I find I am constantly asking myself the question, Does one adopt and accept the mannerisms of the rig to 'fit in', and become 'one of the boys', not causing waves by accepting the status quo? Or should I, and other women, stick to our guns and demand change, that the men working in these isolated and testing environments change their culture and mannerisms in order to incorporate women?

It is not easy to answer. My mother sat me down before I left for my first 'hitch' and gave me some advice. 'Don't forget, Yassmina, that you are not a boy, and you will never be "one of the boys". At the end of the day, you are and will always be a woman, and a Muslim woman at that, so you must act like one and guard yourself.'

At the time, the advice jarred. I had always been 'one of the boys'. It was difficult to understand why this had to change now.

The more I work in the field, though, the more I realise that things are different. Being 'one of the boys' may have been appropriate at university. In the field, no matter what I do, my gender will never be forgotten. This was one of the reasons the rig manager refused to have women on his crews. 'The guy that was pushing for this woman to be hired, he had hired his twin sister way back in the day on the rigs so had a soft spot for women on crews. He ended up having to fire her, though, because she hooked up with another crew member. What does that tell you?'

We are faced not only with entrenched attitudes within the industry of what women are capable of, but also individual prejudices. In an industry where it seems every second man is going through or recovering from a divorce (partly due to the lifestyle), the cocktail of emotion and misunderstanding can be toxic. If I had a dollar for the number of times a co-worker has said, part mirth and part seriousness – 'All you damn women are the same' – I could probably retire.

Even as I write this, I feel I should apologise and add a disclaimer. Not all the oil and gas fields are like this.

Or is this just me, explaining away behaviour that is common on rigs so I don't 'rock the boat' or disturb the peace and become an unwanted entity? I haven't been able to answer these questions yet. Working on the rigs has, however, allowed and forced me to reinterpret my understanding of what it means to be a strong woman.

I was always one for doing things differently, partly because I could, and partly because I just did what I wanted. Being the first girl at a Christian ecumenical school (the largest in Queensland) to wear the hijab when I started there in 2002 was pretty exciting. Being the first woman in my company's department in Australia was even better. I broke the bench press record for girls at school, topped the two male-dominated classes of graphics and technology studies (woodwork) and I prided myself on being able to 'hold my own among the men', physically and in banter. Although I was proud to be a woman, I had always been even more proud of my 'masculine' qualities. Perhaps this is what frustrated my mother the most.

In the rigging world, though, there is no mistaking the fact that I am a woman. I am not as strong as all the guys, though I can hold my own. I am not as foul-mouthed, but I can come back with a quip to keep them quiet (or laughing, depending on the situation).

'Gosh, you've got it pretty good, don't you? You get your clothes washed, your bed made, your food cooked for you and on top of that, your choice of twenty-five men! With no competition!' John, the campie, chortled as he opened the crib room door.

'What more could a woman want, eh?'

His lined, weather-beaten face flashed a grin, showing off his multiple silver fillings as he left the shack. I shook my head slowly and laughed. What more indeed . . .

This job has made me realise that it is actually okay to be a woman, and being 'strong' doesn't necessarily mean being 'masculine'. It's ironic that it has taken a world renowned for its toughness to make me appreciate my femininity.

—

There is no doubt that it is a man's world, but it is changing. Australia is lagging behind other countries – in Norway and other parts of Europe women are much more routinely employed on rigs. How women change the field or change ourselves to fit in remains an unanswered question, but it will be exciting.

On another rig, I need to find the amenities. 'Are the loos working?' I ask the leasehand in charge of keeping the rig clean.

'Nah, they're probably filthy. I haven't been in there in ages, I just piss in the paddock!'

I laugh as I walk towards the amenities shack.

'Hover!' he yells faintly.

Hover I did. As I push down the pedal of the portaloo and the stench wafts up, I shake my head and wonder: *Why did I choose this job?*

But I do remember. I chose this job because I love a challenge, I love working in the field and I thrive on being forced out of my comfort zone and into environments where I have to prove myself. If I manage to smash a few stereotypes along the way, so much the better.

Summernats of '09

Published in November 2014 by Affirm Press in the anthology It Happened in a Holden.

'Hey, you—', the portly figure across the road called in my direction.

I looked around. Was he talking to me?

'You, over there!' He was now pointing at me, through the throng of people walking across the road intermittently blocking my view.

'Who, me?' I mouthed, pointing at my chest, bending the vinyl 'Summernats' logo printed on the shirt.

'Yeh, you! Come over here!'

I hesitated. The man was bald, sporting a biker's beard and a t-shirt with some sort of a naked lady on the front. The market store he was standing in front of wasn't much better and cheeky sloganed t-shirts were just the beginning. Every piece of Summernats paraphernalia from stubby holders to novelty pens seemed to have found its way into this guy's tent.

Oh, what the hell, I thought, as I made my way across the road, ignoring every 'don't talk to strangers' lesson ever taught. Weaving in and out of the crowd, I strode in front of a gorgeous

69

Camaro parked out the front of the store and only just resisted the urge to stroke its bonnet. *Control yourself, girl!* I reprimanded myself silently. The late-sixties model stirred something in my chest that gave me the jitters.

'Hi,' I said on my approach, grinning like a kid in a candy store. 'What's up?'

'How ya doing, gurl? My name's Geoff, I run this place,' the man's gruff, surprisingly warm voice greeted me as he motioned to the store behind him.

I nodded, still slightly bewildered as to why he was talking to me.

'Hey, uh, we heard you came to the festival all by yourself! That's a bit hardcore, isn't it?'

My head snapped back in shock. How on Earth had this old mate heard anything about me?

'Huh?' My face clearly betrayed my confusion.

'Oh yeah, word's gotten around that you're here by yourself. It's a small place. Look, if you need protection or want to stay with us or anything, let us know. We've got a real big tent and it's all decked out, we'll protect you.'

I looked at this man, flabbergasted. Word surely travels fast in this hood . . .

I thanked the man for his offer, unsure if it was out of a place of protection or sleaziness, and made my way back to the drag strip. The smell of rubber hung in the air like an oppressive cloud. A wonderful, adrenaline-pumping hell of an oppressive cloud.

It was my first Summernats experience. The 'Festival of Bogans', some may call it, but I loved every inch. The muscle and drag car festival runs every year in Canberra, over the new year and into the first week of January. I was seventeen and in love with V8s of every shape and size. It wasn't just V8s either, it was any growling, thundering engine that drew excitement from my bones with every rev. Mum had moved down to Canberra for work and that presented the perfect opportunity to make my Summernats debut.

The storeowner's heart was in the right place, and I had misjudged a book by its cover. Although it was a haven for motoring enthusiasts, the festival wasn't particularly known for its friendliness to women. There had been rumours of rapes and the only other women I had seen while walking around the grounds were mothers, girlfriends and older ladies who had perfected the 'take no prisoners' face. I never paid much attention to rumours, though, and wasn't about to start.

I wore skinny jeans, my boxing boots, a regular top and my white hijab. The plain white scarf looked rather conservative, and the cotton billowed in the wind while I walked. Being a Muslim girl who has fallen in love with all things cars was unusual, or so I was constantly being told. I was about to find out that being visibly Muslim, a female and into cars was definitely not the Summernats stereotype either.

My mother dropped me off at the front of the festival grounds. She drove a funny little Ford Capri, a white piece that was straight out of the Aqua 'Barbie Girl' song and constantly needed its radiator replaced. It wasn't muscle, but it was a convertible and we felt awfully cool driving across town with our hijabs flapping behind us in the wind. 'Like superwoman capes, right Yassmina?' Mum always laughed.

I bought tickets at the door, not knowing what to expect. The first day of 2009, and what a way to welcome in the new year – it was a V8 lover's dream! Hundreds of cars lined the streets:

Holdens, Fords, Corvettes, Shelbys and everything in between. There was a loop of cars doing a circuit around the grounds, and you could jump into any one (as long as the owner agreed). The rumble of the engines, the coughing of the turbos, the smell of fuel . . . It was intoxicating.

I wandered around in hubris. That is when I first laid my eyes on her. For the first time in my young life I thought, *Yup, we Aussies know our muscle*.

'Her' was a HQ 1971 Monaro GTS350, meticulously maintained, with its lines gleaming in black. She was parked underneath a tent in a display area next to the drag strip. She sat low, with attitude and an assurance that spoke of the quiet confidence of a big, cast-iron block. I was later to learn it was a Chevy Small-Block, 5.7 litres of goodness.

Nostalgia I didn't even know existed within me rose up, evoking images of stretches of Bruce Highway and leather seats sticky with heat. Next to it sat a HJ One Tonner Ute, the flatback a polished wooden mahogany, classic and commanding. Camaros stretched beyond the pair, but I only had eyes for the Holdens. The love affair had been sparked.

I meandered through the early seventies models, chatting to owners, admiring intake systems and being blown away by the amount of cc's these chassis could handle. One day, I thought. One day, I'll own my very own HQ. With that promise made to myself, I found a spectator's spot right behind the start line of the drag strip and settled in for an afternoon of burnouts and quarter miles. The best start to the year a woman could want!

—

So how had the storeowner found out? It turned out that the owner of a certain 1969 Corvette Stingray had been talking. One of the perks of Summernats was the 'ridealong'; owners of the various cars volunteering to drive other enthusiasts around the festival grounds in their precious steeds. I naturally gravitated towards my favourite, the little red C3 Corvette of my dreams. The silver-haired owner took a little convincing, but after winning him over with my gushing over his long-bonneted machine, I hopped into the left-handed passenger seat, and off we went cruising, joining the train of gleaming machines snaking their way around the marked-out circuit. We made small talk over the roar of the engines, him sharing the car's origin story, me sharing the origin story of my love of cars. Sometime during the twenty-minute ride, weaving through narrow streets crowded with festival-goers, I mentioned that I had come to the festival by myself. An innocent, naive thing to do perhaps, but I got lucky.

He had told the organisers that there was some teenage Muslim girl wandering around by herself at the festival. I can only imagine what that conversation had looked like.

'A what? A Muslim chick walking around this festival? Now I've heard it all . . .'

As Lionel Shriver made light of identity, I had no choice but to walk out on her

First published on my Medium page, and later republished in the Guardian *on 10 September 2016, this essay was the first of many things I would write that would get me into, as US civil rights activist John Lewis would describe it, 'good trouble'.* I wasn't planning on penning anything at all, but when a fellow writer expressed their confusion at my walking out of Lionel Shriver's keynote speech at the 2016 Brisbane Writers Festival, I figured a piece might help explain how I felt, illustrate the emotion powering my actions. The Medium piece did numbers, but it was not until the* Guardian *republished that it truly went viral. The Brisbane Writers Festival director, poet Julie Beveridge, swiftly organised a 'right of reply' session, inviting me, Sri Lankan Australian novelist Rajith Savanadasa and Korean American author Suki Kim to 'answer' the opening address, which, as Lionel Shriver herself admitted, did not adhere to the brief.[1] But the*

---

* Representative John Lewis used this phrase a number of times, including in a 2018 tweet: 'Do not get lost in a sea of despair. Be hopeful, be optimistic. Our struggle is not the struggle of a day, a week, a month, or a year, it is the struggle of a lifetime. Never, ever be afraid to make some noise and get in good trouble, necessary trouble.' John Lewis, Twitter, 28 June 2018; twitter.com/repjohnlewis/status/1011991303599607808?lang=en (accessed 24 January 2022).

impact was felt far beyond my home city limits. My words sparked responses in the New York Times,[2] *the* New Yorker,[3] *think pieces in the* Conversation,[4] *and even an interview with Shriver in* TIME.[5] *Of course, the lion's share of airtime was given to She Who Hath Most Power, most notably when the* New York Times *published Shriver's mocking opinion piece in full on 23 September 2016;[6] then, after asking for a piece from me in reply, pushed it by weeks, cutting it by half and placing it in the Letters section of the paper on 5 October.[7] It was ironic that even in my own hullaballoo, I found myself squeezed to the margins.*

More than five years on, I have little interest in dissecting the topic of cultural appropriation. I include this essay in the collection as a way to mark a moment, the beginning of the end of my age of innocence.

I have never walked out of a speech.

Or I hadn't, until last night's opening keynote for the Brisbane Writers Festival, delivered by the American author Lionel Shriver, best known for her novel *We Need to Talk About Kevin*.

We were twenty minutes into the speech when I turned to my mother, sitting next to me in the front row.

'Mama, I can't sit here,' I said, the corners of my mouth dragging downwards. 'I cannot legitimise this ...'

My mother's eyes bore into me, urging me to remain calm, to follow social convention. I shook my head, as if to shake off my lingering doubts.

As I stood up, my heart began to race. I could feel the eyes of the hundreds of audience members on my back: questioning, querying, judging.

I turned to face the crowd, lifted up my chin and walked down the main aisle, my pace deliberate. 'Look back into the audience,' a friend had texted me moments earlier, when I messaged them for moral support, 'and let them see your face.'

I took my friend's advice, and the faces around me blurred. As my heels thudded against the grey plastic of the flooring, harmonising with the beat of the adrenaline pumping through my veins, my mind was blank save for one question.

How is this happening?

So what did happen? What did Shriver say in her keynote that could drive a woman who has heard every slur under the sun to discard social convention and make such an obviously political exit?

Her question was – or could have been – an interesting question: What are fiction writers 'allowed' to write, given they will never truly know another person's experience?

Not every crime writer is a criminal, Shriver said, nor is every author who writes on sexual assault a rapist. 'Fiction, by its very nature,' she said, 'is fake.'

There is a fascinating philosophical argument here. Instead, however, that core question was used as a straw man. Shriver's real targets were cultural appropriation, identity politics and political correctness. It was a monologue about the right to exploit the stories of 'others', simply because it is useful for one's story.

Shriver began by making light of a recent incident in the United States, where students faced prosecution for what was argued by some to be 'casual racial and ethnic stereotyping and cultural insensitivity' at a Mexican-themed party.

'Can you believe,' Shriver asked at the beginning of her speech, 'that these students were so sensitive about the wearing of sombreros?'

The audience, compliant, chuckled. I started looking forward to the point in the speech where she was to subvert the argument.

It never came.

On and on it went. Rather than focus on the ultimate question around how we can know an experience we have not had, the argument became a tirade. It became about the fact that a white man should be able to write the experience of a young Nigerian woman and if he sells millions and does a 'decent' job – in the eyes of a white woman – he should not be questioned or pilloried in any way. It became about mocking those who ask people to seek permission to use their stories. It became a celebration of the unfettered exploitation of the experiences of others, under the guise of fiction. (For more, Yen-Rong Wong, a volunteer at the festival, wrote a summary on her personal blog about it.[8])

It was a poisoned package wrapped up in arrogance and delivered with condescension.

As the chuckles of the audience swelled around me, reinforcing and legitimising the words coming from behind the lectern, I breathed in deeply, trying to make sense of what I was hearing. The stench of privilege hung heavy in the air, and I was reminded of my 'place' in the world.

See, here is the thing: if the world were equal, this discussion would be different. But alas, that utopia is far from realised.

It's not always okay if a white guy writes the story of a Nigerian woman because often the actual Nigerian woman can't get published or reviewed to begin with. It's not always okay if a straight white woman writes the story of a queer Indigenous man, because when was the last time you heard a queer Indigenous man tell his own story? How is it that said straight white woman will profit from an experience that is not hers, and those with the actual experience never be provided the opportunity? It's not always okay for a person with the privilege of great inherited wealth to write the story of a young working-class man in poverty, filtering the experience of the latter through their own skewed and biased lens, telling a story that likely reinforces an existing narrative which only serves to entrench a disadvantage they need never experience.

I can't speak for the LGBTQI+ community, those who are neurodivergent or people with disabilities, but that's also the point. I don't speak for them, and should allow for their voices and experiences to be heard and legitimised.

So access – or lack thereof – is one piece.

But there is a bigger and broader issue, one that, for me, is more emotive. Cultural appropriation is a 'thing', because of our histories. The history of colonisation, where everything was taken from a people, the world over. Land, wealth, dignity . . . and now identity is to be taken as well?

In making light of the need to hold on to any vestige of identity, Shriver completely disregards not only history, but current reality. The reality is that those from marginalised groups, even today, do not get the luxury of defining their own place in a norm that is profoundly white, straight and, often, patriarchal. And in demanding that the right to identity should be given up, Shriver epitomised the kind of attitude that led to the normalisation of imperialist, colonial rule: 'I want this, and therefore I shall take it.'

The attitude drips of racial supremacy, and the implication is clear: 'I don't care what you deem is important or sacred. I want to do with it what I will. Your experience is simply a tool for me to use, because you are less human than me. You are less than human . . .'

That was the message I received loud and clear.

My own mother, as we walked away from the tent, suggested that perhaps I was being too sensitive. She had followed me out of the event, much less conspicuously through a side flap, and caught up with me in the darkness as we left the venue. Perhaps she was right . . . or perhaps, I thought, my mother's response was the result of decades of being told to be quiet and accept our place. Was I being harsh? I couldn't decide. Soon, our conversation turned to intent. What was Shriver's intent when she chose to discuss her distaste for the concept of cultural appropriation? Was it to build bridges, to further our intellect, to broaden horizons of what is possible?

Her tone, I fear, betrayed otherwise. Humility is not Shriver's cloak of choice.

The kind of disrespect for others infused in Lionel Shriver's keynote is the same force that sees people vote for Pauline Hanson. It's the reason our First Peoples are still fighting for recognition, and it's the reason we continue to stomach offshore immigration prisons. It's the kind of attitude that lays the foundation for prejudice, for hate, for genocide.

The fact Shriver was given such a prominent platform from which to spew such vitriol shows that we as a society still value this type of rhetoric enough to deem it worthy of a keynote address. The opening of a city's writers festival could have been graced by any of the brilliant writers and thinkers who challenge us to be more. To be uncomfortable. To progress.

A Maxine Beneba Clarke, who opened the 2016 Melbourne Writers Festival by challenging us to learn how to talk about race in a way that was melodic and powerful. A Stan Grant, who will ask us why we continue to allow our First Peoples to wallow in inhumane conditions. An A. C. Grayling, if you really want the international flavour. Anyone who will ask us to be better, not demand we be okay with worse.

Asking to be respected – is that asking for too much? Apparently, in the world of fiction, it is.

What are they so afraid of? I'm just speaking my mind.

The first version of this essay was written for the 56th edition of the quarterly Australian publication Griffith Review. *Penned after my appearance on the current affairs show* Q+A, *the initial piece reflected my shock at the reactionary vitriol caused by the debate, my visceral fear of a life unravelling before my eyes. In those early months of 2017, however, I had supporters willing to speak publicly in my defence, opinion pieces slamming the witch hunt printed in sympathetic media publications. After my Facebook post on 25 April 2017, the tenor of the attacks became increasingly indefensible, and the support slowly petered out. Somehow, I had become contagious, the confected outrage so ludicrous, so bizarre, it felt almost impossible to fight in any coherent manner. 'It's like shadow-boxing,' a friend said to me at the time. 'How do you fight an accusation that is made of nothing?' It achieves no outcome other than exhausting you.*

This piece was then edited to reflect my post-Anzac Day frame of mind and appeared in the Guardian *on 6 July 2017.*

Given that I am now the most publicly hated Muslim in Australia, people have been asking me how I am. What do I say? That life has been great and I can't wait to start my new adventure in

London? That I've been overwhelmed with messages of support? Or do I tell them that it's been thoroughly rubbish? That it is humiliating to have almost 90,000 twisted words written about me in the three months since Anzac Day, words that are largely laced with hate.[1]

Do I reveal that it's infuriatingly frustrating to have worked for years as an engineer, only to have that erased from my public narrative? That it is surreal to be discussed in parliamentary question time and Senate estimates for volunteering to promote Australia through public diplomacy programs? That I get death threats on a daily basis, and I have to reassure my parents that I will be fine, when maybe I won't be? That I've resorted to moving house, changing my phone number, deleting my social media apps. That I need bodyguards for any events that haven't been cancelled. That journalists sneak into my events with schoolchildren to sensationally report on what I share. That I've been sent videos of beheadings, slayings and rapes from people suggesting the same should happen to me. That I wonder if the only thing that will stop them is my death.

Do I reassure my parents, or do I tell them the truth? I have yet to decide.

Whatever one thinks of my seven-word Facebook post, and the subsequent apology posted mere hours after the original deleted statement, isn't really the point. The reality is, the visceral nature of the fury directed at my person – almost every time I share a perspective or make a statement in any forum – is more about who I am than about what is said. My statement was hardly radical, but that I – a young, migrant, hijab-wearing proud Muslim woman – deigned to speak as an equal, was. We should be beyond that but we are not. Many, post-Anzac, said the response wasn't about *me* but about what I represent. I am still not sure what that means. Or perhaps I do, but I do not want to accept it, for that would mean seeing myself on their terms, and not my own. Whatever people are afraid of, it has affected my life, deeply and personally.

———

'Ah, the worst that can happen is someone sending you an angry email,' my father says. 'Just don't read it, you will be fine.' My mother's concern is more corporeal. 'Don't forget to take your vitamins. Have you checked your iron levels? You know your anaemia makes you tired.'

Modern-day activism does not garner much sympathy from my migrant parents. Looking at it objectively it's something I can understand: in Sudan the kinds of fights they were involved in had much higher risks. Their friends were jailed, tortured, killed. My mother faced off an army who wanted to storm her university's dormitory during Colonel Omar al-Bashir's coup of 1989. My father would regularly tell my younger brother and me stories of what kind of dangers people faced as they fought for their political ideals.

'One of our friends was taken by police during a protest, for no apparent reason,' Dad recounted one evening at the dinner table. 'We all knew that if we did not get him back in time, he would be killed. So we kicked up a huge fuss to get him back, stormed the police stations, got in the media . . . We did not hear anything back by the evening, and thought that all was lost. The next morning, the man's mother heard a knock on the door. Someone had dumped a body at the foot of the gate, bloody and beaten beyond recognition. It was our friend, so badly tortured that his own mother did not recognise him. Subhanallah, though, he was still alive.'

Such stories are not uncommon for anyone who has lived in a nation cursed by conflict. In fact, violence can become so normalised that it can be an expected consequence of pushing for social or political change, and there are no systems of protection in place to guarantee a person's physical safety. It's no wonder, then, that the battles of a young 'keyboard warrior' in Australia do not seem quite so serious to my war-weary parents. Compared with what they moved away from, the 140-character threats of 'Twitter trolls' seem almost quaint.

There is one major difference, however. Although the ideas we are fighting for – human rights, social justice, equality – have not necessarily changed, the ways those battles are fought certainly have. My parents' activism was localised, speaking to issues that at most would affect the surrounding region and segment of Sudanese society. Theirs was a fight for just governance within a single country, rather than an ideological battle across nations. It was also an analogue challenge. The nature of communication meant that individual reach was limited and therefore individual exposure somewhat throttled. This lent itself to a collective front, and though not always enough of a protection, there is certainly solidarity in numbers.

Today a public advocate's platform is digital and greatly magnified. An issue or debate unfolding in one place can be amplified through a video or tweet to gain international support or condemnation – sometimes both – simultaneously. News travels almost instantly, and the feedback is equally as swift. Individuals can be rewarded with incredible highs – a following that spans the globe, the ability to easily create content that reaches millions, membership of an online community that 'gets it' – but also with floods of criticism, personal, pointed abuse and threats of worse.

The way this feedback is delivered is also incredibly isolating – abuse appears in an individual's inbox, Twitter feed, Facebook page. And while the inverse to this – retweets, likes, positive comments and messages – does give some sense of solidarity and a collective front, that front as a number on a screen rather than the physical presence of others can only go so far towards steeling your resolve. There is little shared experience to commiserate upon. We might all be fighting the same fight but we have our own demons that divide us for easy picking.

Furthermore, an individual's online presence creates a safety concern that is different from those experienced by previous generations. Whereas my parents would have feared government retribution in the form of being detained, disappeared or killed, the threats faced by activists and advocates today are not nearly as organised. They are amorphous, overwhelming and seemingly impossible to defend against. Imagine every single piece of information about you, accessible online, in the hands of someone who does not know you, does not like you or does not care what happens to you – either a teenage hacker or a national broadsheet – and few rules or consequences if that information is used against you. It is almost enough to terrify an activist into silence. Almost.

'You should just get offline!' I am regularly advised by well-meaning friends and acquaintances, after explaining what it is like to be a commentator in the public space, advocating for ludicrous concepts such as the right to be heard or the seemingly radical ideal of equality. Asking us to go offline is like asking us to leave the streets. Sure, it's the safe thing to do, but it ignores the importance of the online in any struggle today. The online and offline worlds are inextricably linked; in 2017 they are simply different dimensions of the same reality.

———

I learnt these realities in a baptism of fire in September 2016 after I walked out of a speech and accidentally picked an ideological fight with a well-known North American literary figure. What I did not realise at the time was that this is something a young, brown Muslim woman simply must not do, particularly if the conflict is even vaguely connected to the nebulous concept dubbed 'identity politics' – a phrase coined, seemingly, to dismiss or disregard anyone asking for their oppression, historical context or personal reality to be recognised and respected.

How silly of me to miss the memo. Respect is so passé.

Put simply, I had flown a little too close to the sun. I'd been given my wings, told I could fly with the flock and contribute to the discussion as an equal, told I could be a part of 'us'. No one mentioned the feathers were fixed in place with wax, and the sun wouldn't hesitate to strip them away.

Walking out, and then writing an (admittedly) emotionally charged piece* about my reasoning, led to an unexpected – and global – ideological hammering. Criticism and ad hominem attacks were levelled from all over the world, starting with

---

* See 'As Lionel Shriver made light of identity, I had no choice but to walk out on her', p. 74.

Australia's national broadsheet and stretching all the way to the *New York Times*.

Not only was the outcry overwhelming but the commentary it unleashed was merciless. Breitbart, the (fake?) news site and platform of the 'alt-right' – formerly chaired by Steve Bannon, who went on to be Donald Trump's chief strategist – featured an article on the encounter. It was not as cruel as it could have been, if I'm honest. But it was certainly deeply convinced of its own righteousness:

> 'Everyone's entitled to their opinion' ... But if that opinion happens to be so ill thought-through, poorly argued, whiny, needy, constrictive, selfish, ugly, ignorant, flat out wrong and probably quite dangerous too, then they deserve to be called on it and relentlessly, mercilessly mocked till they never spout such unutterable bollocks ever again in their special snowflake lives.[2]

I had messages from friends in India, Italy and Indonesia whose friends and family had been discussing the affair. For a brief moment it became the topic of dinner-table conversation. The result of that spotlight, though, meant that for the next three or four weeks my life was overwhelmed by this story. I had hundreds of emails a day, to the point where I began to automatically delete them and avoided my multiple inboxes completely, to the chagrin of those who were trying to connect for non-Shriver-related business. I deleted Twitter from my phone, deactivated Facebook and wrote almost nothing online for an entire month. Which, for me, is a pretty long time.

But because the online is not truly separate from the offline in our lives, it wasn't truly an online coma. The modern-day equivalent of a pack of citizen paparazzi, perhaps, were still on the front lawn, constantly slipping notes under the door, knocking on the windows, yelling obscenities. While I couldn't hear or see them, I knew they were there.

For a modern-day 'snowflake', as folks interested in social justice are often pejoratively named, being attacked online comes with a sense of being desperately alone. It was me and a glowing screen, the dings of messages, tweets and emails sent by strangers reminding me of my place in the world.

Drip by drip, message by message, it's the water torture of the online age.

———

The weeks rolled by. The influx of messages eventually slowed and a semblance of normality was restored. It seemed the storm had passed.

Months later, at the Jaipur Literature Festival in January 2017, I bumped into another well-known literary figure. Tall, imposing and very British, he was the type of high-level agent who wouldn't normally bother with someone like me – save for the fact that I too am tall, and our eyes met briefly as he crossed the lawn. He slowed as he approached me, then stopped as his face brightened.

'Oh, I know you,' he said. 'You're the girl they're all talking about!' I assumed he was referring to the elite group of global literary stars gathered at the writers party that evening.

'Good things, I hope?' I said, glibly.

His response was emphatic and, in a typical English fashion, faintly apologetic.

'Oh, no, no, I'm afraid not. They all disagree with you, really.'

'Oh!' I feigned shock, though of course I was very well aware. The next line was much more genuine: 'I do wish they would disagree to my face! I would love to have a conversation with them.'

The agent shook his head. It was late and he looked slightly intoxicated, which was probably why he was more forthright than Englishmen usually seem to be.

'Oh, no, no one would do that. You're very intimidating! We're all a little frightened of you.'

I flashed my biggest, pearliest smile and pointed at my teeth. 'Look at this face, hey? How could I possibly be intimidating?'

But it seems there is something incredibly intimidating about a young, brown Muslim woman who is unafraid to speak her mind. This became clear again in February 2017 when I was invited to join a panel discussion on the ABC's *Q+A*.

You may have seen the video – after all, it took only a week for the clip to reach 12 million views on Facebook. In essence, I challenged Senator Jacqui Lambie's views on sharia and Islam, loudly and passionately. The immediate response online was incredibly positive, bolstering my confidence – but that was short-lived. My head above the parapet, I then became the subject of an unexpected and unnecessary character assassination by the national broadsheet. *This is it*, I thought. *I'm never going to get a corporate job again. Who will employ me after the things that have been said?*

But this time around, I would be pleasantly surprised. Within a week, voices of support made themselves heard: radio presenters challenged the criticisms levelled against me, breakfast show hosts defended my reputation, and much ink was spilt in calling out the bullying and canvassing for a more considered and egalitarian response. I could not believe it, to be honest: the articles and columns laced with hatred I had come to expect – but others putting themselves on the line to offer their support? It was a humbling and fascinating experience. Perhaps, on reflection, I was not in this alone after all.

—

The irony in all this, of course, is that I am no one very important. I did not, and do not, hold an elected office, I do not officially represent any racial or cultural group, and I have never been part of a political party, union or even political student organisation. I am a twenty-five-year-old Muslim engineering chick, born in the Sahara desert, whose words occasionally find themselves in the public arena. And if a few words that I put together are enough to terrify establishment figures into attacking me, stumbling over themselves to demonstrate why 'people like her' are wrong and why we should not be listened to because our words are oppressive, then one has to ask, What are they so afraid of? Why are they so afraid? For if the argument was truly as irrelevant as so many claim it to be, then surely it wouldn't be worth all this energy.

As I understand it today, identity politics are about power – but not 'real' or 'traditional' power. The reality is, real power – that which lies in financial resources, the mainstream media and politics – is held by hands similar to those of fifty or a hundred years ago: white, male hands. Not much has changed. Sure, there are several women and people of colour fighting the fight, and many more making their way up the ranks, but look at the true hallmarks of power. Who owns the media companies, controls the big corporates, runs the countries? If the real, hard power is still in the hands of those who have always had it, why are they so worried?

Part of me suspects that the reason these attacks are so vitriolic, swift and all-encompassing is because they are about identity. Identity is personal, and that's why people take it so personally. By asserting my identity in a way that challenges my 'place in the world', I inadvertently challenge the place of those who feel entitled to their privilege and status. That feels not only wrong to such people, but deeply, personally offensive – because what is at stake is who they are in the world. And so they fight viciously, because if privilege and status and wealth and whiteness define who they are, what else could be more valuable?

Those who lack a definitive 'place' in society have little to lose by calling out injustices and structural inequalities, and much to gain by disrupting the status quo. For those with something to lose in that disruption, this can be a terrifying prospect. For everybody else, it is a reminder of the strength and conviction that is needed to fight for a more just world. On that, my parents and I agree.

Leaving. For good.

Published on 1 December 2017, in Meanjin. *I was wary of writing anything in the Australian media shortly after my departure in 2017, aware that my words were susceptible to misrepresentation, to feeding an ever-hungry media maelstrom. However, when the offer from* Meanjin *came to write a piece about leaving, it felt like the perfect note on which to mark my departure.*

This isn't the only time I've planned to leave Australia, though it has certainly been the most contested. My mother says fate has something to do with it. I was young the first time; I was only nineteen.

The dream was to work in motorsport, a fantasy sparked after watching the B-grade film *Catch That Kid*. The movie featured a much younger Kristen Stewart, and that guy from *High School Musical* who wasn't Zac Efron (Corbin Bleu?). The film was picked out by my younger brother, Yasseen, in our local Blockbuster knock-off. It was part of a short-lived family tradition of hiring a movie once a week, for all of us to enjoy. Yasseen's choices were often eccentric at best, but this movie introduced me to the world of go-karting, and the idea of driving fast. I fell in love with the sport, and with the *High School Musical* guy who was not Zac Efron (Corbin Bleu). My parents were less in love with the idea of funding a career driving fast, so I turned my attention to a more realistic option: designing the cars. Studying for my undergraduate degree in mechanical engineering and learning about the career paths available, it soon became clear: if I wanted to design cars, I needed to move to England.

Specifically, the not-London parts of England. How does a Sudanese-born, Australian-bred teenage Muslim woman with no contacts in motorsport get a job in this industry in the not-London parts of England? Well, the cool kids call it 'the hustle'.

In practice that meant 'talking to everyone with even a vague connection to England'. This was generally a fruitless exercise, save for a chance encounter with an engineer from the British Institution of Mechanical Engineers. This man had only the slimmest connection to the world of motorsport, but I knew he would be my way in. My small talk got me nowhere, but my connections to Rotary succeeded where my conversation skills failed. Complimenting his Rotary pendant, I asked the engineer if he had connected with any local clubs. I've never seen an Englishman's face transform from bored to boisterous so rapidly.

'No, I haven't yet, but would love to next time!'

'Fabulous, I know a few folks at my neighbourhood centre who can host you . . .' I beamed with victory as he eagerly pushed his business card into my hand.

I never did introduce him to my Rotary Club acquaintances, although I swear, I fully intended to. I instead emailed him once a month, every month, for the better part of a year, asking if he knew of any internship opportunities for a young upstart like me. Eventually, through sheer frustration perhaps, his assistant put me in touch with a motorsport design company doing just that.

It was the dream gig. I packed my life, my savings and my parents' worries in a bulging suitcase. My new home was to be Shoreham-by-Sea, tucked between Portsmouth and Brighton. Shoreham, as it was known to the locals, reminded me of the town featured in *Midsomer Murders*, but I was not going to let such a minor detail dissuade me. This was exciting! *Impress them enough*, I thought, *and you're in, on the doorstep of a career you have always wanted.* Designing and building machines that would go fast. Yes!

My first day at Ricardo was the best half-day of my life. I walked past two McLaren F1s, my favourite car at the time, on the way to the office. The hallways were filled with the delightful sounds of English accents. My new boss was friendly and had already set up a project on renewable car design for me to work on. My bottom had just warmed the seat when my phone rang. It was a lady from administration.

'Hello, love.' Oh, her accent. So joyous!

'How can I help?'

'We were just wondering if you could bring us your work visa?'

My stomach dropped, slightly. 'My what? Oh, I thought you'd deal with the visa situation?'

'Oh no, love, sorry. You are here on a tourist visa. You need a work visa, and we don't have anything to do with that. If you don't have a work visa, you're not going to be able to work here, unfortunately.'

Her voice was chipper. Her English accent, moments ago, seemed so enchanting. Now it began to sound like shards of glass, forcing their way into the cracks appearing in my seemingly flawless plan.

'Oh well, that's okay then! I can just work for free, you don't have to pay me . . .'

'Oh darling. In order to be on the premises you need to be an employee. I'm sorry, we're going to have to escort you out.'

And that was the end of that. It appeared that in order to apply for a work visa I would need to fly back to Australia. My measly student budget wasn't going to cut it, and my parents saw it as a sign from above, not a mistake they would fund fixing. My first attempt to leave Australia was a false start.

—

My second attempt seemed more promising. I had finished my degree and turned my mind to a job where I could save money for an eventual opportunity in motorsport. A job that involved adventure was preferable. What better option for a young Queensland engineer than a role on the oil rigs? Schlumberger, the oilfield services business, seemed to have all the answers. A great record in gender equality (or so they said), the best technology in the business, and all the location options. You're an impressive graduate, I was told, so you can choose where you want to work.

The list they provided was exciting: Argentina, Malaysia, Indonesia; offshore locations in places I'd never been to or ever imagined working in. Indonesia won out, partly because I'd be close to my parents in Brisbane (who weren't convinced by this 'oil rig' thing), but mostly because Indonesia was a majority Muslim country, and all the food would be halal. A girl has priorities.

The departure date was soon after my twenty-first birthday. I was faced with a dilemma: throwing a going-away party and a twenty-first, entirely without alcohol. Many of my non-Muslim friends hadn't partied without alcohol in their adult lives. I knew it was a big ask for them to stay sober, particularly at a twenty-first. Many of my friends were also engineers, and drinking was part of their identity: in my first lecture at university we were told by the professor, 'If you don't drink beer, you can't be an engineer.'

My salvation was to do things the Sudanese way: mountains of food. A hall was booked, a lamb spit borrowed and jumping castle hired. I *fed* my friends drunk instead, announced my departure, and waited for my flight details to arrive. Two weeks from my presumed start date, I sent my supervisor an email, inquiring about details. In typical oilfield fashion, everything had changed. *Sorry!* the email sang. *Visas are tricky to nail down and you've just missed out. You will now be starting in Alaska in October 2012.* Eight months away.

Alaska was one step too far. My family was fresh with Sarah Palin anecdotes, and my mother was adamant she was not letting me go to the 'middle of nowhere, where there are racist people with guns'. I was also jobless and penniless. I couldn't wait until October.

What other options were available? Roma. Not Italy, but Western Queensland, in a newly acquired company called PathFinder, a department with no other women, and a town that was only six hours drive from my parents' house. My father? Delighted. Me? Devastated. I bought an Akubra hat and acclimatised. Bull riding, deep-sea fishing, dirt bikes, cattle. Asking a former farmer how many head of cattle he had, I quickly learnt that question was an invasion of privacy, an indirect inquiry about this man's bank balance. Once he'd calmed down, though,

Gaz was happy to introduce me to Robbo from down the road, who had a healthy farm and was looking for a wife . . .

It would be two years before I made the move to another oil and gas major. Again, the promise of an overseas posting was made on hiring. It was my (verbal) condition on taking the role: six months in Perth then a posting on a rig in Malaysia. Choice.

Six months rolled by, as did a cold Perth winter. Home, for the time being, was a studio in Fremantle: beautiful for the ocean views, but too far away from town to have any friends. I refused to buy a doona, seeing it as an investment that was more than my six months required. I watched the 2014 FIFA World Cup on my laptop, shivering and curled up in bed, wrapped up in colourful headscarves that were not appropriate rig-sanctioned work-wear.

I was glad to be leaving, as the weather crept towards doona. The movers were coming on Friday. On Thursday, I checked in with my supervisor. His tone was careful, careless. Scottish. Oh, sorry, we should have let you know earlier . . . At that point I tuned out. Thwarted, again?

My mother wondered if this had something to do with a radio appearance I had made a few days earlier. Had it caused consternation in the organisation? It couldn't be that. Surely my technical work, which had received only positive feedback, was all that mattered. We lived in a meritocracy, I reminded her. It was just bad luck the plans for the rig had changed and that visas were difficult to come by.

March 2016, and the song of my year is by the Propellerheads. Something about history repeating? It was a double promotion, a reward for passing my technical exams. I would supervise my own rig, in offshore Brunei. The visa was secured, the flights booked, and I was on my way . . . Then: 'Yassmin, we will need you to return to the office before you leave, urgently, thank you.'

Leaving, this time, had coincided with the publishing of my memoir. A memoir that did not mention said oil major's name, but made them uncomfortable enough to dock my promotion, reduce my ranking and formally discipline me. I was out of control, non-compliant. Brunei would have to wait. Fate was not quite ready for me to leave.

The same company offered me a position in London in April 2017. Perhaps this time I really would be gone. But April rolled around too soon. The furore around a certain *Q+A* appearance involving Jacqui Lambie had left me unsure, and I had personal matters still to resolve. Leaving would have to wait a few months more.

———

If I am honest with myself, every time I tried to leave and failed, part of me was quietly relieved. There was always something that drew me back to this sunburnt country in which I never saw myself reflected. I had always had unfinished business: whether it was running the organisation I founded, Youth Without Borders, a new city to explore, or service on a board, council or sports team. But this time, the sixth time in as many years, is the first time I feel free to go. How do you leave a country that has abused you? Quietly, or with feeling? By the time it came to it, nothing I did happened without a splash.

In June 2017 the sunshine in East London was tanning the little strip of my forearm bared as I defied traditional hijabi norms. I was here on business, a short trip to appear at a writers festival and deliver a keynote. In Shoreditch, a nail technician, applying a bright yellow gel to my claws, asked me if I was 'that lady who yelled at that white politician'. I smiled. Although Londoners might have seen my viral video, here nobody really knew who I was. You should move here, another friend laughed, when I explained the reaction to the video in Australia.

That phrase bounced around my skull. What did I have left in Australia? I landed back in Canberra and spoke at a small event at the Australian National University. There was a photographer in the front row, the camera flash a little too bright. The next day, the papers reported that I had attacked democracy. Later, an elected official suggested I move to an Arab dictatorship. What did I have left in Australia? Maybe it was time to leave.

I resigned from all positions, the first time I would be without a board or council position since the age of fourteen. Over the past decade I had served on the board of the Queensland Museum, the Queensland Design Council, the Australian Multicultural Council, Queensland African Communities Council Advisory Board, the Australian Youth G20 Planning Committee, the National Youth ANZAC Commemoration Advisory Committee, United Nations Youth Australia, the Council of Australia–Arab Relations, ChildFund Australia, OurWatch, and my own Youth Without Borders and Mumtaza, among others. Twelve years of board experience is not bad for a twenty-six-year-old, but how to read papers while backpacking is not something they put in the guidebooks. I expected I would feel empty, a shadow of my former self. Who was I, if not the young brown Muslim woman who had more board positions than prospects for marriage?

I expected to feel changed. I did not. If I am honest, by this point the tanks were empty. There was nothing left with which to feel. How are you meant to feel about a country that has abused you? Do you turn away and not look back? Tell the country they don't know what they had, that you deserve to be treated better, that there are many other countries in the ocean? What do you do when that country is home? Do you make home elsewhere? Or do you just make peace with what home has become?

'Public opinion', which never really matches the opinion of anyone I know, says I am ungrateful towards Australia. Some folks, typically online, say that I have more support than I know. Others, usually Australians I bump into on the street, or at literary events, tell me they think I should have stayed. I understand why people think that. I would probably have thought the same thing, had I not been in my shoes.

I leave Australia different to the person I would have been, if I had left any earlier. My mother says it was meant to be. She says that Allah needed me to go through this experience. That I was being prepared for something. That I need to be who I am now for what lies ahead.

I believe in fate, so I believe that there might be some truth in that. Leaving is how I fight what is too big for me to face front on. When a large, powerful force comes up against a small, passionate dissenter, a face-to-face confrontation will always favour blunt, brute strength. One of the most effective options the dissenter has is to disengage and find another angle of attack; one that favours her, the smaller, nimbler actor.

When the game is rigged, perhaps you're playing the wrong game. Leaving, for me, is not an act of giving up. Leaving is strength.

It is reclaiming my time. It is choosing the game I want to play.

Life was easier
before I was 'woke'

Published in 2019 as part of the British anthology It's Not About the Burqa.

When the opportunity arises to be part of an anthology of essays by Muslim women, it's impossible to resist the call. Our cups are overflowing with life to explore, but there are so few occasions to do so wholly on our own terms that to squander the chance would be folly. Yet, the prospect presents an unanticipated obstacle. When writing as a Muslim woman among other Muslim women, one is no longer bound by the broad, representative, generic sentiments so often expected of us and that, despite our best efforts, we often find ourselves sticking to. Being among peers asks us instead to delve into the granularity of our experiences as Muslim women beyond the obvious. In some ways, the obvious conversations are the easy ones. We know what is expected, and what an audience unfamiliar with nuanced perspectives of Muslim women will be comfortable with. Though that narrative is achingly tired, alternatives are few and far between. The space we are allowed to take up is so limited, it leaves little room for the ribbons of our voices to unfurl.

With that in mind, I have decided to take this opportunity to not talk to an 'issue' per se, in the same way I usually choose to, when speaking to a non-Muslim audience. Instead, I'm interested in meandering through my personal journey as a Muslim woman in a non-Muslim (and often a non-female) world. Because, I am the holder of an unpopular opinion: things were a lot easier when I wasn't 'woke'.* Or perhaps they were easier because of this.

What was easier? What am I talking about? Well, perhaps to explain, we need to take a few steps back. Let's set the scene.

My name is Yassmin Midhat Abdel-Magied, of the Hassan Bey Abdel-Moniem family. I was born in the year 1991, in Khartoum, Sudan, as the city was reeling from its most recent (and most recently successful) coup. By 1992, my family had made the move to a small city in Australia: Brisbane. Faiza and Midhat, my parents, were part of a wave of educated Sudanese that had left their nation due to the change of government. My parents' move, though new and life-changing for our particular family, was nothing unique. We were part of the quintessential migrant phenomenon: the search for a new life beyond a repressive post-colonial regime.

My family were one of the first few Sudanese in Brisbane, and with that came privilege: we were a 'founding family' for the North African migrant community. A number of things reinforced that position of privilege: our early arrival, mama and baba's thriving in a system not built to support them, and qualifications that included an advanced diploma, two undergraduate degrees, four master's degrees, and a PhD (mashallah!). Although

---

* I've never self identified as 'woke', despite the worthy origins of the term (see 'Words mean things', on p. 6). However, for the purposes of this piece, 'woke' is the past tense of 'awake', and also a little tongue in cheek!

we may not have been afforded traditional positions of authority and esteem within broader mainstream society, we were creating new traditions and developing a sense of belonging in a new home. Unbeknown to us, that is one of the ways communities and individuals heal from intergenerational trauma. By taking an active role in defining who we now were, my parents were creating a blueprint for my brother and me to follow: you can choose how to live your life, even when you are completely different from the norm. The method was simple: *Don't pay attention to your difference. Do what you want to do.*

I absorbed this slightly naive lack of self-awareness and in essence, it became armour. I truly believed that I was an equal in all the spaces I entered. Being female, a migrant, an African and a Muslim meant I was often the only one deviating from the norm in a room. And yet I believed that all the stereotypes, biases and assumptions associated with those identities were irrelevant to me. That is why, when, during university, I decided my dream was to work in Formula 1, it seemed like an entirely plausible endeavour. I found people's excitement about the novelty of it all quite humorous. And anyway, my ambition bore fruit: I was accepted onto an exclusive Master's in Motorsports program and offered work experience at Mercedes F1 in the United Kingdom. Unfortunately, the pesky reality of unpaid internships and the appropriate visa nipped that dream in the bud, and so I found myself back in Brisbane, the possessor of a first-class honours engineering degree and a virtual Rolodex of contacts in the motorsport world, but no income stream and no foreseeable way to a job in my industry of choice. The only answer that seemed obvious and within my control? A job on the rigs.

I knew I wanted to work on Australia's oil and gas rigs from the day I saw the stall at my university's careers fair in my first year of study. As a budding mechanical engineer, it appeared to combine all my loves: enormous equipment, adventure, travel. Four years later, when the time came to apply for that 'real job', I emailed the man I had met at the fair and asked if his company had any positions for someone like me: smart, accustomed to working with their hands, willing to travel anywhere in the world. My heart leapt when his reply included an invitation to an interview.

'You know you're our first female field engineer?' my new boss said to me at the end of the interview. We were sitting across the desk from one another, and he'd just offered me a job. I nodded, unfazed. Cool . . .?

'Do you need any . . .' he hesitated. 'Specialist equipment, seeing as you're a woman?' His thick Glaswegian accent did not hide his discomfort, though I wasn't sure why he would be feeling that way. I laughed in response. 'Yeah, I mean, do you have women's clothing? I hate having to fit myself into men's trousers, they don't really work for my body.'

My manager's face creased into a frown. He clearly wanted to show support but didn't actually have the capacity to follow through on any request I might have. I picked up the standard men's uniform a few days later.

The second conversation of this sort happened on the drive to my first rig, my colleague behind the wheel. Earl looked at me out of the corner of his eye. He opened his mouth to start a sentence, then closed it. A moment later, he tried again. No sound. 'Earl, are you okay?'

'Yassmin . . . listen. I've never worked with a woman before.'

Again, I laughed. These men were so worried! What for?

'I mean . . . we work with pretty heavy equipment. Are you going to be able to . . . lift the tools?'

I looked at Earl, throwing some of the shadiest side-eye I've ever thrown. I'd been going to the gym and lifting weights since I was twelve years old. I'd held the bench press record for my age group at school. I was much, much larger than Earl.

'Earl . . . You're a Filipino man half my size. I can lift you up!'

Earl smiled, uncomfortable and tight lipped, then fell silent.

I looked out of the window at the desert passing by, my eyes unfocused, the conversation almost completely forgotten. *This is going to be fun*, I thought. *I can't wait to show them how wrong all their assumptions are!*

I had no reason to believe that I should be treated any differently from my co-workers, no reason to think that my experience in the workplace would be any different from my life in school and university. Boy, was I wrong.

The rigs were a different world. During my undergraduate studies, I felt the power dynamic between my peers and me was fairly even, or at least manageable. Ultimately, I was competing with my fellow students on grades, and I'd spent enough quality time with professors, tutors and classmates to create the human-to-human connections needed to overcome any bias and prejudice they might have had. At work, however, who I was came with no inherent power. I was a young, female graduate in a hyper-masculine working environment, and a clear deviant from 'the norm'. It was becoming obvious that there was a chasm between my understanding of my place in the world and the reality of it. Here, on rigs in the middle of the desert and ocean, my process of awakening would begin. This change would take time.

Anne Summers, a prominent Australian feminist, once said to me that young women don't think they need feminism until they have a child. The implication was that having a child is a life stage when the difference between women and their male colleagues becomes irrefutable. The conversation occurred a number of years ago, before feminism enjoyed the resurgence in the popular consciousness that it's going through today. Her statement bore some truth, but in my case, it wasn't having a child that spurred my belief in the cause. Rather it was my entrance into a space where my gender was inescapably obvious and so unarguably different from the accepted norm that something was going to have to change. To nobody's surprise except my own, the environment I moved into didn't change; I did. I fell into the pattern of so many female engineers before me, who did what they could to survive.

Research by Deneen M. Hatmaker at the University of Connecticut published in 2013 shows that women in engineering tend to fall within two main categories when dealing with the male dominance of the workplace: coping mechanisms and/or impression management.[1]

Internal coping mechanisms include 'blocking' and 'rationalising'. Blocking involves using verbal blocks of any kind to stop any mention of gender or gender identity. This serves the purpose of bringing one's professional identity to the foreground, and attempts to prevent any gendered biases, expectations or stereotypes affecting an interaction. Rationalising is a more cognitive process whereby female engineers convince themselves that they're 'okay with' unfair or discriminatory behaviour. Importantly, these techniques help with coping (they help the engineer – me – feel better about the situation), but rarely change long-term behaviour in any substantive manner. 'He's an old man, of course he would say that about women,' I'd say to myself. 'Oh, they didn't mean it like that!' 'They're teasing me because I'm now part of the group.' 'I'm not like other girls, I can hack it!' 'It's no big deal . . .'

I fell into the rationalising category, hard. It was easy to do: when trying to fit into a group, where you're the only one who is 'different' and when your income is dependent on being accepted, there is an enormous amount you can rationalise to yourself. It also helps if you're unaware of the biased dynamics at play. Only in the years since I left the rig have I been able to consider – and admit to myself– that some of the behaviour I encountered was unprofessional and inappropriate at best, and sexual harassment at worst. At the time, I was able to rationalise almost all of it away.

Impression management, the second category of survival strategy, I also used in spades. The two techniques within impression management, according to Hatmaker, are 'proving oneself' and 'image projection'. Both of these are 'external facing' strategies that try to influence the perception of others. Proving oneself is as simple as it sounds: being so good that you outperform your gender, or, ostensibly, your entire identity. The ultimate achievement is to be recognised as a technical expert.

On the other hand, image projection involves women typically choosing to project a 'gender neutral' version of themselves. Hatmaker did identify some cases that provided hope: when impression management embraced 'gender ownership', the women were coping by owning their gender and projecting positive aspects of being a 'woman engineer'.

This, of course, is the most successful strategy in the long term. Women feeling comfortable enough to project an image that being female is positive, where it is currently seen as a negative, or at best neutral, can only be beneficial. However, it requires a lot of work – internally and externally. 'Identity work' is an extensive and exhausting process, and many women – and any group that doesn't enjoy the power and individuality of being in the dominant demographic – are doing this work at all times. It is no wonder that the retention of female employees in STEM (science, technology, engineering and mathematics) is dismal: after twelve years, 50 per cent of women in STEM will have left their jobs, compared to 20 per cent of women in other professions. Most of those leave in the first five years.[2]

It's much simpler to navigate a world that you believe is level, and where your individual actions define the opportunities you have to progress and succeed. It gives you a sense of power, and control. Choosing to see otherwise – to think of yourself operating within a system that sees you as a sum of one-dimensional, inferior identities – can be, and often is, overwhelming. So, I resisted.

I pushed back against the idea that I might be faced with racism, sexism or discrimination. Look at my privilege, I would say. My education, my class, my lightness of skin tone. If people pointed to the specific experiences of others, I believed that I could continue to do what I had always done: rise above. Naivety, arrogance, or an unexpected blessing in disguise? Either way, the belief took root because I wasn't aware.

I was unaware of the impact of history on my current existence. I was incognisant of the systemic inequalities that exist. I was ignorant to the cunning adaptability of the system, which learnt to use the example of the exception to make liars of those who dare shine a light on the true nature of the rules. Oh, how I believed! I was curious, but not curious enough: I had yet to entertain the thought that I should never need to earn my equality. I was starting from a basis of believing that I needed to earn my right to be seen as equal. A heartbreaking admission, in hindsight. But alas, we all start our journeys into consciousness at different points, and my time was fast approaching. I distinctly remember the moment I began to realise 'gender ownership' was an option for me, marking the beginning of my journey of awakening. At the time, I was a year and a half into working as an operator on rigs in Western Queensland and the South Australian desert. It was hot – temperatures above 40°C were typical – and grittily dusty. Insects thickened the air, colliding into us and each other with pure abandon. I was sitting next to a colleague of mine in our 'donga', a refurbished shipping container that doubled as our office while we were on site. My colleague, an old friend from university, was a jovial and straightforward character. Although I was in a supervisory role on site, our relationship was friendly and collegiate.

Our conversation had turned to a comment one of the men had made about me, somehow referencing my gender. I couldn't tell you what the remark was; all I remember was being furious that he kept mentioning the fact that I was a woman. 'Why do you get so mad anytime anyone mentions that you're a chick?' my mate asked, abruptly. 'Like, I mean – you are one, right?' I nodded, unsure where the conversation was turning. My forehead creased as I tried to parse the meaning behind his words.

'Well, why don't you just, I dunno, embrace it or something? I mean, I don't know what it's like to be a woman, but surely there are some advantages to it? Why don't you, like, just focus on them?'

The question stunned me. Bizarrely, I had never thought to see my gender as an inherent advantage before. Paradigm-shifting moments don't often come in a neat package, yet mine came in the form of a simple question from a Measurement-While-Drilling operator on a rig in Western Queensland. It planted a seed: perhaps I didn't need to think of my difference as something needing to be compensated for. I could be proud of my difference, wholly and fully. In a way where I wasn't confined by borders drawn by others, but where I took ownership and chose to define the space I wanted to take up myself.

As I would later learn, this idea was dangerous. Fully taking up space, in a way where my equality was not conditional on good behaviour – oh! This belief would lead me down the most diffi-cult path I'd ever walked.

As for the details of that story? Ah ... there are a number of other essays in this collection dedicated to what happened to Yassmin Abdel-Magied in 2017. I had, up until then, been the Model Minority™, but with a single Facebook post I suddenly became the Controversial Muslim Activist™. To say it was a shock to the system would be like calling Hurricane Katrina 'a bit of a breeze'.

Mine was a virtual public lynching, constituting a Murdoch-press character assassination and months of attack by the conservative government, ostensibly on the basis of my identity as a Muslim migrant. And I faced it without the backing of my employers, my university or any of the major organisations for which I had volunteered or that had given me awards over the years – the very same institutions that had benefited from my Model Minority™ performance to date. The people who did have my back were the creatives – writers, artists – those who were already awake.

For me, 2017 fed the seed of change planted on the rigs with steroid-infused fertiliser. The kernel grew into a thick stem of understanding, irrevocably transforming my conception of the world. You see, although I'd had a paradigm shift with respect to gender, I had yet to apply that perspective to other facets of my identity treated with bias: faith, migration status, race. It took losing everything – my public standing, my job, my safety – to fully comprehend the scope of the lesson I had learnt. I could no longer accept the conditional equality that I had been socialised to be grateful for. I would accept nothing less than substantive, transformative and unconditional equality, for myself and for others. If we are equal in the eyes of the Lord, how can anyone allow otherwise? This was what I would now fight for, until my dying day, inshallah.

Once you have begun the journey of awakening, there is no turning back. Your eyes have been opened to the ways of the world. These are forces not easily unseen. With the burden of knowing comes a freedom, bittersweet. At least, it did for me. The pressure to be enough: gone. The pressure of earning equality: lifted. I realised by accepting this reality I had unknowingly centred somebody else's rules, instead of following my own. My rules are those of my faith, and they require me to answer to nobody except the Almighty. Sweet, these freedoms, yes. But the aftertaste is bitter, because in order to undergo the process of change, one needs to recognise and name the problem. Constantly doing that is exhausting. Engaging with and understanding the structural nature of inequalities in the world is crushing, and it's not just the weight on one's shoulders. Sometimes it feels as if my very bones are heavy; the marrow weighed down with lead. Truth has turned my soul's light spirit into the viscous tar of molasses. Opening your eyes to the light can help you see, but it can also blind you. That is not the fault of the light, but our bodies can only carry so much, and our eyes cannot continue to see without blinking.

And so, I search for the middle ground. Seeing, with the respite of the blink. And my journey is not nearly complete – for that would mean a finished product, which I am far from being. I am on a journey of awakening to the world around me; a constantly evolving project taking into account where I have come from and where I might, inshallah, go. That's why the space to talk about different realities for Muslim women is so important. Our lives are not uniform. My story is not representative; it is simply my own. It is not a reflection of anyone else's truth. It does not cancel another's pain or want to be seen as more than what it is.

Mine is one person's lived experience. An experience full of contradictions, imperfections and incongruities, but my lived experience nonetheless. Part of the journey, for me, is owning these inconsistencies in myself and my stories – we cannot change our past perspectives, but we can certainly reflect on them, own them, and commit to growing from them. We must cultivate compassion for our past selves, trusting that we did the best we could at the time, while simultaneously striving to do better.

I did say it was easier, back when I wasn't awake. I didn't say it was right.

I wanted to make jokes
about my destroyed career,
but all I felt was grief

This is an edited version of a speech given at the Melbourne Writers Festival event 'Eulogy for My Career' on 26 August 2018.

I recently spent some time in my childhood home of Brisbane, returning for the first time since I'd moved to London in 2017. As we drove around the soft bend leading up to my family's double brick house, I couldn't help but reminisce. I'd travelled on this road many a time on almost all forms of transport: driving in my new Alfa Romeo at 3 am, sneaking back into the house from a late-night session (and by session I mean study session, okay?), walking to the bus stop when that Alfa Romeo lived up to its reputation by inevitably breaking down, running two-kilometre loops around the block when I was in that short-lived 'maybe-one-day-I'll-do-a-marathon' phase.

Sitting in the passenger seat of the family car, my younger brother grown and behind the wheel, watching the familiar houses and trees glide by, I grew nostalgic.

How was fifteen-year-old Yassmina to know, running around this block, that a decade later, these streets would hold more than simple, happy memories of early morning jogging sessions accompanied by the soundtrack of feet lightly padding along the pavement, neatly wrapped in the still silence of suburbia?

How was twenty-year-old Yassmina to know that five years later, her hard-won engineering degree would be the last thing that people knew about her, not the first? That six years later, she would have walked away from her dream of working on a Formula 1 team, been ushered out of her job on an oil rig, squeezed out of her newfound role as a TV broadcaster, her mental health spiralling, reputation in shambles, and with a Wikipedia page that mostly talked about 'controversies'?

How was twenty-six-year-old Yassmina to know that a year later she would be returning to the country of her citizenship to eulogise a career she didn't even know was coming to an end?

As my brother parked the black Honda Civic, I was overcome with a tidal wave of heaviness, a blanket made of lead that seemed to smother my soul. There was a strange metallic taste in my mouth that I couldn't quite name, and it wasn't until I lay in my bed that evening, the single bed I had lain in every night for over a decade, that it hit me. Moonlight was shining through the blinds, glinting on tears that threatened to spill. The weight was more than just jet lag – I was in mourning. What a strange feeling indeed.

I could feel my face furrowing as I tried to make sense of my emotions. I swallowed, allowing my tears to run down my cheeks and turn the pale pillow cover a darker shade of blue, and I attempted to reckon with reality. What was this deep, cavernous sense of loss that had opened up in my chest? What was this ache in my lungs, making every breath feel like I was drowning, trying to take in air through a snorkel that was rapidly filling up with water? Why did this whole house, this whole street, this whole city now feel foreign to me, like it was only a place I'd visited in my dreams?

This was grief, but it was not just my career I was grieving. I was grieving my past self. It was the baby Yassmina I had lost, a resolutely positive and perhaps mistakenly optimistic young person, a soul unburdened by the knowledge of what the world does to people who don't quite fit the mould and who want us all to be a little better. I had lost an innocence I didn't even know I had.

Is it better to have been innocent and lost it, than to not have been innocent at all?

I wanted this eulogy to be funny. I wanted to bid farewell to a Formula 1 career that waited for all the lights to turn on but never quite got off the starting mark. I wanted to say goodbye to a professional engineering pathway that many don't know the details of, but that makes me very proud. I wanted to commemorate a broadcasting job that took us all by surprise, as it turned out that I was halfway decent at it. I wanted to talk about the highs and the lows, the bits that make me laugh, the times that gave it all meaning. And there are lots of those moments. But when I sat down to write this eulogy, all that came out was grief.

It poured out of my fingers and soaked these pages, like rainwater in a drought-stricken desert. It's actually annoying, really. I'm quite tired of this grief business. I thought I had bid farewell to this traveller. But grief is a visitor that overstays its welcome, and no matter how much subtle hinting at the time, it's still splayed out on your couch, eating nachos and getting guacamole on your carpet. Turns out grief does what it wants, and pays no attention to schedules or social niceties.

Grief will turn up when you least expect it – you're on your way out to a dinner date, and ding-dong, there it is, at your door, walking in uninvited. You're having lunch with friends, and then poof! It apparates next to you and dominates the conversation for the next hour, paying no attention whatsoever to what you were talking about before. Hell, you could be watching *Happy Feet 2* on a plane, and grief will pop out of the oxygen compartment above, wave its hands in your face and make you miss the rest of the damn film. Not that I'm speaking from experience or anything.

Part of me also doesn't want this eulogy to be about anything at all, because that would be admitting that those past versions of myself are gone. Done, dusted, finito. I'm not sure I'm ready for that. Are we ever really ready to let go? That's the thing about death. It's kind of like grief. A terrible houseguest. It just turns up, and you're expected to have the kettle on and the right kind of biscuits on hand. I mean, c'mon man. Cut a sister a break! Send me a calendar invite or something at least, so I can make sure I'm presentable. But no. Death, pain, grief: the bloody three musketeers that they are, they give zero fucks about your plans. It's brutal, but I guess it's the only way to ever really level up in this life. If you don't know, now you know, sister.

In Islam, when someone dies, we say 'Ina lilahi, wa ina lani rajiun'. It roughly translates to: We are for Allah, and to him we shall return. I wondered if I could apply this to my past self, or my various iterations of careers, and then I mentally slapped myself for my indulgence. Girl, get a hold of yourself! You ain't dead yet! This is a eulogy for your career, you indecisive millennial, not you. You're still here, alive and kicking, Alhamdulilah, no matter how much some may wish otherwise. So act like it.

I got an Instagram direct message on Friday, just before I got the plane from London to Australia. It read as follows: 'My Name Is Nelson, and I'm a big fan. Do you mind if I ask just one favour? Please Reply, I love You.'

Then: 'Go to Flinders St Station, Cut Your Wrists and Let them bleed out so we can all watch you die. Lest We Forget. Hopefully I'll be able to distinguish you from all the other Sudanese Niggers, but I know you'll be the only ape wearing a ridiculous towel over your head.'

Nelson, I'm sorry to inform you that this specific favour will not be granted, darling boy, though I may be wearing a ridiculous towel on my head, because well, that's very on-brand. My past lives might be thoroughly dead, cooked, roasted, their remains served on a platter for all to feast on, but in this moment, I am not. I'm very much still alive, and that is a gift that I cannot bear to waste, and in the words of the great Hannah Gadsby, there's nothing stronger than a broken woman who has rebuilt herself.

I now think of the death of baby Yassmina as a controlled burn, in the tradition of the First Nations people who are the custodians of the land I once called home. They understood that sometimes for change and regeneration, you have to raze the existing growth to the ground and let the new take root. And oh, yes, those flames are searing and yes, sometimes, I still hear the crackle and pop of burning flesh.

But I'm starting to get used to it, as my careers have a habit of going up in flames. So why do I keep playing with fire? Well, perhaps my previous analogy was slightly off. This is no controlled burn, no regenerative wildfire. It appears that I live in a burning house. Death lives down the road, pain is my roommate and grief is always turning up uninvited. But we're friends now. We bicker, we fight, we make each other laugh. And I wouldn't be who I am today without them.

So bye bye baby Yassmina. Bye bye, straighty-180 engineer, toothy-smiled TV presenter, giggling Good Muslim Girl who thought that her trio posse of innocence, positivity and optimism were all she needed. I've got new friends now. But your old friends are welcome to visit, of course. Maybe, maybe they can even stay. Maybe, we can get to know each other. Come through, I'll put the kettle on.

Nostalgia, solastalgia

9 AUGUST 2021 08:41 AM – Paris, France – Sent from iPhone
@yassmin_a: COVID has messed w my friendships something fierce. I haven't seen some people for nigh on two years. So much has changed in their lives, and I haven't been there, really, for any of it. 1/?

9 AUGUST 2021 08:41 AM – Paris, France – Sent from iPhone
@yassmin_a: Friends in new relationships, their lustful crushes ripened beyond the initial excitement into mature partnerships, mundane routine; in love with people I've never met. New babies, no longer simply sleeping and suckling, now walking with words and wonder. My friends' infants are suddenly little humans. 2/?

9 AUGUST 2021 08:42 AM – Paris, France – Sent from iPhone
@yassmin_a: I speak not of the sharp edge of Covid loss, I know, but the accumulated grief of 'ambiguous loss', a quiet thief of joy . . . 3/?

9 AUGUST 2021 08:44 AM – Paris, France – Sent from iPhone
@yassmin_a: I miss my loved ones; their presence, laughter, the intimacy of knowing their everyday. I miss not worrying about

them, not reading between the lines of their messages, not creating storylines in my mind that drive wedges between us, hewed of problems that don't exist. 4/?

9 AUGUST 2021 08:45 AM – Paris, France – Sent from iPhone
@yassmin_a: I miss the friends that you meet at events or parties; never hanging out one on one, but in the right social setting . . . magic. 5/?

9 AUGUST 2021 08:45 AM – Paris, France – Sent from iPhone
@yassmin_a: I miss the colleagues who you bump into at a workplace, w little in common apart from a shared hatred of the printer or love of niche bikes, but whose quick hallway chat always brought sparks of light to your day. 6/?

9 AUGUST 2021 08:45 AM – Paris, France – Sent from iPhone
@yassmin_a: The coffee mates, the house party hosts, the gossip in the green room before an event . . . and everything in between. 7/?

9 AUGUST 2021 08:46 AM – Paris, France – Sent from iPhone
@yassmin_a: I fear I will be returning to friendships with folks whose lives have changed so much that it is almost as if we are starting anew. 8/?

9 AUGUST 2021 08:51 AM – Paris, France – Sent from iPhone
@yassmin_a I know that life is not meant to be easy, we are taught to ride the waves of change. But this? This unyielding tsunami, leaving us each isolated, all on our own journeys . . . that wasn't

how it was meant to go. Not even Frodo faced the darkness alone. 9/9

—

Sometime in the last two years, a seed lodged itself into a nook in my sternum, feeding on the loneliness that prolonged uncertainty brings. The seedling has since sprouted, its roots reaching down around my ribcage, whispering quietly, dangerously, towards the bloody, pulsing muscle nestled in my chest. I am afraid, it would seem. Of what, I do not know.

I tell myself I should have seen it coming.

It had warned me, gently, of its impending visit. It had sent messengers, coded canaries in various forms. Untimely tears bubbling to the surface in anodyne conversations on a recent film, a children's book. Unpredictable, crackling snaps of frustration that charged the air like static. The moods, swinging; a pendulum of serrated edges and unreasonable anger.

Have you ever been afraid of your own grief? I hadn't known I should be. I hadn't known it wasn't the loss that would hurt most, but what came after.

—

This was not the grief of a single, cavernous loss, a silent lightning strike that shatters foundations, cleaving your world in two. There was no beauty in this grief, no honour in facing it, no spectacle to be seen. Ambiguous grief, arising from a loss without closure, brought with it a quieter remorse, cloaked in velvet shadow, unnoticed by most. The slow leaking of my reserves of resilience, the dull throb of stolen time, of memories never made.

How do you speak of missing years of shared moments, from the intimacy of knowing the minutiae of your colleague's daily routine, to the transcendence of cradling your best friend's newborn, whispering in half-awed, half-joking tones: 'Can you believe we're the adults now?' The same best friend whose hair you held back as they discovered the limits of their alcohol tolerance over a chipped toilet bowl (your teetotaller duty) is now a mother. You beam. *Look how far we've come.*

But when you look around, you haven't gone anywhere at all. You *couldn't.* You saw only pictures, after, through a glowing screen, oceans away. It is all there is, you console yourself. It must be enough.

It is not.

A few more get married, another couple buy a house – a home? Some you have known almost all your life, others you have only just met. You watch from your studio, alone in yet another foreign country, wondering if they know you think of them, wondering if this counts.

What do you call the loss of something you never had, the nostalgia for something that never happened?

In Arabic, a word for 'love' and the word for 'seed', use the same two letters, 'ح' and 'ب'. The inflection varies slightly: 'حب', for love, asks you to pucker your lips into an 'o' shape, elongating the vowel before the word ends gently as your lips meet. With 'حب', your lips are to draw back, tongue pressing into your bottom teeth as you let out the first puff of a laugh before your lower jaw rises up, cutting the sound off with a bounce. The two words' roots are shared, as both a seed and love are inert pockets of potential without adequate nourishment to coax the beauty out of their shell. Water, soil, sun. Time, together.

What is friendship, if not bonds forged through experience and shared memory? What is there to remember in the absence of this essence?

—

At first, I chose not to pay attention. Perhaps I did not yet know how. But as the days melted into weeks, sliding sloppily into months – longer – the gnawing at the edge of my consciousness grew urgent, all-consuming.

The world narrowed, multilane highways becoming worn, one-way country lanes. 'We', who could afford to stay home, shared air with those we lived with, kept within walking distance of our front doors. 'We', who had access to the internet, stayed in contact via screens, telling ourselves this was just fine, just like before. 'We', who had a before, wept for what we had lost, consoling ourselves with the hopes of going back to 'normal'.

On occasion, I found myself silently, unexpectedly furious. *Why haven't they reached out*, a voice raged inside the chamber of my skull, not pausing to ask why I hadn't picked up the phone to check up on anyone myself. In quieter moments, I berated myself for this double standard, knowing my self-righteousness was cruel, unfair, born from the exhaustion of seclusion rather than any genuine injury. *I must try to be better* . . . but I did not know where to draw energy from. My cup had dried out, cracked, unfit for its primary purpose: holding water. In this grief, I was drained, rendered powerless.

Did they know I missed them, even if I did not call?

It had been so long since I hugged my mother, squeezed her thin frame, pressed her spectacled face into my chest, my chin resting on her oiled curls.

Does she know I think of her?

(Even when I do not call.)

(Especially when I do not call?)

I shared my grief on social media, beamed my emotions into little rectangles of light across the globe. 'It me', people said, sharing my words on their rented slips of the internet. Soon though, other perspectives joined the chorus; folks with disabilities, chronic illnesses and more, some of whom have never had the 'before' time that I so keenly cried out for. 'You know this is how we have always lived,' one commented, their rebuke deservedly sharp, pricking me with the needle of its truth. 'This just shows how much the wider world sees lives like ours as undesirable,' another said. My father reminded me the family in Sudan only got twelve hours of electricity that week, and there hadn't been running water for days. I swallowed the shame rising up my oesophagus. My desperation to not be wrong was cloying, but I had learnt to temper its excess. On this, I knew, I must pause. On this, I must resist the indefatigable desire to be seen as *good*. On this, I must listen.

'I'm sorry,' I say.

What else is there to say? Anything else seems trite.

I am yet to make sense of my own pain, but to be reminded that for others this has always been the way, there is no 'return' in sight to speak of . . . the taste of shame is burnt cardamom, bitter on my tongue.

A little perspective never hurt.

I am grateful, for their honesty.

Two gleaming drops form in the well of my cup.

—

Solastalgia.

I swirl the syllables in my mouth, the portmanteau of Latin *sōlācium* (comfort) and Greek *-algia* (pain).

Sol-as-tal-gia.

The last syllable comes out in a rush, my corrupted Australian accent flattening the modulation. Coined by philosopher and academic Glenn Albrecht in 2005, 'solastalgia' is described as 'the homesickness you have when you are still at home', the distress of our local habitat changing around us, primarily as a result of environmental change. I am introduced to the word in a conversation with a fellow resident at the Cité Internationale des Arts in Paris. We are both here for artist residencies, seeking time and space in the heart of the city to work on our craft. As a visual artist, she shares how she uses light, sound and other media to illustrate our connection with the natural world, or as her bio describes, 'creates moments of reflection regarding human agency within the built and natural environment'.[1] I later visit her exhibition at the Cité, titled 'Against our better nature'. The gleaming white walls display the uncanny-valley prints of seeds, digital records created through a study of electromagnetic radiant imagery, a process known as 'photogrammetry'. Whether the hyperreal details of a seed or the messages a tree sends to its shrubby neighbour, her work makes the natural world visible in new ways for our short-sighted selves.

Sol-as-tal-gia.

If our scientists are right, this is only the first global pandemic of the twenty-first century. There will be more, we are warned on our newsfeeds, these desperate calls presented alongside weight-loss advertisements and the latest viral TikTok dance, all judged equal in the courtroom of the algorithm. Although there is no direct evidence, the World Health Organization states, linking climate change and the emergence of COVID-19,[2] a clearer argument can be made for the link between the scale of the pandemic and globalisation, the very interconnectedness that allows me to live the kind of life I do. 'Globalization has emerged as an essential mechanism of disease transmission,' note researchers in a COVID-focused scientific journal edition published in December 2020.[3] That said, we don't yet know what the longer-term impact of this pandemic will be on our current economic, political and social world order.

It might be a stretch to say this modern plague has presented me with my first real taste of solastalgia, for the concept of 'homesickness' has never quite made sense to me in the first place. I have never quite known what 'home' I should be longing for. Yet the term has buried itself in the folds of my mind, wormed its way into my dreams. It speaks to something profound, the nebulous sense of grief, sorrow and heartache that we are collectively facing, in profoundly different ways. Perhaps 'homesickness at home' is the best fit for when home is everywhere and nowhere, simultaneously.

It dawns on me that the 'after' I am looking forward to might no longer exist. Too much has changed, our planet amongst it.

Homesickness while one is still at home. And yet . . .

I speak to friends and family, leaning on their expertise as climate scientists, nurses, doctors. I am struck, time and time again, by their optimism, their hope. I wonder, can they face all the types of grief there are and not fold at the knees, folded in two, three, more, by the weight of what we must do?

—

10 AUGUST 2021 07:31 PM – Paris, France – Sent from iPhone
@yassmin_a: I have been making the same three dishes
since March 2020
the taste of red lentils
just doesn't hit like it used to
my mother lives too far away

I share my grief on social media, and my friends call.

I watch their names light up through the block of aluminium, tempered glass and rare earth metal I hold in my palm.

I answer.

I fold, in two, three, more, as we hold our small 'g' grief together.

A few more drops form in my cup.

Sometimes I dream

Sometimes I dream
but
this is no March on Washington

I dream of the mob
but
this is no family affair

I dream of
being run over
as I stand in an empty road
(they made good on their word)
I dream of
bonnet colliding with legs
as I stand   alone   in an empty road

it's silent as I
replay the moment, my dream   g l it chin g

the crashing into the back of my knees
  buckling
    shattering
      splintering of bone

their faces behind the wheels

    smiling

    is a smile always sunnah?

Sometimes
the dream is different

Now
there are two cars
coming from   either side, they
        squeezeme
between their bumpers, then e s r e v e r
round two

I see them in my mind's eye, as I lay spread eagled

then—

there are no cars, only the mob, r
                                  e
                                   i
                                    g
                                     n
                                      i
                                       n
                                        g
                                         d o w n

they punish me for
   speaking
      believing
         existing?

their fists and fits and bats and stabs, I
feel their   hunger (saliva, dripping)
hear their   bellows (dark, braying)
smell their   bloodthirst (scarlet, scorching)

as they beat me, I
curl up into a tight ball, I
bury my face in my stomach, I
pray
protect my vital organs
prepare for death

Ashadu (I bear witness)
Ana la ilaha ilaha ila Allah
Ashadu (I bear witness)
Ana Mohammed rasul Allah

I bear witness

I feel no pain in my dream, only relief
maybe if I die at the hands of the mob,
maybe they will finally believe it was real
maybe if my body lay bruised, bloody, burnt
maybe it won't happen again?

in my dream, I argue with myself
you have delusions of grandeur, I say
no one cares enough to want to kill you (anymore)

it's only when I wake up that I wonder
why I think care only shows up in the clenched fist of death

even in my dreams, no one is coming   to save me.

PART TWO
Systems
and Society

Empowerment v Power

My father was always a believer.

'Empower the people,' he would say, between mouthfuls of rice and mula7*, the red mincemeat stew we had for dinner anytime my mother chanced upon the secret ingredient in a local store (dry okra powder was a rare treasure in the 2000s Brisbane burbs). 'Empower the people and they will do the rest,' he preached from his dinner-table pulpit. Whether the issue was youth unemployment, mental health or poverty, *empowerment* was my father's magic salve to heal all wounds.

I would nod, listening attentively to his nightly sermons, sitting between my unimpressed mother ('He's been saying the same thing for the last twenty years') and a younger brother itching to escape ('Mama, can I go now?'). I, on the other hand, couldn't get enough of The Midhat Show. Whether it was the United States's invasion of Iraq in 2003 ('Mark my words, this will come back to bite them in ten years, fifteen max!'), Sudan's complex political landscape ('Never trust al-Akhwaan'**) or how much one should

---

* When Arabic words are written with the Roman alphabet, numerals are used to translate sounds that don't exist in English.

** Arabic for 'the Muslim Brotherhood', a political movement founded in Egypt.

save of their pocket money every fortnight, my father's analysis served as my true north, his words all but unimpeachable.

It wasn't quite 'pull yourselves up by your bootstraps' rhetoric, but the concepts were close cousins. For a man born in Dresden, spending his formative years under the bite of East German communism while his own father completed an engineering doctorate, the individualistic emphasis is perhaps of little surprise. That said, my father understood that resources were required: community support, government funding, a mentoring system, *something*. Teach a woman to fish, then empower her to feed herself by gifting the fishing rod (what use is the knowledge without the tools?). But if she knows how to fish, and she's still hungry – in my father's reading – then that was her responsibility.

This concept became the keystone to my understanding of social change, so embedded in my approach that it emerged in my organisation's mission statement for the next decade. When I founded Youth Without Borders at sixteen, our mission was to 'empower young people to work together for the implementation of positive change in their communities'. *Empower* took pride of place, front and centre. I had not yet learnt to question it.

We empowered young people in Indonesia and Sudan by giving them access to books through mobile and school libraries, supporting their access to literature and educational resources. Through the Shinpads and Hijabs program, we worked with Football United to connect young girls at the local Brisbane Muslim school with Australian national champion soccer and futsal players, empowering them to pursue a sport regardless of stereotypes internalised or imposed. We set up a fully funded week-long experience known as the Spark Engineering Camp, where young people from historically marginalised backgrounds around the country were flown in for a fun week of learning and horizon-broadening.

It is likely of little surprise that for a bunch of teenagers, changing the world began with changing our local communities. The concept of 'structural' change hadn't entered our lexicon, and though I didn't quite believe that the world was fair, I did believe that we could trick it into working in our collective favour. It would be sometime before I learnt that we could not, in fact, *empower* ourselves out of every disadvantage. You can be the world's finest fisherwoman, with a state-of-the-art rod and the freshest bait in town, live worms like mie goreng in your tackle box, but if the river is poisoned, or turned into a dam, or made into private property, all your 'empowerment' is for nought.

Can you be blamed for your hunger? No.

But if people don't believe (or don't want to believe) the river has been contaminated, if they get electricity from the dam's hydropower, or they are made wealthy by the profits from selling the land, suddenly it becomes politically expedient to blame your fishing skills, your fishing rod – ultimately, you – for your hunger.

The existential challenge of climate change is a classic example of this dilemma: even if every single person in the United States became vegan overnight, left their trucks in the garage to go à pied, and only bought second-hand clothing, corporations would still be left producing the vast majority of global emissions. We cannot *empower* our way out of the climate crisis. We cannot *empower* our way out of white supremacy, heterosexism, patriarchy. We cannot *empower* our way out of systems of oppression, because by its very definition, oppression is 'the unjust or cruel exercise of authority or power'.[1]

As I wrote the first draft of this essay, news came in of the Taliban entering the presidential palace in Kabul. An old friend messaged me about her partner, stuck in the capital's airport, among fear, chaos, pandemonium, with thousands unable to leave, abandoned. History will judge, but it is moments like these, moments where personal empowerment is as significant as a flea in a firestorm, that remind me why focusing on the individual alone can never be enough.

My friend's partner was safe, in the end, Alhamdulilah. But many others were not. I found myself weeping for those I did not know, hot tears blurring my vision, dampening my face mask as I wandered through European streets in comparative safety. My privilege was jarring. How was I meant to make sense of the luck of the draw?

I shared my worries with another friend, a lawyer made pragmatic by family circumstances unimaginable to me. Her perspective took the long view, inspired by science fiction's hypotheses of humanity's state in the coming millennia. 'In the grand scheme of things, aren't we all insignificant?' she mused. 'We should just focus on being good to those around us, living good lives. Isn't that enough?'

She was not wrong, per se. In some ways, this position is even supported by my understanding of Islam. Our actions will be judged on intention, through what we can control, by how ethically we have lived our lives.[2]

But why, then, does focusing on my intentions, on my immediate surroundings, not feel enough?

There is a part of me that cannot sit with the inequality of the world, cannot abide simply accepting how the cards fall, without at least trying to do something about it. Even if my footprints in the sand are smoothed away by the tides of time, at least I will know I tried. So, the calculation becomes thus: if we accept our individual insignificance, how do we create any change? As the saying goes, 'If you think you are too small to make a difference, try sleeping with a mosquito.' The question is not if change can be made, but how.

Let us start, then, with the mechanism for change-making, with my father's favourite word. *Empower* clips the old French prefix 'em' (meaning in, into) to the front of the heftier, meatier *power*, a slippery word that defies glib, simple definition. Two letters, and whole worlds, separate the two.

In her recent book *The Purpose of Power*, co-founder of the Black Lives Matter movement Alicia Garza frames power as 'the ability to impact and affect the conditions of your own life and the lives of others'. She clarifies that it is an entirely different beast to the more individual form of the term. Empowerment, she says, 'is feeling good about yourself, akin to having high self-esteem ... unless empowerment is transformed into power, not much will change about our environments'.

In a keynote address to the Center for Justice and Peacebuilding at Virginia's Eastern Mennonite University, Garza framed power as the 'ability to make the rules, and the ability to shape the rules'. The idea stayed with me, marinating.

Power: the ability to affect the conditions of your own life, and the lives of others. Real life, tangible change, that is not situated only inside our psyches, but rather focused on material conditions, physical safety, deciding how we want to live our lives, on not being *controlled* by others. For someone for whom independence is part of their personality, for whom options in life have been narrowed and redirected by the bowling-alley gutter rails of historic structures and systemic oppressions, the idea of building power is . . . intoxicating.

But there is a part of me that fears being *too* powerful. I am not naive enough to believe that I am somehow immune to its corrupting influence. I come from Sudan, a country that has suffered from abuses of power by people who share my skin tone, mother tongue, and call themselves followers of my faith. Oppression has no preferred host, finding comfort in any warm fold of organic matter, its dark tendrils beguiling and strong. It bends itself into forms the host will allow, whispering sophistries, cogent and compelling: *If you don't do this, someone else will . . . It will be worth it in the end . . . Only the impotent are pure . . .*

My reticence towards building power also cloaks a trickier, uglier truth. It allows me to remain 'virtuous', wearing my self-righteousness like a warm blanket, wrapped and comfortable in my moral superiority. But like many ugly things in this world, my pharisaic leanings are born from fear: fear that I will try and fail, fear of turning into the very being I vow to oppose, fear that nothing will ever change.

My fear is natural. It would be arrogant to believe I am inherently predisposed to make better decisions than any other human. My fear arises from an understanding of the cruelties of the world; the depths of the challenges; the corruption, malice and greed hidden in almost every dark crevice, if you just go looking. Of course I am afraid. And yet, the blanket of self-righteousness grows heavy and ill-fitting; it itches on my skin, reeks of damp fur. What use is moral superiority in a flood? Isn't one of the marvels of humanity feeling afraid, and acting anyway?

Despite my stated fear, I am often told that I *have* accumulated significant swathes of power, and I wonder how the perception of others jars so sharply with my own. I see my precarity, whereas others see my stability. They focus on the beautiful cladding, while I obsess on the bamboo scaffolding propping up the façade. Both things can be true; in some ways power is both fragile and infrangible. It can seem permanent, then be extinguished in an instant. But, like dull embers, mere kindling can coax it back to roaring life. If we cannot empower our way out of structures of oppression, if we need *power*, how do I build it without being immobilised by my very own trepidation?

The dinner table sermons come flashing back. For all my parents' community work, for all their organising, debating and cajoling, the community meetings, the fallouts and the reconcili-ations, the disagreements, and the excitement, for every minute of every hour of every day I sat in an uncomfortable chair in a nondescript community hall, swinging my legs with a child's boredom and impatience, I do not remember my parents ever being interested in power for personal gain. Individual awards and recognitions were of little interest – even the ones I received – unless they came from peers, within the community, recognising a tangible impact in our people's lives. My reflections remind me of British psychotherapist and scholar Gail Lewis's remarks in a recent collection, *Revolutionary Feminisms*. She noted that 'even when [the young generation] do organise collectively, it's to gain a capacity to be more self-actualising in a neoliberal individual sense rather than actualising in a collective sense'.[3] Her diagnosis is damning, as she ascribes this shift to 'a marker of the success of the Thatcherite project, and of the success of "integration" at one level, ideological integration, even though they're still minoritised, still othered ... in terms of the indices of tribute, applaud, success, failure, they're just transformed'.

I think back to Youth Without Borders, and the joy of communal progress. We may have named it 'empowerment', but the culture within the organisation was resolutely collective, accumulating power between us in a flat hierarchy, profoundly uninterested in sophomania. We may not have had the sophistication required to campaign for long-lasting structural change, but we understood the symptoms of systemic injustice with the intimacy of those who lived it. On some level, we knew we had to be in it together.

When did that change for me? When did I start fearing power the way I fear it today, reluctant to be in its vicinity, lest I am contaminated by its festering tentacles? I wonder whether it began when I moved cities for the first time at the age of twenty-two, losing connection to a place that had grounded me for so long. I consider if it was linked to the rise of individualised technologies: social media platforms asking us to present versions of who we are to the world, incentivising self-centred versions of power through the attention economy. Conceived in 2007, Youth Without Borders never quite got the hang of social media, and although today, many collectives have found success through these ultra-modern digital technologies, they are not the intended users. These platforms are not designed around the needs of those who want to share power. But blaming digital platforms is easy.

They are amplifiers of pre-existing symptoms, magnifying an infection that has already taken root.

You want to know the real truth about Youth Without Borders? Running a volunteer youth organisation was *chaotic*. I have spoken of what we pulled off, but there was so much more that didn't quite pan out, or that blew up in our faces in fantastic, disastrous fashion. I would often be embarrassed that the collective we built was not one of perfect order, of enviable efficiency. But who among us has built power collectively with 'enviable efficiency'? In life, as in complexity theory, 'nonequilibrium is a source of order'. As physicist Fritjof Capra theorised, 'in living systems the order arising from nonequilibrium is far more evident ... Throughout the living world chaos is transformed into order.'[4]

And it is here, in complexity theory, that I find the beginnings of the answers I seek. Contemporary political scientists like Michael F. McCullough,[5] building on the work of 1977 Nobel Prize winner Ilya Prigogine, draw the physical and social sciences together to help us better understand the world we inhabit. A complexity theory of power offers an alternative way to understand the concept, for the simple binary has often felt deeply insufficient. How do I feel incredibly empowered in some ways, but profoundly powerless in others? On one hand, I am socially mobile, educated and assured. I work for myself and have my own voice. On the other, I am beholden to precarious visa conditions, legislated Islamophobia, entrenched misogynoir. I have hundreds of thousands of online followers, and yet still sometimes struggle to pay the rent. My Australian passport opens borders, while my Sudanese one does the opposite. How do I make sense of, as a comrade put it, being 'a complex intersection of privileges and oppressions'?

When thinking about power, I have often found myself trapped in the traditional, linear approach. Party A has power *over* party B, and for anything to change, party B needs to acquire power, likely directly from party A. In this Newtonian approach, order is based on an equilibrium. Order exists, but it is a mechanical, inhuman form, founded on an assumption of the *absolute power* of party A, and the *absolute obedience* of party B. Is this sustainable?

McCullough argues when there is no choice from party B's perspective, party A's exertion of power is in fact a *disorganising* process, akin to increasing entropy in a closed thermodynamic system. The implication is damning, suggesting that any order arriving from one party having total control over another is inherently unsustainable. The lack of choice itself disorganises. A linear expression of power will always have a shelf life.

If 'power-*over*', the lack of choice, controlled equilibrium, is unsustainable, what happens if you flip it; if you allow for choice, for the system to be open? Here is where complexity theory shines, encouraging us to think beyond nineteenth-century mathematical approaches and embrace the non-linear, the interconnected, the interdependent.

Prigogine's concept of the 'dissipative structure' demonstrates the possibilities. A 'dissipative structure' is simply one that is far, far from equilibrium, with both open and closing potential. Think: a hurricane. When travelling across land, a hurricane operates as an open system, constantly exchanging energy, matter and information with the external world. Prigogine would argue that this system has the ability to 'self-organise', by virtue of its openness, choice and state of non-equilibrium. You can see this when, eventually, hurricanes sort themselves out. They 'self-organise', turning a chaotic weather system into one of order.

So how would this work with people? Take, for example, a group of teenagers trying to tackle climate change. They start as individuals, spread across the world, loosely connected through similar actions. It's an open system: far from equilibrium, with plenty of choice. The openness and lack of order, rather than being a hindrance, is in fact what may allow them to succeed. This group of teenagers is constantly changing, learning, leaving, joining; the group boundaries in constant flux. Through this process, they learn to self-organise, adapting through feedback to each other and the world, regulating themselves, undergoing phases of stability, ever evolving.

In some social justice organisations, such as British trans-formation educators Fearless Futures, effective versions of self-organising are known as 'power-*with*': a shared process of collaboration, solidarity, influence and collective action. But power-with is not for the faint-hearted. It requires skill, self-awareness and a commitment to maintaining a delicate dynamic, instead of slipping into the linear, choice-less, power-over frame-work. The temptation to control is strong, but power-over is, and will always be, disorganising.

In this process of self-organising – or in a thermodynamic sense, as entropy (disorder) decreases – some systems can reach 'bifur-cation points', forks in the road in the journey towards organised complexity. If the group maintains power-with, they can evolve into 'more complex, more self-organised structures', i.e., they level up. If, however, they yield to the power-over temptation, things don't go as well. Scientifically, it is known as breaking down through 'thermodynamic closure'. The system stops interacting with the outside world in an enhancing way, becoming less self-organised and less complex. Put plainly, things fall apart.

But even in an open system that contains choice, self-organising is not automatically guaranteed.

We see bifurcation points like this all the time in systems, Tuckman's 'stages of group development' at scale. First proposed by American psychologist Bruce Tuckman in 1965, the model theorises the four phases a team inevitably goes through if it is to function effectively: forming, storming, norming and performing.[6] After the team forms, it 'storms', a process through which power and status are assigned. Here, disagreements and conflicts may arise, and we find the moments of bifurcation, potential forks. If all goes well, the group moves on to 'norming'[7] and 'performing'. The dust settles, and the group turns to focus on achieving their common goals. If it doesn't, the team will disorganise and will likely eventually fail.

One such bifurcation point occurred in Youth Without Borders, after our second successful year of running the Spark Engineering Camp. There was a moment of potential mutiny, where a particular volunteer's actions threatened to break the organisation down, split it into pieces, diminish its complexity and therefore its potential. By working through it, by ensuring we remained open and adaptive, and resisting the temptation to punitively shift to power-over, we were able to keep the project together. The process itself strengthened our ability to self-organise, and ultimately, grow.

The process was both an exercise of power-with, and also *empowering*. We worked together to shape the rules of the organisation, to achieve the results we wanted for our community: a certain (in both meanings of the word) exercise of power. In doing so, I felt *good*, confident, grounded: undeniably empowered. Indeed, reflecting on it now, it made me wonder if my binary approach and perspective had been missing something all along.

Rather than unilaterally decide on the destination, decry the idea of 'empowerment', or dismiss individualisation as inherently incompatible with social progress, I wonder if it is more useful to zoom out every so often, and reflect on the dynamics of each particular system. Rather than asking, Are they doing it the way I think is right? – a desire borne of power-over – I should ask, Is this still an *open system*? Are we still learning and evolving? Is there still choice, collaboration, a functional feedback loop that is enriching?

Thinking of power as the energy which pulses through a system in flux, self-organising through complexity, I find myself unexpectedly reassured. This is not a power to be feared, not the pressure cooker of a closed thermodynamic system reliant on control and obedience. This is more a reflection of the natural world, the shifting of the tides and the cycles of the seasons. There is no 'destination'; instead, there is the constant exercising of choice, the understanding of our role in the system, and a responsibility to stay *open*. That, I can certainly do.

What does my headscarf mean to you?

Originally performed at TEDx Brisbane in December 2014, the talk I am perhaps most well known for today was never planned. On my way to meet the organiser of the event at the bustling café next to the recently renovated State Library of Queensland, I had become irritated by an experience that I needed to get off my chest before I could begin to pitch my idea. Throwing myself into the too-small seat, I shook my head.

'You won't believe it,' I muttered. 'I got on the bus this morning to do an errand, and I was wearing this exact same scarf, but wrapped in a turban. Everyone was so nice to me, you know? And then, I got on the same bus, at the same bus stop, wearing the same scarf but just wrapped differently, wrapped like this—'

[my hijab was tied in a traditionally Arab manner, the long rectangular cotton piece wrapped around my head leaving my face framed in a neat oval]

'—and everyone treated me completely differently! The bus driver didn't even smile, the shop keeper turned his eyes away from me . . . I'm wearing the same piece of cloth, but I'm seen completely differently!'

I grumbled for a few more minutes, and then, rant over, I filled my

*belly with air and let it out in a huff. Turning to the official business,
'So, about my talk—'*

The organiser interrupted me. 'Yassmin, that is your talk!'

I didn't understand her point. 'Excuse me?'

*'That is your talk! You can tell that story, about how people see you
so differently based on the way you tie your scarf, better than anyone
else. That's your talk . . .'*

*I raised my eyebrows, pondered, then left to put together a thirteen-
and-a-half-minute TEDx talk that would have transformative power
far beyond my imagining. A few months later, it would be selected for
the global TED platform, then chosen as one of TED's Top Ten Ideas
of 2015. At the time of writing, it has been viewed over 2.5 million
times and helped usher the idea of 'unconscious bias' into mainstream
conversations around the globe.*

—

*[I walk onto the stage wearing an abaya, the long plain black flowing
gown favoured by Arab women in the United Arab Emirates and
Saudi Arabia. It is my mosque outfit.]*

Someone who looks like me walks past you in the street. Do
you think they're a mother, a refugee or a victim of oppression?
Or do you think they're a cardiologist, a barrister or maybe your
local politician? Do you look me up and down, wondering how
hot I must get or if my husband has forced me to wear this outfit?
What if I wore my scarf like this?

*[At this point, I pick up the edge of my scarf, hanging loose, and use
it to cover my nose and mouth, resembling a niqab.]*

I can walk down the street wearing the exact same outfit and
what the world expects of me and the way I'm treated depends

on the arrangement of this piece of cloth. *[I point to the hijab on my head.]* But this isn't going to be another monologue about the hijab, because Lord knows, Muslim women are so much more than the piece of cloth they choose – or not – to wrap their head in. This is about looking beyond your bias.

What if I walked past you dressed like this and later you'd found out that actually I was a race car engineer, and that I designed my own race car and I ran my university's race team? Because it's true. What if I told you that I was actually trained as a boxer for five years? Because that's true, too. Would it surprise you? Why?

Ladies and gentlemen, ultimately, that surprise and the behaviours associated with it are the product of something called unconscious bias, or implicit prejudice. And that results in the ridiculously detrimental lack of diversity in our workforce, particularly in areas of influence. Hello, Australian Federal Cabinet.

Let me just set something out from the beginning: unconscious bias is not the same as conscious discrimination. I'm not saying that in all of you, there's a secret sexist or racist or ageist lurking within, waiting to get out. That's not what I'm saying. We all have our biases. They're the filters through which we see the world around us. I'm not accusing anyone; bias is not an accusation. Rather, it's something that has to be identified, acknowledged and mitigated against. Bias can be about race, it can be about gender. It can also be about class, education, disability. The fact is, we all have biases against what's different; what's different to *our* social norms.

But if we want to live in a world where the circumstances of your birth do not dictate your future and where equal opportunity is ubiquitous, then each and every one of us has a role to play in making sure unconscious bias does not determine our lives.

There's a really famous unconscious bias experiment in the space of gender in the 1970s and 1980s. Orchestras, back in the day, were made up mostly of dudes. Up to only 5 per cent were female. And apparently, that was because men played music differently, presumably better. Presumably. But in 1952, The Boston Symphony Orchestra started an experiment.[1] They started blind auditions. Rather than having a face-to-face audition, you would have to play behind a screen. Now, funnily enough, legend has it no immediate change was registered until they asked the auditioners to take their shoes off before they entered the room, because the clickety-clack of the heels against the hardwood floors was enough to give the ladies away.

Now after this, researchers looking at blind auditions on the gender composition of five major US orchestras (through data from auditions and rosters) found that using a screen led to a 50 per cent increased chance a woman would progress past the preliminary stage. And it almost tripled their chances of getting picked at the final round.[2] What does that tell us? Well, unfortunately for the guys, men actually didn't play differently, but there was a perception that they did. And it was *that* bias that was determining their outcome.

What we're doing here is identifying and acknowledging that a bias exists. And look, we all have bias. Let me give you an example. A son and his father are in a horrible car accident. The father dies on impact and the son, who's severely injured, is rushed to hospital. The surgeon looks at the son when they arrive and says, 'I can't operate.' Why? 'The boy is my son.' How can that be? Ladies and gentlemen, the surgeon is his mother. Now hands up – and it's okay – but hands up if you initially assumed the surgeon was a guy? *[Hands go up in the audience.]* There's evidence that unconscious bias exists, and we all have to acknowledge that it's there and look at ways that we can mitigate it, work through it, find solutions.

Now, let's talk about quotas. Something that's often brought up is this idea of merit. People say, 'Look, I don't want to be picked because I'm a chick, I want to be picked because I have merit, because I'm the best person for the job.' It's a sentiment that's pretty common among female engineers that I work with and that I know.

And I get it, I've been there. But if the merit idea was true, why, in identical résumés sent out for a lab technician job, would there be a difference in perception between a 'Jennifer' and a 'John'? In an experiment done in 2012 by Yale, researchers created a fictional student and sent out said student's résumé to science professors at the top research-intensive universities around the United States for a lab manager position.[3] Participants in the study rated 'John' as significantly more competent, likeable and hireable than 'Jennifer'. 'John' was also offered a higher starting salary, and more career mentoring than 'Jennifer', who, remember, has *exactly the same résumé.*

The unconscious bias is there, but we just have to look at how we can move past it.

And, you know, it's interesting, there's some research that talks about why this is the case and it's called the 'merit paradox'.[4] And – this is kind of ironic – in organisations that talk about merit being their primary value-driver in terms of who they hire, they were more likely to hire dudes and more likely to pay the guys more, because apparently merit is a masculine quality. But, hey.

So you guys think you've got a good read on me, you kinda think you know what's up. Can you imagine me running one of these? *[I point to a photo of a large offshore oil rig.]*

Can you imagine me walking in and being like, 'Hey boys, this is what's up. This is how it's done.' Well, I'm glad you can. Because ladies and gentlemen, that's my day job.

[At this point in the speech, I take my abaya off, and reveal I am wearing an orange jumpsuit – my oil rig uniform – underneath. I take off my hijab, and there is a bandana that I then cover with a green hardhat. I am 'transformed'.]

And the cool thing about it is that it's pretty entertaining. Actually, in places like Malaysia, having Muslim women on rigs isn't even comment-worthy. There are that many of them. But, it is entertaining.

I remember I was telling one of the guys on the rig, 'Hey, mate, look, I really want to learn how to surf.'

And he's like, 'Yassmin, I don't know how you can surf with all that gear you've got on, and I don't know any women-only beaches.' And then, the guy comes up with a brilliant idea. He says, 'I know, you run that organisation Youth Without Borders, right? Why don't you start a clothing line for Muslim chicks at beaches. You can call it Youth Without Boardshorts.' *[Laughter.]* Thanks, guys. I remember another bloke telling me that I should eat all the yogurt I could because that was the only 'culture' I was going to get around there.

Bit cheeky maybe, but the problem is, it's kind of true because there's an intense lack of diversity in our workforce. Now, in 2010, the Australian National University did an experiment where they sent out 4000 identical applications to entry-level jobs.[5] To get the same number of interviews as someone with an Anglo-Saxon name, if you were Chinese, you had to send out 68 per cent more applications. If you were Middle Eastern – Abdel-Magied – you had to send out 64 per cent more, and if you're Italian, you're pretty lucky, you only have to send out 12 per cent more. In places like Silicon Valley, it's not that much better. Google put out some diversity results in March 2014 and it was 61 per cent white, 30 per cent Asian, the rest was a bunch of Black people, Hispanics, that kind of thing.[6] And the rest of the tech world is not that much better. They've acknowledged it, but I'm not really sure what they're doing about it.

But the thing is, equity doesn't trickle up. A study done in 2014 by Green Park, a British senior executive supplier company, found that over half of the FTSE 100 companies don't have a non-white leader at their board level, executive or non-executive.[7] And two out of every three FTSE 100 companies don't have an executive from a minority. Most of the minorities that are at that level are non-executive board directors, so their influence isn't that great.

I've told you a bunch of terrible things. You're like, 'Oh my god, how bad is that? What can I do about it?' Well, fortunately, we've identified that there's a problem. There's a lack of opportunity, and that's due, in part, to unconscious bias. But you might be sitting there thinking, 'I ain't brown. What's that got to do with me?' Let me offer you a possible answer. And as I've said before, we live in a world where we're looking for an ideal. If we want to create a world where the circumstances of a person's birth don't matter, we all have to be part of the solution. And interestingly, the author of the lab résumé experiment offered some sort of a solution. She said the one thing that brought the successful women together, the one thing that they had in common, was the fact that they had good mentors.

Mentoring. We've all kind of heard that before, it's in the vernacular. Here's another challenge for you. I challenge each and every one of you to mentor someone different to you. Think about it. Everyone wants to mentor someone who is kind of familiar, who looks like us, who has shared experiences. If I see a Muslim chick who's got a bit of attitude, I'm like, 'What's up? We can hang out.' You walk into a room and there's someone who went to the same school, plays the same sports, and there's a high chance that you're going to want to help that person out. But for the person in the room who has no shared experiences with you, it becomes extremely difficult to find that connection.

The idea of finding someone different to mentor, someone who doesn't come from the same background as you, whatever that background is, is about opening doors for people who couldn't even get to the damn hallway.

Because ladies and gentlemen, the world is not just. People are not born with equal opportunity. I was born in one of the poorest cities in the world, Khartoum. I was born brown, I was born female, and I was born Muslim in a world that is pretty suspicious of us for reasons I can't control. However, I also acknowledge the fact that I was born with privilege. I was born with amazing parents, I was given an education and had the blessing of migrating to Australia. But also, I've been blessed with amazing mentors who've opened doors for me that I didn't even know were there. A mentor who said to me, 'Hey, your story's interesting. Let's write something about it', so that I can share it with people. A mentor who said, 'I know you're all those things that don't belong on an Australian rig, but come on anyway.' And here I am, talking to you.

And I'm not the only one. There's all sorts of people in my communities that I see have been helped out by mentors. A young Muslim man in Sydney who ended up using his mentor's help to start up a poetry slam in Bankstown and now it's a huge thing. And he's able to change the lives of so many other young people. Or a woman here in Brisbane, an Afghan woman who's a refugee, who could barely speak English when she came to Australia. Her mentors helped her become a doctor and she took out the Young Queenslander of the Year Award in 2008. She's an inspiration.

[At this point, I disrobe one more time, taking off my offshore outfit to reveal a plain white blouse and blue trousers underneath. I am wearing khaki-coloured Nike wedge heels and earrings, the hardhat removed to leave the bandana and turban visible.]

This is me. But I'm also the woman in the rig clothes, and I'm also the woman who was in the abaya at the beginning. Would you have chosen to mentor me if you had seen me in one of those other versions of who I am? Because I'm that same person.

We have to look past our unconscious bias, find someone to mentor who's at the opposite end of your spectrum. Because structural change takes time – and I don't have that level of patience. If we're going to create a change, if we're going to create a world where we all have those kinds of opportunities, then choose to open doors for people. Because you might think that diversity has nothing to do with you, but we are all part of this system and we can all be part of that solution.

And if you don't know where to find someone different, go to the places you wouldn't usually go. If you tutor high school students in fancy private schools, maybe devote some of your energy to your local state school or drop into a local refugee tutoring centre. Or perhaps you work at an office. Take out that new grad who looks totally out of place – 'cause that was me – and open doors for them, not in a tokenistic way, not because we're victims and need to be saved, but because sometimes you have access to doors we don't even *know* exist. Whether it is vouching for someone in a promotions meeting, writing that reference letter or introducing them to a prospective new employer they wouldn't have met otherwise, sharing opportunities and opening up can truly change someone's world. You also just might realise how much exists in your world that so many others don't have.

Ladies and gentlemen, there is a problem in our community with lack of opportunity, exacerbated because of unconscious bias. But each and every one of you has the potential to change that. I know there are so many challenges in the world, and so much to do, but I implore you to find it in yourself to take on just this one piece, this one action item. Find someone in your world who is different from you, who you can open doors for, and do it. Do it without expecting gratitude, without expectation, but do it because well . . . diversity is magic! And there is something incredible about opening doors for folks and seeing what wonderful things can happen when you share opportunity.

And if that is too much to ask, then I will leave you with this: the next time you meet someone who dresses anything like me, try to look past your initial perceptions. Because, I bet you, they're probably wrong.

To the moon

A young woman's journey
into the world of cryptocurrency

Published in April 2019 in Griffith Review.

I'd like to believe that I wasn't jumping on the bandwagon. But don't we all tell ourselves little white lies to keep our self-worth intact?

It was November 2017. I was jolted awake by the rousing sound of a deliciously obnoxious four-stroke engine. The alarm clock sound, 'Motorcycle', blared out of my iPhone's speakers, an inch from my ear. I smiled sleepily to myself, my petrol-head craving pleasingly sated before I'd even thrown off my doona. Opening my eyes provided a little less joy: still dark outside. The jury remained out on whether my Sudanese-born, Brisbane-raised body would ever become accustomed to the European winter's apparent allergy to light. Sunlight – if any would be able to make its way through the dense layer of grey draped over the city – wouldn't make an appearance until well after 8 am. By then, though, it wouldn't matter much: I would be deep in the throes of my daily cryptocurrency market routine, a habit that had kept me company for the best part of six months.

My what?

You may have heard of cryptocurrency before. If not, you have probably come across a headline with the term 'bitcoin', the original 'crypto'. (I use 'crypto' for short, while knowing that cryptographers dislike the term because it confuses their profession with the volatile electronic asset class.) You may have even considered dabbling in investing yourself, and then talked to a financially savvy mate of yours who dismissed the whole thing as a fad.

So, what is bitcoin even about? Why would anyone be interested? And how on Earth did I, a woman with next-to-no interest in the financial sector, end up being a person with a morning cryptocurrency market routine?

It started with $200, curiosity, and a little too much spare time.

The end of 2017 marked a pivotal moment, both for me and the world of cryptocurrency. The bitcoin price was skyrocketing, making it nigh on impossible to escape the hype. Its reach was so absolute that my own financially disinterested mother was asking about buying bitcoin in the family WhatsApp group ('Do I keep them in the house?' she asked). I was on a wild ride of my own: coming off an incredibly tumultuous year and having recently arrived in London, I was settling in and up for trying new things. It was either get a haircut or start investing in cryptocurrency, I thought to myself, and figured I needed all the hair I could grow to keep me warm in the winter months. Cryptocurrency it was.

I really wanted to believe that I wasn't just following a trend; after all, I had heard about bitcoin in university circles way back in the early 2010s. But, like every other boisterous internet user who began buying bitcoin in the latter half of 2017, I was intoxicated by the promise of a bit of online magic that would – apparently overnight – make me rich. I had just moved to London, had no idea what I was going to do with my life, and the promise of an income that wasn't connected to an employer who could fire me or a state who might reject me was quite something. What made it even more fascinating was the core technology behind it all: blockchain. Not only was bitcoin going to make us all monied, but blockchain technology seemed to hold the key to solving many of the wicked, systemic societal problems that were, until now, proving intractable. Bitcoin and the blockchain design behind it were therefore not mere novelty, but transformative technologies that held the promise of getting us out of the mess we were in.

—

Bitcoin was developed after the global financial crisis of 2008, as an alternative system of currency that did not depend on financial institutions. It should come as little surprise that by 2017 – a year notable for the lowest recorded levels of trust in institutions across the world[1] – a decentralised system that eschewed all traditional forms of governance and regulation had risen to such sweeping popularity.

Bitcoin's story is as compelling as it is mysterious, imbuing the entire technology with Netflix-worthy novelty and intrigue. In August 2008, the URL bitcoin.org was quietly registered, and two months later a nine-page white paper titled 'Bitcoin: A Peer-to-Peer Electronic Cash System' was circulated on a cryptography mailing list by ... who? Even today, the identity of bitcoin's developer is known only by the author's alias, 'Satoshi Nakamoto'. Nakamoto's vision for bitcoin was laid out in the paper: it was to be 'a purely peer-to-peer version of electronic cash [that] would allow online payments to be sent directly from one party to another without going through a financial institution'.

Although the white paper didn't make headlines at the time, it did pique the interest of Hal Finney, a console-game developer and an early member of the 'cypherpunk' movement. Cypherpunks comprise programmers, engineers and activists who advocate for a digital world free of corruption and manipulation from governments, and promote enhanced privacy as a means of achieving this. Finney wrote on a bitcoin forum of Satoshi's announcement four years later: 'He got a skeptical reception at best. Cryptographers have seen too many grand schemes by clueless noobs. They tend to have a knee jerk reaction.'[2] Finney was more optimistic, immediately offering to work with Nakamoto.

On 3 January 2009, the bitcoin network came into existence with the first block – the 'genesis block' – being created by Nakamoto. Hal Finney was the first recipient of a bitcoin transaction.

Think of the genesis block as the first loop in a chain or the first living organism on Earth. Every bitcoin transaction can be traced back to this single block, like an online 'foundation stone'. Inside this digital container, Nakamoto left fifty bitcoins (BTC) and the following text:

> The Times 03/Jan/2009 Chancellor on brink of second bailout for banks.

The text was the headline of London's *The Times* paper that morning, interpreted by cryptographers as a timestamp of the origin date. It is also seen as a commentary on the state of the banking system, ostensibly bitcoin's raison d'être. The revolution had begun, and it was not being televised, but broadcast on a network of nodes, via the internet, in a way that history could never rewrite.

—

So how does bitcoin work, and what makes it revolutionary?

It's helpful to think of bitcoin as 'electronic cash' or an 'electronic asset'. It is a unit of value that can be bought, sold and exchanged for other currencies. As per the white paper, a maximum of 21 million bitcoins are allowed in circulation (at the time of publication, 17.5 million had already been 'mined' – stay tuned for an explanation[3]). This makes bitcoin a scarce and limited resource: digital 'gold', if you will. It is entirely virtual – there is no 'coin', per se – but the value is implied in the transaction that is then recorded on a distributed, public ledger. As a user or 'owner' of a bitcoin, you own a private key (a string of random numbers and letters) that is able to unlock the value of a particular transaction, signed with a public key.

In essence, the public key is like the number of a safety deposit box and the private key is like the physical key you keep for the box. The blockchain 'ledger' is then like a room full of folders (or 'blocks') that are all connected to each other with a unique 'padlock' (based on the timestamp of the transaction), making a 'blockchain'. Inside each folder is a bunch of transactions that say 'X has transferred Y BTC to Z', where X and Z refer to safety deposit box numbers. Once your transaction is in a block, and attached to the chain, it can't be changed, because to access it you would have to open every single digital 'padlock' in front of it.

Every single bitcoin transaction ever is in this same room, so there are a lot of digital padlocks to open, and every time a new block is added (every ten or so minutes[4]) you would have to start again. Also, you would have to open all the digital padlocks in all the rooms at the same time, because all the copies have to be exactly the same. This chain, or ledger, sits on nodes (powerful computers) around the world. Some of these nodes are in the bedrooms of individuals like me, some are huge set-ups run by teams in Russia and China. All of these nodes have the exact same copy of the ledger (thus, it's distributed), and anyone – including you or me – can see all the transactions that have ever occurred (thus, it's public).

Like gold, bitcoin is 'mined'. Unlike gold, this process exists entirely digitally: 'mining' is the process whereby computers compete to solve a mathematical problem while processing bitcoin transactions. The difficult mathematical problems are part of what makes the whole network secure: this 'proof-of-work' required to add a block to the local blockchain (that is, add a new folder with a digital padlock to the room) is resource intensive, requiring substantial computer power and electricity. The bitcoin network is essentially impossible to hack because there is literally too much work to do. However, as an incentive to do the work of processing transactions, miners are rewarded with new bitcoins. So, bitcoin mining allows the network to be safe while also adding new coins to the system.

What does this look like in practice? Well, say I want to send *Griffith Review* 0.1 BTC for this edition of the publication (given that 0.1 BTC was valued at US$3500 in 2017, I would be drastic-ally overpaying, but let's leave that aside for now[5]). I would open my bitcoin wallet through a web browser or app (using both my public and private key) and enter *Griffith Review*'s bitcoin address, a secure version of their public key/safety deposit box number – like an email address. My transaction (a digital note that says: 'Yassmin sends 0.1 BTC to *Griffith Review*') would be broadcast to all nodes on the network for validation. The computers would run some basic tests on the transaction, like checking that the code is technically correct (have I spelt everything correctly?), that the file is not too large (right paper size?), and that the transaction is unique (have I sent the same 0.1 BTC to anyone else?). Once the nodes have validated that it is a legitimate transaction, my transaction sits in a pool of transactions, waiting to be recorded on the bitcoin blockchain. This is the open and distributed ledger saved on nodes around the world. Every ten minutes or so, each node collects a group of transactions – including mine – into a block (like putting a set of those digital notes into a new folder) and then starts to solve the computational problem (proof-of-work) required for that block to be added (attached with a digital padlock). The first node to solve the maths problem 'wins', adding the block to the chain and being rewarded with a bitcoin – essentially being paid by the system for its effort. My transaction is now part of the bitcoin blockchain, and the additional 0.1 BTC will now be reflected in *Griffith Review*'s bitcoin account.

It wasn't until 2010 that the implications of the bitcoin network started becoming apparent. Initially, it was predominantly used as an alternative payment system for the anonymous purchase of drugs and weapons on the dark web. This changed over time, and cryptocurrencies began to be used as capital-raising mechanisms. Similar to an initial public offering on the stock market, initial coin offerings began to be promulgated widely, although the entire landscape was highly unregulated.

In early 2017, the use cases of cryptocurrencies began to evolve. Bitcoin began to be seen as an alternative to gold as a store of value, and some cryptocurrencies were utilised as a stopgap against a depreciating currency. Venezuelans, for example, were rumoured to be some of the largest and most active purchasers of crypto, using it in place of the hyperinflated local currency. There were also stories of refugees converting their money into cryptocurrency before fleeing their homes, holding it in an online wallet and then converting it back to a local currency when they got settled into their new home. Whether or not these rumours were true, crypto-hobbyists like me ate them up with relish: they made us feel like we were really on the cutting edge of something that was changing the world. Bitcoin was designed to make transactions immutable (unable to be changed), public (so fraud would be impossible) and anonymous (no personal information on the network). The network is also decentralised and trustless: no third party (like a bank or government) could hold total control, and none was required for a transaction to occur. Finally, the system is secure and essentially unhackable. The bitcoin white paper had introduced a possible framework for an entirely new financial system.

But the revolution extends beyond bitcoin. Blockchain technology is a whole new way of recording information. It means computers can talk to each other directly and record transactions efficiently, verifiably and permanently without needing a 'trusted third party'. This has implications beyond just the financial world: it affects logistics, insurance, contracts – any industry that records transactions. Total adoption of blockchain could eliminate the need for 'trusted third-party' services like lawyers, brokers and bankers. It's a foundational technology, like the technology behind the internet. It's a new way of thinking about trust, and it is here to stay.

—

Reading bitcoin's birth story, snuggled in bed one afternoon in a dark London flat, had me enthralled. A new piece of technology with an unknown creator, founded with something called a 'genesis block', potentially revolutionising the entire financial system and the concept of trust, all complete with cryptic messages left in the code? Dan Brown had met the utopian version of *Black Mirror*, and I couldn't get enough of it. I loved the story behind bitcoin and the promise of blockchain technology. This was the answer, I thought. This would lead us to secure financial futures, a world where we could remain private and protected, free from the world's current structural inequality and hierarchy of wealth. This would allow us to buy a house with a single avocado.

I drank the Kool-Aid – gulped it without taking a breath – and jumped right in.

I started humbly, buying the cryptocurrency basics through my online bank. I wasn't ready for the public key/private key/bitcoin wallet business just yet. The app made buying the three biggest currencies at the time super easy: bitcoin, ether and litecoin. The process was just like converting my dollars into pounds – something I could do with the tap of a button. In late 2017, £200 bought me 0.01818 BTC, and within a few days, my portfolio had grown 7 per cent. That would be a decent quarterly return on an investment (I was told, given this was my first time independently investing), let alone the return after less than a week.

If it continued to grow this quickly, I could double my money in a fortnight, I thought, falling into the same trap that many bitcoin newcomers had before me. I felt the rushing thrill of fast money, and a sense that maybe I had become part of something wild, something big. A few days later, I sat down and set myself up on the major cryptocurrency exchanges, conducting my first proper fiat investment and beginning to trade in earnest. ('Fiat' is a currency that doesn't have intrinsic value, but has value because a government has declared it to be legal tender. I'd converted $1000 into BTC.) I was officially crypto obsessed.

In early December 2017, I had invested $3000 and my portfolio value was $6000. I had doubled my money in less than two weeks. I was on a high. My mornings had become a whirlwind.

Step one: check portfolio for any movement. After trialling various applications that claimed to have the most intuitive user interface or the most comprehensive portfolio options, I settled on the industry standard: Delta. The Delta Crypto Portfolio Tracker famously gives you 'all you need to know about your whole portfolio at a glance'. As such, it would be mere moments after I silenced my alarm clock's blaring that I'd tap on the little black icon on my phone's home screen to open the app and begin my crypto-routine. I'd squint to make out whether or not my investment had grown or shrunk in the five or so hours since I'd fallen asleep. A little green arrow underneath my total portfolio figure would tell me my investments had done well overnight and grown. That would mean I could begin my day with a sense of calm. An upside-down red triangle, on the other hand, would cause my heart to plummet like a lead balloon and would often be followed by a squeal and slight panic. But no matter: given the state of the market in the fourth quarter of 2017, there were rarely any red arrows . . .

Step two: check individual investments.

Scanning down the screen, I would take in the individual movements of each crypto to check their overnight performances. My portfolio was mixed: like most, a percentage of my investment sat in bitcoin and ether (ETH), while the rest was a random mix of solid bets and odd hopefuls. It was wise to always have a stash of BTC as a base investment, like gold. ETH was the best 'liquid' cryptocurrency: it had a faster transaction time, and new cryptos were being built on the Ethereum network so one could easily exchange ETH for other cryptocurrencies directly. The rest of my crypto investments held various levels of risk; some I'd chosen after serious consideration, and others were total punts. XRP, DENT, NEO, RaiBlocks, Oyster, Propy and more: any one of these coins could grow fifty- or a hundred-fold overnight, taking my investment, as they say in the crypto world, 'to the moon'.

Step three: check the socials.

Most of my information about crypto came from the same place that fed the Arab Spring: the internet. Whether you preferred Reddit, Discord, Telegram, WhatsApp, Facebook or Twitter, online was the place to get your crypto-info fix. My first stop was usually the Reddit crypto front page, where I would spend fifteen minutes or so scanning for any serious news, before falling into a hole of memes and videos about the latest ICO (Initial Coin Offering*) or the next crypto that would go to the moon.

---

* An initial coin offering, or ICO, is somewhat like the cryptocurrency version of an IPO, initial public offering. It is a way to fundraise for a new cryptocurrency – the main difference is, you don't get a stake in the company, like you would in an IPO. You are buying into a new 'crypto' and hoping that the 'BabyCoin' you purchase now with your bitcoin or Ethereum will one day be worth something. It's a risky business!

Step four: Get out of bed. It's gotta happen at some point, right?

In mid-December 2017, I had invested $5000 into a portfolio valued at $11,000. I was starting to write a wish list of the things I would buy when I hit six figures.

—

With unabashed enthusiasm, I threw myself wholeheartedly into the world of crypto. It helped that I had found myself in London, a particularly finance-obsessed city. By pure luck, I'd also booked a long-term Airbnb in the perfect spot to take advantage of this crypto-wave. The landlord, James, had a London-sized one-bedroom apartment in East London near Old Street, or what is quite geekily known as the 'Silicon Roundabout'. And by London-sized, I mean tiny. The kitchen doubled as the dining room, and the bathroom doubled as a laundry, linen cupboard and plant nursery. As we stood in his cramped kitchen one day in mid-December, I asked James for his advice on getting involved in the crypto world in London IRL (in real life). He worked in FinTech, and seemed fairly trustworthy (if you're thinking, *That's a risky move, Yassmin*, you are right). 'There are lots of meet-ups you can go to,' he told me. I trusted his word, signing up for every meet-up in a one-mile radius. And oh, was the world of crypto meet-ups fascinating!

My first crypto meet-up was relatively modest: a nondescript café in the Old Street tube station. The sky outside had already resigned itself to an exhausted grey; inside, the café was stiflingly warm. There was something poetic about the choice of location: we were in a place of transition, a spot where people pause in the middle of a journey but which never counts as the final destination.

That's where we crypto-hobbyists felt the cryptocurrency/block-chain world was: in a state of transition, before it got onto the tube to its next destination of total domination.

I had found the meet-up quite quickly: they were the only group in the café, three men sitting together awkwardly around a long table. I joined them tentatively, and after fifteen minutes or so of stilted conversation I asked the man immediately to my left, dressed in green khakis and a large, black jacket, what we were waiting for. 'Oh, we're waiting for Vlad! He's the one who set this meet-up up. We're waiting for him.' One of the other men murmured in agreement and began telling me about Vlad in a reverent tone. He was one of the Originals, I was told. He'd been involved in bitcoin for years, since maybe 2009! He's the guy to talk to about the bitcoin price. He will know what's going to happen! He even mines bitcoins! He has his own nodes, mining cloud, everything!

The famed Vlad eventually arrived, half an hour after the agreed meeting time. He strode in with an agitated gait and the demeanour of a man who believed in his cause but was paranoid that everyone was out to get him. He spoke rapidly, in a thick Russian accent, about the recent upheaval in the crypto-currency world. He seemed only mildly interested in asking others their opinions. He dismissed all crypto except for bitcoin – but this was a specifically bitcoin meet, not a general cryptocurrency event or blockchain bash. Of course, this kind of hang-out would be geared towards the purists, the 'true believers' who thought bitcoin was the only cryptocurrency worth its server space.

—

My next few weeks were full of random crypto meet-ups in unusual settings and with unique characters. This included 'When blockchain rules the world!', an event held at the local WeWork with hundreds of attendees crammed into the co-working space's ground-floor lobby. This WeWork meet-up was a classic 'techbro' bash: beer and pizza were free, the room was full of young white men in hoodies and Converse shoes, and the stench of unfettered capitalism hung in the air. See, while block-chain and crypto hold revolutionary potential for many social issues, what people really love about it is the potential to make a lot of money, very rapidly. Nothing like a get-rich-quick scheme to get the masses frothing. Me too, apparently? I liked to think I was different . . . but perhaps I was telling myself another little white lie.

I began to see familiar faces at these events, and they would recognise me. Fair enough: there weren't loads of turbaned Sudanese women at these soirees. I started getting invited to private crypto events, although I stayed away from those, slightly unsure of the men's intentions. But I continued making my way around the public meet-ups, including an event with a crypto trader who presented his predictions for the year wearing cowboy boots and a cowboy hat. It was a look made even more striking by the fact that he was a young man of East Asian appearance, who spoke almost exclusively in memes and crypto jargon. Almost everyone in that room had owned bitcoin for longer than five years; I felt strangely proud for having made it onto the guest list. I wasn't like one of those 'newbies', I told myself, as I ate another slice of free pizza (techbros don't know how to order any other type of food) and looked at the enormous line-up to get in.

But of course, I was exactly like all those other newbies. I was only in the room because I'd signed up to the event ridiculously early; I wasn't ready to admit to my self-delusion just yet. And it wasn't only my place in the crypto world that I was deluding myself about. I was unwilling to ask myself any of the tough questions: What was all this really built on? Was there even substance to the hype? Was I truly in this because of the revolutionary potential, or because I liked the idea of fast money?

My faith system, Islam, forbids gambling. And there were moments when I wondered if I was flagrantly disregarding this edict by participating in the wildly volatile and speculative game that was the cryptocurrency market. There seemed to be no real logic to what assets would do, no sense to what would rise and fall, no reality to what people were even selling. And that's an important point to note: the way that things worked meant that you didn't even need to have a workable product yet to set up an ICO and start making money by selling the 'coins' for fiat. An ICO, like an initial public offering, is a way to raise money for a project. Companies were starting with the idea of building apps based on blockchain technology (typically on top of the Ethereum network). Once they came up with an idea, they would set up an ICO and sell coins, or 'tokens', to raise the money to build the technology. Due to the unregulated nature of the market, though, anyone could make anything up, sell the idea, take people's fiat for tokens and then disappear. That was the risk you took when you invested in a new currency. Sometimes they grew a thousand-fold in a month; sometimes they were a total scam. Sometimes they would grow a hundred-fold overnight and they were still a scam. It made no sense. It really was the wild, wild west.

I became addicted. Crypto took up all my time. I tried to convince my little brother to put his savings into bitcoin. I spoke about it to anyone who would listen, checked the market obsessively. When not trading, I spent time on the online platforms that would give me more information. There were secret Facebook groups and chat groups where people would share information about new currencies (coins or tokens) hitting the exchanges, price predictions, and the coordination of 'pumps and dumps', in which groups of users would all buy a currency to raise its price then sell it all at once to crash it, making a healthy profit along the way. I spent New Year's Eve with a group of friends in a house near Lake Como in Italy, standing on the balcony over one of the most beautiful scenes in the world, unable to resist the urge to refresh my Delta portfolio. That trip, I sold $5000 worth of RaiBlocks to a friend, a process known as 'taking out my principal'. I had now made my fiat investment back, and anything I was now making was 'free money' – and gosh, who doesn't love free money?

But alas. What's that saying? Something about glitter and gold . . .

—

January 2018 was not a good month for the cryptocurrency market. Compare this: BTC hit US$20,089 on 17 December 2017. By 17 January 2018, the price was almost half that, at US$11,431. It was a slow, inexorable downhill run from there.

Opening my Delta app became increasingly dispiriting: the happy green arrows were completely replaced by sad, upside-down red triangles. One day, in mid-March, I woke up, fumbling with my phone to switch the damn alarm off, and decided to go to the bathroom and brush my teeth instead of checking my portfolio. The next day, I did the same thing. I felt a sliver of guilt, an urge to check the bitcoin price, but it was a slight tug rather than the irresistible pull I had become accustomed to.

When I did eventually check my portfolio, it was valued at $600. Not quite enough for a house deposit yet. Not even a week's rent, if we're being perfectly honest. If only I could pay in avocadoes. A month later, I deleted the app from my phone. Crypto slunk out of my life, replaced with real-life friends and an obsession with privacy that coincided neatly with the Cambridge Analytica scandals of early 2018. I'd found something else to fill my time.

I wish I could say that I didn't jump on the bandwagon – but by god, I did. I hopped right on with the rest of the impressionables, hungry for easy money and that bloodless revolution. I could cloak my brief obsession in all sorts of moralising reasons, but the reality is perhaps much simpler: history is replete with get-rich-quick bubbles, and this was one that fitted our world perfectly. It was based on new technology, built on online hype and sustained by dark internet humour – all with the promise of a solution that was also making the world a fairer place. And why did 'fairness' matter? Yes, there was an element of anti-establishment rhetoric that wanted anarchy for the sake of it. But I was also part of an entire generation that had been burnt by a neoliberal, capitalist system that wasn't setting us up for a life of stability or success. We were the generation that had been told that working hard would get you far, and then popped out of colleges and universities to find ourselves steeped in austerity, uncertainty and unemployment. Our democratic governments seemed deeply uninterested in our welfare, concerned more with maintaining power and their own legacies. Our parents had expectations that were formed in a world very unlike the one we were currently living in. And don't even get me started on the financial sector. Blockchain technology held a promise of something else. Of a parallel system we could design and no one else could control. It smelled like freedom.

Where has that promise gone? Ultimately, blockchain technology, of which cryptocurrency is one part, is revolutionary – but it's in its nascent stages, although things are changing. Think of it like the early days of TCP/IP (transmission control protocol/ internet protocol), the technology behind the internet. TCP/IP was developed in 1972. The world wide web was not developed for public use until the 1990s, and it wasn't until the early 2000s that we began to see the possibility of things we take for granted now, like social media and digital maps. Facebook would have been impossible to conceive of in 1972. But decades of development allow for all sorts of new applications of a technology to be dreamt up and created.

Personally, that's where I think we're at. As a technology, blockchain is in the 1970s stage of the internet: we have no real idea what applications it may have just yet. The difference with blockchain is that institutions have a lot more to lose. The political implications of a system that cuts out the middle man, or of a currency that governments cannot control, is destabilising for those in power. So, this revolution, like almost all before it, will face immense resistance to widespread adoption. Where does this leave us? Time will tell. I'm not necessarily going to throw any more of my fiat at any company with 'blockchain' in its name just yet, though I'm still pretty pumped. To the moon with us all.

—

2022 update:

I took the remainder of cryptocurrency out of their various wallets later that year, as my savings ran low and I had yet to find a source of income in my new city. Since, I have occasionally bought some Ethereum and deposited handfuls of savings into a bitcoin wallet for safekeeping, but my interest never quite regained its fervour, even as the price of bitcoin peaked again, and again. Indeed, I find the world of crypto borderline repulsive today, and I cannot put my finger on whether it is due to a change in me, or them. Certainly, it has become increasingly institutionalised, discussed in finance media instead of underground tech forums, more likely to be the subject of conversation in a dreary finance-bro networking event rather than among a group of social change-makers. The community is no longer full of wild and wonderful characters, but teems with blue suits and sharpened teeth, talking of markets and regulation and using jargon that, frankly, sends me to sleep. Somehow, in transitioning to the mainstream, being controlled and co-opted by the same forces who already hold the levers of power, cryptocurrency became unfair, and unfun. Perhaps it was always a matter of time.

Whose borders are they anyway?

If I give up my citizenship, will I finally, truly become 'un-Australian'?

I fantasise about giving up my Australian passport. My dreams are filled with warm, golden hues, the imagined release of renunciation the moment I hand in papers and walk away. Away from the country responsible for trauma that still wakes me up in sweats. Away from the false promise of fairness and equality I had so wholeheartedly bought into. Away from what had been my parents' safe harbour, turned personal Taiji cove.* I had swum into cool, calm waters, trustingly and willingly, only to be taken to slaughter. *If I hand in the little blue book*, I think, *I will at last be free.*

Maybe if I walk away, I can breathe again.

My mother, on the phone from the family home in Brisbane, says I shouldn't be too hasty. As local rainbow lorikeets chatter

---

* The Taiji dolphin drive hunt is a practice based on luring dolphins into a small bay to be captured for sale or killed for their meat. A 2009 documentary, *The Cove*, focused on traditional Japanese hunting practices, through an American ocean conservationist perspective. It was critically acclaimed by the film industry establishment, caused controversy over the secrecy of its filming and production, and was poorly received by the population of Taiji.

noisily in the background, she suggests my feelings towards the land down under may change, eventually. *Life is long*, she reminds me, followed by the obligatory *inshallah*. I nod, wordlessly.

She's right. These feelings will evolve, as emotions are wont to do. What they will become, I do not know. I may indeed regret voluntarily relinquishing my legal status, especially one as powerful as Australia's. My dual Sudanese citizenship means avoiding the purgatory of statelessness, but gaining little else: the modest green document with golden Arabic emboss is typically ranked in the weakest ten passports globally.[1] By virtue of my father's mixed southern Egyptian ancestry, the ID card I hold labels me 'mawaleed', Sudanese by birth, not by tribe. If you are deemed an outsider, not even birth can secure your 'right' to belong. This is as true in Sudan as it is in Australia. It seems I cannot escape being a second-class citizen.

My dream replays, looping in my head, kamikaze-esque. *Is betrayal enough for such drastic action?* I wonder in my more lucid moments, when the sharp edges of pain feel less urgent. The voices of friends and family argue compellingly in the chamber of my mind. *Don't you know how lucky you are? How much you would lose? How much you owe this country? You should be grateful.*

It is true. Becoming 'Australian' is an inextricable part of who I am today, and the privileges of my nationality allow me to be sitting here in a studio in Paris, writing essays, while being Sudanese can't even secure me a tourist visa. But what *keeps* me 'Australian'? Is it my fading broad ocker accent, or the pledge of commitment I took with my parents in the early 1990s? Is it my familiarity with long humid summers, or the paperwork allowing me to vote in the elections? Is it my ability to still sing the opening tune to *Blinky Bill* or the ability, passport in hand, to more easily navigate a world order designed to maintain the power of decaying European empires?

Is being Australian a legal identity, or a cultural one? Can they be separated in any meaningful sense? As I reflect on my own relationship to being 'Australian', I consider implications beyond me, the basis on which any belonging is premised.

As Professor Aileen Moreton-Robinson reminds us, belonging's flip side is exclusion. 'In Australia,' she writes, 'the sense of belonging, home and place enjoyed by the non-Indigenous subject – the coloniser or migrant – is based on the dispossession of the original owners of the land and the denial of our rights under international customary law.'[2] Such belonging is neither pure, nor innocent, but inextricably bound to the nation's original sin, the fiction of terra nullius.

Why, if I had the choice, would I bind myself, legally and psychologically, to a nation-state founded on the dispossession of the oldest continuous living civilisation on Earth?

We so often talk about wanting to belong, but what about wanting to *un-belong*?

———

Citizenship, historian Derek Heater[3] writes, is a socio-political identity, one of the many that have existed over millennia. Unlike feudal or monarchical systems, which are specific to individual relationships, citizenship is the relationship between an individual and the *idea* of a state.[4] This is also separate to a system of nations,*

---

* Not to be conflated with the ideology of 'Nationalism-with-a-big-N'.

whereby the relationship is between individuals and a broad cultural group. Political scientist Benedict Anderson describes the nation as an 'imagined political community, both inherently limited and sovereign'.[5] A community, he said, because regardless of any inequality or exploitation, 'the nation is always conceived as a deep, horizontal comradeship'.[6] Citizenship, in Heater's expression, differs from nationality in that it is less comradeship and more allegiance, a bond to the state rather than to one another.[7]

—

I grew up a true believer. Becoming a citizen was a rite of passage for migrants like myself, an official declaration and mutual acknowledgement of our new home. The Australian Government's Department of Home* Affairs[8] website reads: 'Making the pledge is a public commitment to Australia. It means that you are accepting the responsibilities and privileges of citizenship.' The pledge itself says:

> From this time forward (under God),
> I pledge my loyalty to Australia and its people,
> whose democratic beliefs I share,
> whose rights and liberties I respect, and
> whose laws I will uphold and obey.

---

* It is always interesting to me that the department is named 'Home' affairs, rather than 'State', both in Australia and the UK. Although the USA has the 'Department of State', after 9/11 President Bush created the 'Department of Homeland Security'. One could argue the more a department title centres 'home', the more violent and protectionist it actually is. It is only in these department names that 'Home' can be found in state affairs.

As an Australian citizen, you *must*: obey the laws of Australia; vote in federal and state or territory elections and in a referendum (a globally unique requirement!); defend Australia should the need arise; serve on jury duty if called to do so.

As an Australian citizen you *can*: apply for children born overseas to become Australian citizens by descent; apply for a job in the Australian Public Service or in the Australian Defence Force; seek election to parliament; apply for an Australian passport and re-enter Australia freely; ask for consular assistance from an Australian official while overseas.

Most Australian citizens,[9] born in Australia or to an Australian parent, would have never seen, let alone explicitly accepted, these pledges.

I understood citizenship as an exchange. Act as a 'good' citizen, engage with the system in good faith, contribute to the community and work to build a better nation, and you would be afforded the state's safety and protection. This was no hare-brained idea plucked out of thin air, but what we were taught at school and what my parents regularly reinforced. 'Here, the system works,' my father would exclaim proudly, as the rubbish bins were collected on time every Thursday morning. For a man who found joy in simple pleasures, like the local Member of Parliament catching the bus to work, Australian citizenship was – and remains – a privilege.

I do not remember my father asking how we were afforded these Australian rights, nor for whom the system didn't work. First Nations people only attained the right to citizenship in the late 1960s, and non-Indigenous citizenship continues to be predicated on their dispossession. 'Should we do something?' I asked my father one afternoon, as we watched debates on the Northern Territory Intervention.[10] 'We can't help them,' he replied, 'because we are not a part of their community.' His remarks were not meant unkindly but drawn from a reflexive suspicion of imperialist intrusion. Interference in a community that was not his was anathema to him. But we were Australian citizens, weren't we? Why wasn't that enough? This was an early case of my father understanding citizenship as allegiance to the state, and my misunderstanding it as to *one another*.

—

Although around since the Ancient Greeks,[11] citizenship's modern conception can be drawn back to English sociologist T. H. Marshall's 1950 essay 'Citizenship and the social class'. The state has *social* responsibilities to its citizens, Marshall wrote, from 'economic welfare and security, to the right to share to the full in the social heritage and to live the life of a civilised being'.[12] Rights had been acquired through citizenship over the centuries: civil in the eighteenth century, political in the nineteenth and social in the twentieth; and Marshall posited they would naturally continue to expand and evolve. Although critiqued for his focus on only the white working English *man*, 'social citizenship' is useful in describing the concept's theoretical benefits. Indeed, the privileges my father enjoyed by virtue of his newly minted legal Australian status included all three of Marshall's categories: civil (a justice system), political (voting) and social (access to welfare); rights that were being eroded in Sudan, the country he had just left.

Hannah Arendt also spoke of citizenship's importance. Arendt fled Hitler's Germany for Paris in 1933, and two years later, the

Nuremberg Laws formally confirmed she and all other German Jews were now officially stateless refugees. By 1951, she had received political asylum and become a naturalised citizen of the United States. For Arendt, this experience reinforced her view of humans needing to be more than just 'human' to guarantee their rights. For individuals to enjoy legally protected rights to education, to healthcare, to work etc., they needed to be members of a political community. They needed to be *citizens* of a nation-state. Before we speak to any specific civil, political or social rights, Arendt argued in 1949,[13] there needs to be 'the right to have rights'.

But in 1949, many nation-states that exist today were years away from independence. Is it therefore still true to say that citizenship guarantees the right to have rights? What of those nation-states who do not have the ability to secure for their citizens the most basic of rights, whether due to the legacy of historical foreign invasion and imperialism (like my birth country Sudan) or other contemporary calamities (like the impacts of climate change)? What of those who *chose* not to, actively oppressing the very citizens they are meant to protect, or alternatively, those who may have never accepted the framework of human rights in the first place, due to the critique that they are a 'Western construct'[14] or otherwise? It is worth remembering that although no nation voted *against* adopting the Universal Declaration of Human Rights in 1948, eight did abstain, including the Soviet Union, South Africa and Saudi Arabia. Are we satisfied as a global society that the only viable political community one can belong to is that of a nation-state? What happens if the nation-state does not hold up its side of the bargain? When the fit isn't quite right anymore, as in the case with me and Australia?

184 TALKING ABOUT A REVOLUTION

Arendt's framing assumes that the category of citizenship is honoured, that the nation will in fact uphold the rights it claims to bestow. Reality shows us this is far from the case. The current nation or supra-state is not there for citizens, but for itself. The citizen who threatens that project is expendable.

The modern state is no generous fairy godmother, bestowing wishes for all in her care, but more Dolores Umbridge:[15] what it says, goes. Today's citizenship is a by-product of the nation-state, not the other way around, as evidenced in the aforementioned 'privileges' of Australian citizenship. They are not guarantees, they are permissions. You can *ask* for consular assistance, *apply* for a passport, *apply* for a job. You are not guaranteed a job, nor assistance, nor entrance into Australia freely (as Australian citizens in India found out in 2021 during the COVID-19 pandemic). The partisan nature of governments is a further complication, as the politics of the day may mean certain citizens find even their *access* to said permissions actively denied. Note also the lack of care, dignity, or respect. It is a curious relationship, that between citizen and state. The power dynamic is clear. You are expected to have loyalty, with no guarantee of allegiance in return.* 'We used to think the state was accountable to its citizens,'[16] Bengali literary theorist Gayatri Spivak dryly puts to an audience of academics at the University of California. 'Look what has happened.'

The modern citizen is not only a citizen but a subject as well, argues political scientist Eric Gorham, required to 'subjugate themselves to the institutions of the modern state and the market'.[17] If you want to enjoy the economic and social security

---

* There is much room to discuss the racialised aspect of this as well, but alas.

that citizenship provides, Gorham points out, you have to agree to occasionally relinquish certain freedoms, like privacy or movement. Indeed, the state does not *ask* the citizen to relinquish the occasional civil freedom but *demands*, requiring no less than unquestioning obsequiousness, especially from those racialised and otherwise historically marginalised. The state is brazen in its willingness to hold civil, political and social rights hostage to this end, as in the case of US citizen Ahmad Chebli, placed on a No-Fly list for refusing to become an FBI informant.[18] Critique is akin to treason.

This has been clear most recently during the COVID-19 pandemic. Reflecting on the public discourse around COVID-19 restrictions in Australia, Professors Tim Soutphommasane and Marc Stears observed in September 2021 that 'anyone advocating for the reopening of Australian borders or society is suspected of . . . revel[ling] in letting people die', despite government restrictions moving from 'necessary and proportionate' into 'something rather more oppressive'.[19] Progressives have supported the 'Fortress Australia' policies,* the authors note, and remained quiet in the face of a militarised lockdown targeting racialised communities in Sydney and Melbourne.[20] In July 2020, 3000 residents of nine public housing tower blocks in Melbourne were placed under a snap lockdown, banned from leaving their homes for up to fourteen days. Those away working when the lockdown commenced were forbidden from re-entering their apartments.[21] Five hundred police officers were deployed to 'guard' the residents, effectively placing some of the most vulnerable and heavily

---

* Stranding more than 30,000 Australian citizens overseas.

policed people in the state under house arrest. Across the border a little over a year later, troops were deployed to enforce stay-at-home orders in Western Sydney, a region with significant migrant, refugee and First Nations communities. Groups pointedly noted the discrepancy between where additional police and army personnel were deployed and where outbreaks of COVID-19 were actually traced to.[22] Australian citizens and permanent residents were also banned from leaving the country until the end of 2021, only able to travel overseas if granted an exemption.[23] Soutphommasane and Stears's article urges a pushback against the country's erosion of rights and liberties. But was this an aberration, or the expected behaviour of citizen-subjects, policing each other on behalf of the modern nation-state?

Twenty-year anniversary commemorations of 9/11 also brought reckonings with the 'War on Terror' and the panoptical security apparatus constructed by the United States, operating unencumbered until today.[24] 'Panic made us politically vulnerable,' whistle-blower Edward Snowden told the *Guardian*. 'That vulnerability was exploited by our own government.'[25] Former FBI agent and whistleblower Terry Albury was part of that apparatus. In an interview with the *New York Times*, released after his four-year sentence for leaking classified information, he said, 'What the FBI was directing us to do was to go into these communities and instil fear and then generate this paranoia within these people [Muslims] so that they know that they're under suspicion perpetually.' The FBI, he added, 'has given agents the power to ruin the lives of completely innocent people based solely on what part of the world they came from, or what religion they practice, or the color of their skin'. Albury's interview with the *Times* is as much about his guilty conscience as it is about the state-mandated mass surveillance he was part of. 'I helped destroy people. For seventeen years.' It is unclear how many people he 'destroyed' have had their rights and lives reinstated after Albury's leaks.

The FBI is just one arm of one state's surveillance apparatus, but it illustrates Gorham's point: the state 'empowers and dis-empowers citizens simultaneously'. On one hand, citizenship is how our modern world confers rights to individuals. On the other, these rights are predicated on states' integrity, on their own self-regulation. Who do we turn to in the face of state-level abuse?

—

In 2015, a young British teenager was groomed to leave England and travel to Syria to join Daesh.* Shamima Begum lived under Daesh's rule for three years, marrying a Dutch man fighting with the group, and giving birth to and losing three children. In February 2019, Begum was found at the al-Hawl refugee camp in Northern Syria, wanting to return to the United Kingdom, as was her right as a citizen. It almost immediately became clear her rights were far from assured. Then Home Secretary Sajid Javid quickly signed an order revoking Begum's citizenship; she was the first ever British-born woman to undergo this exclusion. Although legally, the United Kingdom could not render their own citizen 'stateless', the government argued that Begum's heritage made

---

* Arabic speakers almost exclusively use the term 'Daesh' to refer to the terrorist group, an acronym of the group's initial name in Arabic: 'al-Dawla al-Islamiya fil Iraq wa al-Sham'. Acronyms are quite uncommon in Arabic, and 'Daesh' as an Arabic word doesn't mean anything itself, though it does sound similar to 'da-yis', which means to 'crush underfoot'. The term is also useful in distancing the group from anything to do with Islam, or its self-styled importance as a 'state'. It doesn't hurt that they hate the name, too.

her eligible for Bangladeshi citizenship. Bangladesh, unwilling to play on the United Kingdom's terms, rejected this contention completely. Shamima Begum had never visited Bangladesh, nor applied for citizenship, its Ministry of Foreign Affairs stated. There was 'no question' of her being allowed into the country.[26] At the time of writing, Begum's appeal against losing her citizenship is still in court.[27]

Between 1973 and February 2002, not a single individual was stripped of their British citizenship. Yet in 2017 alone, such deprivation was meted out to 104 Brits.[28] Deprivation of citizenship, the punishment of exile without trial, is back in vogue, *à cause d'un* securitised environment post-9/11, and conditions are only becoming more hostile. In 2021, the UK House of Commons passed the Nationality and Borders Bill, awarding the British government, among other concerning powers, the ability to strip a person of their citizenship *without notifying them*, 'in the interests of national security, diplomatic relations or otherwise in the public interest'.[29] A vulnerable class of citizenship has been thoroughly established. For British dual nationals, or those with potential eligibility for 'nationality' elsewhere, citizenship has been *confirmed* as forever precarious, contingent on 'good behaviour'. This vulnerable class is comprised largely of British citizens from former colonies, Black and brown folk who are historically and presently marginalised, often Muslims. Begum's case laid bare the false promise of citizenship, especially for those of us deemed as 'other'. For all the so-called guarantees of citizenship, the 'right to have rights', the state still retains the power to create and enforce a hierarchy of humanity,[30] where for some, your rights are far from assured.

—

Everyone eventually comes back, my mother reminds me on the phone. The rich and famous, the ones who 'make it' overseas, the young that go on working holidays, everyone eventually returns. It's The Lucky Country, after all. Who wouldn't go back to 'The Lucky Country'?*

But who is Australia lucky for? Certainly not for the First Nations people, custodians and sovereign for millennia. Not for those who are othered on its soil, whether due to their ancestry, gender, class; nor for the ones who sought refuge in a way the state deemed 'wrongful', now left languishing in prisons, in almost indefinite detention, a catastrophe of bipartisan making. Unlucky for some, 'lucky' depends on who you are in the world.

For many, citizenship remains a cudgel of the state, a tool to justify the deprivation of those who sit outside the bounds of a particular (and often powerful) political community. But we do not exist in a world that allows us much other choice. As French philosopher Etienne Balibar writes, 'contemporary citizens will not abandon a status, however insufficient and damaged, which encapsulates certain rights and powers, in favour of another'.[31] Or, as Spivak puts it, we would 'rather have a relationship with a rogue state than no relationship at all'. You're either in, or you're out. And it is this binary choice – or lack thereof – that gets my goat.

---

* *The Lucky Country* is the title of the 1964 book by Donald Horne. Although today the phrase is used positively, in Horne's eyes it was a pejorative, reflecting his belief that all of the country's success was due to luck rather than the strength of its political or economic systems. One could argue this continues today: Australia 'succeeds' in spite of itself.

Arendt's words are still largely true. Being a citizen of (most) nation-states is one of the only ways to even *access* most rights.[32] Our supra-national institutions rely on an infrastructure made up of nation-states, and therefore citizenship, with all the related geo-political power dynamics (you have more power in the United Nations if you are from the United States, say, than if you are from Togo). The European Union is also dependent on the idea of citizenship, though given its primary interest in collective economic security and its fatal weaponising of migration, the Union is more interested in collectively sharing benefits than dealing with burdens.

Writer James Baldwin once said of his relationship to his homeland: 'I love America more than any other country in the world and, exactly for this reason, I insist on the right to criticise her perpetually.' It's a quote often repeated by those who critique the nations of their birth, residency, citizenship. I wonder about the implication. Does one need to 'love' a nation in order to critique it? If so, this seems to me another mythologised example of the fealty nation-states compel. But if Baldwin is suggesting instead critique is *part* of loving a nation, one wonders what he would make of the current resurgence of big-N ideological nationalism that brought us Trump, Brexit and almost elected hard-right French nationalist Marine Le Pen. There seems little appetite for critique of the nation-state today.

Hannah Arendt herself famously said she did not understand the notion of loving a people. She loved her friends, she said; when it came to Jewish people, she 'merely belong[ed] to them'.[33] I feel compelled to shy away from both ideas. A nation-state is an institution that exists to maintain itself and its own power. That is neither inherently good nor bad, but for all the talk about globalisation 'ending' the nation, it is clear that the power of citizenship still prevails.

The political community you are lucky enough to be born or naturalised into still defines so much of an individual's outcomes and chances in life. I can say with almost complete certainty that I would not live the life I do, if it weren't for my parents' decision to pick up and start all over again on the other side of the world in Australia. I *am* grateful, sure. But to my parents, not to the system. And that gratitude exists alongside an understanding that my privilege sprouts from blood-drenched soil in so-called Australia.

For me, wanting to un-belong to Australia is about wanting to divest from a system of borders and frontiers that gives my crested little blue document the power it has, power my green Sudanese passport has never been accorded. It is about wanting to divest from the dispossession of Indigenous people that my citizenship is predicated on. It is about wanting an alternative political community to the nation-state whose modern manifestation, with its immigration controls and obsession with boundaries, reflects more the end of the era of empires in the mid-twentieth century. It is about committing to the search for the 'abstract structure of redress' as described by Spivak,[34] which allows for accountability, but avoids the inherent dangers of ideological nationalism.

Rather than 'Why do you want to give up such a powerful passport?', it should be 'Why do we live in a world where some passports are so much more powerful than others?'

Rather than asking 'Why don't you want to be part of the

lucky country?', we should be asking 'Why is it that so many other countries are "unlucky"?'*

'You want to push the thing you love out of you, as if you can reject Australia like it feels it rejected you,' Australian academic Eleanor Ivory Weber writes from Brussels, on the COVID-19 restrictions blocking overseas Australians from returning home, or flying out again if they make it in. 'But it doesn't work like that, rejection always carries resentment, a plague on any psyche and any state.'[35]

Is un-belonging a rejection? I can understand how it feels that way, I see it in the flickers of betrayal behind the eyes of fellow Australians who ask when I am coming back, hear it in the pitch of their voices, the sudden slips of their smiles. In these moments, I feel compelled to apologise, equivocate, or silently turn away from their naked displays of vulnerability. But un-belonging is perhaps more common than we think: people are constantly and consistently choosing to un-belong all the time; from their religious group, their political party, their profession. Whether it is because their values have shifted, they have become disillusioned or because they simply don't feel the need to belong anymore, there are innumerable valid and perfectly rational reasons to choose to un-belong to a community. Sure, there might be some costs, but most of the time, you are free to go.

If cultural identity is, as British cultural theorist Stuart Hall

---

* British journalist Leah Cowan writes, 'If colonialism involved the imposition of rules, hierarchies and categories, from land borders to the gender binary, where before there were none or less; decoloniality requires the breaking down of borders and these systems of oppression.' Cowan, L., *Border Nation: A story of migration*, Pluto Press, London, 2021, p. 138.

writes, 'a matter of "becoming" as well as of "being"', un-belonging is part of that constant transformation.[36]

———

I visit the Department of Home Affairs website, curious as to what the process of renouncing my Australian citizenship would entail.

On the landing screen of the page in question, it reads:

> We will not approve your application to renounce your citizenship if you do not have another foreign citizenship or it is not in Australia's interests.

I am struck by the fact that even the decision to un-belong to the state is not, in fact, my own.

———

My mother tells me on the phone that perhaps I won't ever move back, but I should come and visit. Of course I'll visit, I say, with the obligatory inshallah.

You know, she says, *maybe it's in your blood.*

Maybe what is?

Moving. Travelling. Your ancestors did it, we did it . . . you know, I think we are descendant from nomads.

I smile, imagining the life these predecessors used to live. Tougher, perhaps, without the creature comforts I am accustomed to today, but with the freedom to travel where they wanted to go, without fear of frontiers. It is ironic that the only way I can do that is by holding on to my Australian passport, and I tell my mother so.

Subhanallah, she says, and I wonder what she knows that I don't.

Tyranny and free speech

First published in the Saturday Paper *on 5 May 2018.*

Call it mass cognitive dissonance. All around us, the loudest proponents of free speech, in politics and the Australian media, are in many ways the most flagrantly hypocritical. These actors set a dangerous precedent: by refusing to acknowledge their double standards, while simultaneously utilising their public platforms to bully and harass those who disagree with their version of the truth, they become the very tyranny they claim to stand against. The hypocrisy is so glaringly obvious that it is almost comical to point it out. It is as if the mere act of highlighting something so clear diminishes the identifier, rather than the perpetrator.

Let's zoom out for a moment and take the broader view. What is the point of free speech? A concept talked about so readily, debated so passionately and defended so feverishly in many ways benefits from an ambiguity of purpose when discussed. Is it the pursuit of truth or the freedom to offend? Each ardent defender sees in the concept what they choose. Is one purpose more noble than another? Why is free speech shared so unequally? And why is it that freedom of expression seems to enjoy an elevated status above all other rights?

The concept of free speech is so deeply misused and mis-construed in Australian public discourse that a key fact is often obscured: freedom of speech in Australia is not explicitly pro-tected. In arguably the only western liberal democracy without a bill of rights, Australians have an implied freedom of political speech, but it is worth noting there is very little protecting us from the *consequences* of said speech.

There is, of course, more than one way of policing a society. The Australian debate is conducted in the context of what is socially permitted and acceptable. It is policed by a concentrated media and a hyper-partisan political system.

I have been thinking a lot recently about free speech, and have been interested in what the English philosopher John Stuart Mill wrote about the danger of limiting expression and 'the tyranny of the majority'.[1] In his opinion, free speech is concerned with the pursuit of truth. He wrote:

> The peculiar evil of silencing the expression of an opinion is, that it
> is robbing the human race; posterity as well as the existing genera-
> tion; those who dissent from the opinion, still more than those who
> hold it. If the opinion is right, they are deprived of the opportunity
> of exchanging error for truth: if wrong, they lose, what is almost
> as great a benefit, the clearer perception and livelier impression of
> truth, produced by its collision with error.

The collision of a true proposition with an erroneous one, Mill argued, is how we get to truth, or the closest possible expression of it. Presenting a hypothesis and then having it tested by others without fear of reprisal is, arguably, how scientists strengthen their research, how engineers iterate a design or how chefs perfect their recipes. In the right environment, it is an undeniably effective method of convergence.

At the civil society end, Human Rights Watch's definition seemingly squares with Mill's. The international non-governmental organisation articulates freedom of speech as a bellwether, stating: 'How any society tolerates those with minority, disfavoured, or even obnoxious views will often speak to its performance on human rights more generally.'[2] What the organisation believes constitutes freedom is less defined; however, it is largely focused on government interference with citizens. This would align with Australia's implied freedoms of political speech. But what about beyond that?

Typical proponents of free speech use Mill's arguments to warn against their 'silencing' – whether Lionel Shriver on cultural appropriation or Margaret Court on Christians being unable to speak against queer rights. Defenders of Shriver and Court might even use arguments based on Mill, announcing that we should always 'err on the side of free speech', and that 'our right to speak our minds is under threat like never before'. Although useful, when Mill's argument is used in today's discourse, it is often stripped of context, applied in a peculiar vacuum and devoid of an understanding of history and power. The colliding of opinions will only lead to the emergence of truth if the force behind both is equal, if the playing field is level, if there is a commitment to truth rather than to an agenda that is self-serving. Herein lies the rub: those who claim to be the biggest proponents of free speech seem uninterested in the pursuit of truth, unable and unwilling to accept any version of truth that is not their own. The cognitive gymnastics that allows those who are the most powerful to persuade themselves and others they are being silenced is remarkable, and, in a perverted way, almost awe-inspiring. To quote an unlikely ally in this, here is Janet Albrechtsen: 'Free speech has become a political smorgasbord where who you defend depends on partisan tastes rather than principles.'[3]

Free speech is shaped and at times distorted by society's informal but powerful mandates and norms, led and bolstered by actors in media, and reinforced by politicians, corporates and influencers online. This, in Mill's writings, is 'a social tyranny more formidable than many kinds of political oppression ... it leaves fewer means of escape, penetrating much more deeply into the details of life, and enslaving the soul itself'.[4] This tyranny rears its head when the sacred cows of prevailing opinion are challenged and existing power structures are questioned: Anzac Day, Invasion Day, the rights of First Nations people, climate change. One does not need to look far for proof: Adam Goodes and Gillian Triggs are two examples of individuals targeted for expressions deemed by a powerful elite as 'unacceptable'. The Adnyamathanha and Narungga man and dual Brownlow medallist Goodes was bullied out of the Australian Football League after pointing to a young Collingwood supporter in the stadium who yelled out a racial slur during a game. For the crime of highlighting racism, Goodes was routinely booed and yelled at by fans almost every subsequent game, mocked by media pundits until he retired. The 'long crucifixion'[5] of Australian Human Rights Commissioner Gillian Triggs, who dared to do her job and challenge the government on its human rights record, also made her target. Life for these figures, and for anyone who chooses to speak outside socially acceptable norms, is made deeply uncomfortable through the use of overwhelming social pressure and the concentrated fury of a public shaming. Believe me: I know through personal experience. As *Crikey* journalist Guy Rundle wrote in a piece on what he called my 'lest-we-forget saga', 'practically no one, no matter how strong, can go through being on the front page, day after day, as a hate figure, and come through unscathed'.[6] That is precisely what is intended.

The positions taken by these interests are the very operation of the social tyranny that Mill warns against. On some issues, public sentiment has changed over time: marriage equality is a fine example of how the agenda of some media and conservative politicians was deeply out of step with the electorate. However, there are still some issues on which there is little appetite for an alternative perspective.

The danger here is twofold. First, Mill's concern becomes prophetic: the tyranny of prevailing opinion limits us as a society from achieving our fullest potential and leads us to a place of political despotism. Less obviously dire, but perhaps more urgently, is that the way in which power is exercised in today's public arena frightens those without traditional forms of power into actual self-imposed silence. The examples of Goodes, Triggs and even former Prime Minister Julia Gillard are often used by marginalised voices to explain why they are afraid to speak out about issues that are important to them. Scores of young people contact me and share their concerns, stonewalled by their fears of voicing them too loudly, lest they attract the ire of media dragons lying in wait. 'Look at what happened to you,' they whisper. 'What chance do I have? I need to pay the rent.'

Is this a society that we believe is truly free? Is this the world that proponents of freedom of speech want to build? Because if their objective is 'truth', they are doing quite a poor job of securing it.

The other peculiarity in the furore around free speech is why it is that those who have access to the largest platforms feel so disproportionately injured by any questions around their ability to say as they please. The answer seems impossibly simple: they already have everything, but if they give up any of that space, if their opinions are questioned or even usurped by people who look and think differently to them, the systems of oppression on which their power is built could come crashing down. If you live emboldened by the power of patriarchy, racial supremacy, ableism and wealth, you have the power to glide effortlessly where you want. Even the whiff of a headwind, an opposing view, a dissenting perspective, seems personally offensive. This is why freedom of expression takes up so much space in our public discourse on rights, rather than freedom of movement, freedom from torture and inhuman treatment, the right to social security. These are rights and freedoms that are infringed upon on a daily basis by our very governments but are not met with nearly as much outrage by pundits in power. One wonders why.

Why the protests in the US are an awakening for non-Black people around the world

The murder of George Floyd by police on 25 May 2020 sparked protests against police brutality and for racial justice around the United States, then the world. This piece was initially published in TIME *magazine on 5 June 2020, reflecting on how the death of one Black man in the United States of America ignited a global racial reckoning. With reporting by Suyin Haynes.*

The United States is alight with the flame of revolution. Like wildfire, it spreads, and it has been a long time coming. But revolution is borderless, and racism is not solely an American problem.

Though the murder of George Floyd at the knee of a policeman was the most recent spark, the fuel has been pouring for decades. Widespread police brutality in an environment of racialised poverty and inequality has led Black people in the United States to feel there is no option but to overwhelm the streets. Years of peaceful protest and court proceedings brought neither change, nor justice. And so, uprisings; the ferocious cry of the unheard.

Outside the United States, solidarity protests have sprung up in Australia, Britain, Germany, France and beyond. Some have struggled to understand why, blithely suggesting that these protests are due to the United States's cultural hegemony. But as someone who grew up in Australia, lives in the United Kingdom and travels often to work in the United States, it's clear to me that the reason lies under our noses.

The structural racism underlying police brutality in the United States thrives globally, including in Australia and Britain. In England and Wales, young Black people are nine times more likely to be locked up than their white peers[1] and in Australia, Aboriginal and Torres Strait Islander people account for 28 per cent of the prison population,[2] despite only making up 3.3 per cent[3] of the total Australian population. The statistics are devastating in their conclusion: Britain and Australia disproportionally kill and incarcerate Black and Indigenous people. For those whose bodies are not directly violated, equity of opportunity is still a long way off. The system of white supremacy is alive and well.

'I don't know any Black person that would be surprised or shocked by what happened with George Floyd,' says Dr Shola Mos-Shogbamimu, lawyer and women's rights activist in the United Kingdom. 'People suffer from selective amnesia: they forget Grenfell, Windrush, Sarah Reid, Rashaan Charles, Mark Duggan, Stephen Lawrence.'

This 'selective amnesia' conveniently extends back centuries, eliding over the fact that the British Empire was effectively responsible for the concept of race and racism. The Barbados Slave Code of 1661 marked the beginning of the legal codification of slavery, establishing the concept of 'Black' and 'white' races and the racial hierarchy between them. Black people were enslaved, deemed property into perpetuity, whereas white people (Irish, English, Scottish) would be labelled 'indentured servants', property only for the length of their contract. As Barbados was the first English colony to create a set of slavery laws, these laws created the foundation ideology for white supremacy that continues to smother Black lives and dreams today.

Not only are the British often quick to deny their links to the origins of racism and forget their role in pioneering the transatlantic slave trade, they also ignore how they built an entire nation based on the concept of 'whiteness' they so treasured. Australia, the country I grew up in, was that very project. When James Cook declared it 'nobody's land' (terra nullius) in 1770, he erased at least 65,000 years of Aboriginal and Torres Strait Islander inhabitancy. This meant no obligation to get consent to settle, and the freedom to murder Indigenous people with impunity. Those who survived were declared subjects of the British Crown and forcibly 'assimilated'. Whiteness continued to be the nation's aspiration, furthered by the *Immigration Restriction Act* of 1901, a bill that introduced the 'White Australia policy', forbidding non-European migration. The policy was only officially dismantled by 1973.

Australia has never formally acknowledged its racist and genocidal history, and so unsurprisingly, the amnesia persists. 'When I see things like that [referring to George Floyd's death], I'm just very thankful for the wonderful country we live in,' Australian Prime Minister Scott Morrison said in June 2020, warning against importing overseas divisions to Australia while hundreds of protesters gathered in Sydney.[4] He conveniently forgets that the very existence of his 'wonderful country' is contingent on the violent and enduring oppression of Aboriginal people. Too many Australians prefer to live in wilful denial rather than face the brutal spectre of their history.

The British are able to deny their racist history because the worst occurred not on English soil, but in the colonies. They sought to offshore their racist brutality, attempting to buy themselves a semblance of plausible deniability. Out of sight, out of mind. But racism has a long history on British soil too. From Enoch Powell's 1968 'Rivers of Blood' speech in Birmingham, to racism in schools[5] and sport[6] and politics,[7] there is no version of Britain that has existed without it.

There have been countless sparks. Why did this one catch? Why was George Floyd's murder the one to light the fire of sustained protests in the United Kingdom and Australia, rather than Mark Duggan's, the twenty-nine-year-old British man shot and killed by police in August 2011, or David Dungay Jr's, the twenty-six-year-old Dunghutti man who died in police custody in Sydney's Long Bay jail in December 2015? Why now?

I find myself unable to answer. This has long been the lived reality of Black and Indigenous peoples. I've travelled to over twenty countries educating companies and leaders on inclusion, bias and tackling structural inequality, but have often been frustrated by the lack of genuine and sustainable change. People seem willing to accept they might have racial 'unconscious bias', a sanitised way of saying 'internalised racism', but baulk at doing the unlearning, tackling structural change, committing to anti-racism.

Perhaps that is what's changing – or at least, I hope so. These uprisings do not appear in a vacuum. They come on the heels of a devastating global pandemic, a phenomenon that has demonstrated with crystal clarity the failure of states to fully protect their citizens, especially those from Black communities. After months of economically and socially devastating lockdown, there is not only undeniable evidence of systemic inequality. There is also the time and space for people to grapple with the reality of structural racism. In lockdown, there is nowhere else to go, and nothing else to look at.

This is not an awakening for Black people, who have known this reality since we were classified 'Black'. This is a moment of awakening for white people, non-Black people, non-Indigenous people. People who have, through the experience of the pandemic – some perhaps for the first time – an understanding of what it means to be at the mercy of a 'system'. Who now have no excuse for not doing the work they have to do.

What has always been needed is systemic change. Systems and institutions need to become anti-racist. And here's the thing: institutions are made up of people, like you. Systemic change begins with you. It is incumbent on you, reader, to commit to anti-racism, in yourself, your work, your daily practice. The policies and reforms that are required for transformative change need a critical mass of support. To dismantle the system of white supremacy that has killed us and erased our humanity for centuries, we need you to commit to being anti-racist.

Commit to examining your own anti-Blackness and internalised white supremacy. Commit to voting for anti-racist politicians. Commit to actively hiring more Black people and paying them well and giving them the space to make mistakes. Commit to educating yourself on the racial history of your nation. Commit to educating those around you and holding your non-Black friends and colleagues accountable. Consider your anti-racism work a muscle that will atrophy if not exercised. Commit to improving and maintaining your anti-racism 'fitness'.

Commit to doing the work, so we don't have to be here again. And commit to doing it long term, even once the headlines have moved on. Remember the privilege in the choice to learn about racism, rather than live it. I will still be Black after it stops trending – and my life should still matter then.

On abolition

Abolition can seem like a daunting task. We live in a world that is saturated with the assumption that police and prisons are necessary to address widespread problems of violence and harm. Even amongst those who recognise that police and prisons do not make us safe and instead perpetuate inequality, violence and harm, it can still feel hard to imagine life without these institutions

Angela Davis, 2003

It was the autumn of 2017, all leaves of maple and ruby, and pumpkin spice lattes. I was changing with the seasons, gently shedding old ideas, clearing the way for buds of new. In Washington, DC, for a conference, a fellow speaker suggested I visit the National Museum of African American History and Culture on my afternoon off. She promised it would be life-changing. I didn't know her well enough to gauge whether or not her words were likely to be true, but it was a beautiful day and the walk promised to be pleasant. Off I strolled, down picture-perfect boulevards, dry leaves crunching musically under my boots.

Later, I would learn the *Chicago Tribune* said the museum was 'one of the toughest tickets in American culture', perennially sold out and exceeding all of the museum planners' expectations. Nicknamed the 'Blacksonian', there was so much demand when it first opened the previous year, access was strictly limited to those who had booked tickets multiple months in advance. Indeed, this was still the case when I turned up with nervous anticipation at the gleaming bronze building that sunny mid-week afternoon. *You can't just buy tickets at the door*, the security guard said, his genuine contrition at bursting my bubble of excitement not completely hidden. *Try again another time.*

Please, I've come all the way from Australia. There is no other time, I pleaded, but to no avail. The folks in the queue with their tickets and watchful eyes remained silent as I slunk off dejectedly, dumping myself onto a nearby bench, smarting from the public rejection.

Perhaps he had a change of heart, or simply took pity on me. Much to my surprise, once the queue cleared, the uniformed guard waved my woebegone self over and quietly let me in. *Just this once*, he said, smiling kindly.

I wonder if he knew how transformative this act of generosity would be.

Done right, museums are life-changing. Visiting the National Museum of African American History and Culture guided me onto a path I had previously glimpsed, but never ventured along. This was the first time I had seen the history of Black Americans presented with such space and care. The museum stretched over five floors, beginning in a dark, low-ceilinged basement for the intentionally claustrophobic exhibit on enslavement and the Middle Passage, travelling up to the era of segregation, ushering visitors all the way to the civil rights movement and the contemporary racial justice landscape. I learnt about the period of reconstruction, the construction of 'whiteness' in the United States, and activists and abolitionists like Sojourner Truth,

Frederick Douglass and Fred Hampton. Yes, of course, I had self-taught on many of these issues, learnt about John Lewis through comic books, read *The Autobiography of Malcolm X* before I reached double digits, watched any civil rights movie I could torrent or legally stream. But there's a reason the Blacksonian was so popular, forever oversubscribed. *Aussi longtemps que les lions n'auront pas leurs historiens, les récits de chasse tourneront toujours à la gloire du chasseur.* As long as lions do not have their historians, in the words of the proverb a Tunisian French friend shares with me, hunting stories will always glorify the hunter.

For so many of us, formal education systems and institutions have taught us only stories of the hunter, failing catastrophically to teach anything resembling a fuller version of the truth. They have constructed an understanding of the past that reinforces the power of the dominant and elite, uninterested in helping any of us genuinely understand how we have arrived at our status quo.

The Blacksonian poured into the vast lacuna, and as I slowly absorbed the tangle of US history presented there, I wondered what an Australian version might look like. I felt torn between believing it possible and so deeply needed, versus knowing the current political landscape makes it so improbable that I may never live to see such a thing. Then again, a lot can change in a lifetime.

As with most museums of this stature, one visit is insufficient to imbibe the curation's full offering. After spending hours on the first three floors (reportedly, visitors to the Blacksonian stay up to six hours,[1] compared to two in a typical museum) alternating between tears of grief at the centuries of injustice, sobs of pride at generations of courage and resilience, and promises to myself that

I would be back, I found myself approaching the exit. There was just one more little surprise for me in store: the gift shop.

Squeezed in next to the usual museum store paraphernalia of mugs and key rings and black-fist printed scarves stood a book selection beyond anything my Brisbane-bred self had ever set eyes on. Angela Davis and Audre Lorde, James Baldwin and bell hooks, John Lewis and Ta-Nehisi Coates, I bought them all. I bought so many books that the museum offered to ship some back to Australia free of charge. See, these texts were not part of any syllabus I had studied, nor freely available at my local bookstore. They were tickets to a whole new way of understanding the world. And in one of those paradigm-shifting moments, absorbing the analysis and experience of activists and thinkers before me, I was reintroduced to the concept of prison abolition.

I had come across abolitionists before, through my early years of grassroots work in Brisbane. They volunteered with me at the café in Fortitude Valley, supporting locals with no fixed address, a history of incarceration, former wards of the state. They moved through in the heavily postered underground rooms of the Socialist Alliance, who regularly joined our protests supporting Palestine and Lebanon in the mid-2000s. The idea of prison abolition floated around, appearing in snatches of conversation, on pamphlets with crowded text on cheap paper, but the concept remained fringe, fantastical even, to my idealistic teenage self. It would take a book bought from the Blacksonian, Angela Davis's 1981 book *Women, Race and Class*,[2] to bring the idea to life. In it, Davis spoke with characteristic urgency and insight on an idea I had never even dared to imagine: a world without prisons.

Years later, I have the language to understand that Davis was presenting a Marxist feminist analysis of gender, race and class, and talk to you about her critiques of what we would now call 'white feminism'. However, at the time, I didn't have the jargon, the right phrases, or the reading done. I just had a deep curiosity, my lived experience, and a mind critically sharpened on the whetstone of an anti-imperialist father and a fiercely independent mother. Yet still, I was thoroughly challenged by the idea of abolition. A world without prisons, or police? I wondered. *Interesting idea, but no-one will go for that, surely*, I thought. Although I continued to read abolitionist work, I considered it an imaginative exercise, like the broad push for universal basic income, rather than a concrete policy position.

Fast forward a few years to the summer of 2020, and things began to look a little different. Following the murder of George Floyd and the global resurgence of the Black Lives Matter movement in the midst of the COVID-19 pandemic, people seemed ready, for the first time in my memory, to imagine genuinely alternative and liberationary futures. Articles about 'abolishing the police' appeared in the pages of the *New York Times*[3] and radical talking points spilt from the lips of the 'liberal elite' (upper middle-class folks who, ahem, 'read' at Oxbridge or attended Ivy League schools). Discussions about police reform versus abolition bubbled on social media, and folks whom I had never known to engage on 'controversial' topics began posting about their racial awakenings online in an utterly unprecedented manner (like almost everything else in 2020).

The heady, murky months of June, July and August 2020 defy simple summary. Yes, there was a deluge of words of solidarity

from countless corners of society. Companies and celebrities rushed
to perform their support. Institutions announced their desire to
reckon with the past, to do better, to change. Books tackling
racism skyrocketed to the top of best-seller charts,[4] remaining
there for weeks, breaking records in the process.[5] A little over a
year after Derek Chauvin knelt on George Floyd's neck for a fatal
eight minutes and forty-six seconds, he was found guilty of all
charges and sentenced to twenty-two-and-a-half years in prison.

However, much understandable cynicism around any long-
term impact remains, for it is difficult to determine exactly how
much structural and systemic change has tangibly occurred.
Anti-racism books ordered hastily by the thousands languished
uncollected in independent bookstores.[6] Over 1000 people were
killed by United States police officers in the year after George
Floyd's murder.[7] First Nations people have continued to die in
police custody, like Tanya Day and Kumanjayi Walker.[8] Assa
Traoré, the sister of Adama Traoré, who died in French police
custody, was sued for defamation by police officers, only to be
acquitted in June 2021.[9] In 2020, one of Britain's foremost conser-
vation charities, the National Trust, released an 'interim report'
investigating their own 'histories of colonialism and historic
slavery'. The backlash from members was so severe that it is
unclear whether the full report will ever be published[10] and the
Trust seems at a loss as to how to proceed.

It is too soon to say definitively what the long-term, tangible
impact of the 'racial reckoning' of 2020 will be. Only in hindsight
can we join the dots. But it feels safe to say that the racial-justice
Overton window – the range of ideas 'politically acceptable' to the
mainstream[11] – has irreversibly shifted.

The language of change, for example, seemed to stick. Whether it was 'defund the police' or 'abolish prisons', these terms found their way into the mainstream, a positive example of linguistic evolution in a time when words seem to be constantly losing their utility (see: cancel culture, cultural appropriation, freedom of speech). Like genuinely revolutionary language, it reminded us that it is more than a flippant prescription for change.

Abolition forces us to engage with the ills of our society as a whole, pushing us to think outside ourselves as individuals, beyond sharp interpersonal desires. It necessitates a structural and systemic approach; a level of complexity and nuance not so easily boiled down to an op-ed or to-do list. One cannot talk about abolishing prisons, the police or the criminal 'punishment' system* without addressing socio-economic inequality,** the lack of opportunity, employment, and a social safety net that treats people with dignity and respect. As prison abolitionist and scholar Ruth Wilson Gilmore reminds us, 'abolition is about abolishing the conditions under which prison became the solution to problems, rather than abolishing the buildings we call prisons'.[12] British academic and abolitionist organiser Sarah Lamble writes that abolition is 'an ongoing process and practice . . . a way of life

---

* (An alternative to the idea of the 'criminal justice system').

** If anyone has tried to open a bank account without a fixed address, you will understand how difficult the 'system' is for those who are not deemed 'compliant'. You cannot rent a place without a bank account and an accordant credit check, with payslips and proof of previous address. You cannot open a bank account without a fixed address. You cannot get an 'above the board' job, without a fixed address or a bank account. These systems do not need to be this way, but it locks individuals and communities out of financial, housing and justice systems, forcing them to the margins and entrenching the socio-economic inequalities that fuel intergenerational poverty and disadvantage. A simple solution would be to remove the inflexible requirements on basic needs.

and a collective approach to social change'. It is also worth reinforcing that the political conception of 'abolition' is more than simply *dismantling*. 'Abolition is about presence, not absence,' Gilmore reminds us, about 'building life-affirming institutions'. Institutions focused on, for example, housing justice, committed to delivering safe homes for all,* or eradicating family violence, interventions necessarily centred on investing in social and mental health services and strengthening a community's capacity for appropriate intervention. To think of abolition as a 'singular or revolutionary "event"' would be to misunderstand the project.[13]

As I processed the many monumental events of 2020, this idea burrowed its way into my psyche, demanding my full attention. The type of transformation needed was radical, vast, something I could work towards but in some ways outside my control. How could I be more effective? How could I bring this into my life?

I found clues in the writings of contemporaries, like writer and transformative justice practitioner adrienne maree brown. Publishing *We Will Not Cancel Us and Other Dreams of Transformative Justice* in November 2020, brown addressed the culture of disposability she had noticed developing in abolitionist spaces. She shared ways to distinguish between abuse, harm and conflict, behaviours which may overlap and intersect but warrant different responses from individuals and movements. By tackling the concept of 'call-out culture' in movement spaces she had observed, she opened up a space to discuss ways in which we are

---

* 'Safe housing' might mean not only freedom from crime, but also from lead paint, environmental injustice, sudden evictions, etc.: House, S., Okafor, K., 'Under one roof: Building an abolitionist approach to housing justice', nyujlpp.org/quorum/house-okafor-building-abolitionist-approach-housing/

all capable of causing harm (herself included), and how we can potentially move forward with a spirit of love. 'The whole thing was scary,' she said of publishing the booklet, 'but I was curious about the fear itself . . . If there was no such thing as cancel culture or callout culture – in the sense that if you say the wrong thing, you can get disposed of – I don't think I would've felt that I was taking a big risk by speaking about it.'[14] I found her bravery in speaking on challenges within movement spaces humbling and inspiring, a guiding light through an unfamiliar landscape.

Through writers like brown and others, I began to consider what 'abolition' could look like as a way of *life*. If I am truly committed to radically reimagining how society exists, I have to be able to start with myself. What is the link between 'abolition' and my day-to-day praxis? It is in abolishing the conditions which underpin the society we live in, one in which prisons and police are seen as the only way of dealing with harm, of holding a society together. It is about replacing a punitive culture with one of care and support. It reconsiders the manner in which we relate to each other, moves to kindness over cruelty, commits to offering the gift of time and care that healing requires. For as much as abolition is concerned with the very necessary and practical work of dismantling the current criminal 'punishment' system, it also entails reconceptualising how we, individually and collectively, are conditioned to deal with 'problems'.

The conflation begins young. As children, many of us are socialised to listen to and obey authority, without question. We are shown that any 'misbehaviour' (as defined by those with authority) should be *punished*, typically reflecting patterns of historical exclusion and marginalisation. Whether or not a punishment is just, or justified, is of little relevance. We are treated punitively and encouraged to do the same. We grow to understand a single action can become a person's entire identity – 'criminal', 'troublemaker', 'offender', 'slut'. We are urged to involve state power and its accompanying threat of punishment at every level of social, human interaction, in the face of family violence, mental health issues, or a fist fight at school. We are counselled towards a punitive response. We are told that is justice.

In a world where 'justice' and 'punishment' are synonymous, is it any wonder so many of us walk the streets with open wounds?

This 'carceral logic' is something we internalise and carry with us through life. Our partner cheats, so we cut them off completely. An employee makes a mistake, so we dock their pay. A young student is 'disruptive' in class, so they are excluded. A homeless person 'loiters' on your doorstep, so you call the police. A neighbour refuses to cut their grass, so they are sued. An influencer says the wrong thing, and Twitter users call for their 'cancellation'.

Carceral logic tells us that there are 'good people' and 'bad people', 'innocent' and 'guilty', those who are victims and those who should be punished. The reality of course is much more complex. We can be both a victim *and* a perpetrator, innocent *and* guilty, harmed *and* harm others. An abolitionist approach asks us to embrace the complexity and asks us to believe 'no one is disposable'.[15] 'Let them pardon and overlook. Would you not love for Allah to forgive you?' (Quran, 24:22)

We are conditioned to *immediately* respond to any problem that occurs in a society punitively, meting out punishment, including economic and social isolation. There is often little time and consideration given to figuring why something has occurred, or any interest in locating the cause *not* within the individuals themselves, but in the broader, collective context (racialisation, poverty, isolation etc.). Often, our harsh reactions only serve to escalate the harm instead of creating the space to move towards healing, change or resolution. There is no denying that punishment can feel really good, too. If you have been robbed, there is satisfaction in having the thief 'locked up', 'paying' for what they have done. The Venn diagram of holding people to account for their actions and the sweet taste of revenge is sometimes a circle.

Healing is naturally further complicated by contact with the criminal 'justice' system. Any abolitionist worth their salt understands no society can operate safely without proper processes for accountability. However, it is evident that our current 'justice' system is very far from just. It is about 'law and order', control, and punishment. It is a vote-winning strategy,[16] and although research has shown that increased incarceration has a minimal impact in reducing crime,[17] the perception of police and prisons as the trusted force for crime prevention still prevails.[18]

And is it any wonder? We are surrounded by stories and narratives about the moral goodness of the police and state forces. Docu-style TV shows like Australia's *Highway Patrol* and *Border Force*, now in the United States and United Kingdom, show events from the state force's perspective, presenting them as composed and respectful in dealings with a lawless and bellicose public. Our popular culture does the same, whether in *Law and Order: Special Victims Unit*, *East West 101* or *Line of Duty*. The police are the good guys, even when they are investigating themselves. *Mystery Road*, a popular show centred around an

Indigenous cop protagonist, places the 'good' and 'moral' character within the realms of the police force, and asks us to trust in a system the characters themselves understand is flawed. The trope even extends to children's television, like in the popular show *Paw Patrol*,[19] and straight comedy, like *Brooklyn Nine-Nine*.[20] Even when shows acknowledge the problems within the system, the solution is almost always that the main character chooses to operate by their own personal moral code – or throw it out altogether. From Idris Elba as Luther to Jimmy McNulty from *The Wire*, these characters still operate within, and are beholden to, the institution. As the racial justice organisation Colour of Change reports, modern cop shows 'make heroes out of people who violate our rights' and represent police misbehaviour as 'relatable, forgivable, acceptable and ultimately good'.[21] 'Good' only truly exists in a carceral system, operating in the interests of the state.

It might make for compelling TV, but a well-functioning society it does not.

One might argue that the concept of retributive punishment has religious roots. 'An eye for an eye' is certainly a concept found in the Abrahamic tradition, and the phrase is referred to in the Quran. How does the abolitionist way of life fit a faith-based framework? In the Islamic tradition, particularly Islamic liberationary theology, the logic is not the carceral approach to which we are accustomed today. While (proportional) punishment in response to certain crimes might be permissible, it is certainly not considered praiseworthy by leading scholars. And such conceptualisation does not only exist in the contemporary theological landscape, but stretches back hundreds of years. One of the eleventh century's leading Muslim thinkers, Ibn Hazm Al-Andalusi, wrote in *al-Akhlaq wa'l-siyar (In Pursuit of Virtue)*:

> The greatest of good deeds is to refrain from punishing your enemy and from handing him over to an oppressor ... Magnanimity consists not of mingling with our enemies but of showing mercy to them while still not trusting them.

The Prophet Mohammed (SAW) is also reported to have said, 'Do not be people without minds of your own, saying that if others treat you well you will treat them well, and that if they do wrong you will do wrong. Instead, accustom yourselves to do good if people do good and not to do wrong if they do evil.' (Sunan At-Tirmidhi)

The morally aspirational position is, in the language of Al-Andalusi and others, *mercy*. In abolitionist language, it would be considered moving from 'responding to harm with punishment' to 'offering support, healing and connection'[22].

Again, the Prophet Mohammed (SAW): 'Whoever suffers an injury done to him and forgives (the person responsible), Allah will raise his status to a higher degree and remove one of his sins.' (Sunan At-Tirmidhi)

My Islamic liberation theology aligns with an abolitionist way of life. It demands the dismantling of all oppressive systems, carceral logic included. It stands against injustice regardless of the cost. It creates cultures of accountability and reparation, building infrastructures of support and care, individually, interpersonally and institutionally. And it begins with me. For if I can start with myself, practising abolition, the Islamic application of mercy, in my day-to-day life, that may lay the groundwork in a small way for broader social change. If enough of us radically transform our personal worlds, who knows how far our collective ripples will travel?

For me, that looks like resisting the urge to participate in or comment on situations where I feel the approach is harm inducing rather than reducing, especially online. It looks like taking the time to do all I can to mediate between people when conflict occurs, working with folks not from a place of judgement but from a place of respecting and caring for all. It looks like responding in good faith when those who have caused me harm reach out and apologise (like journalists who have abused me in the press), accepting that they have taken accountability and taken steps to alter their behaviour. It is about biting my tongue in a fight with my partner or apologising and taking responsibility if I overstep the mark and cause my loved one hurt. It is choosing to hear a friend out, even if they have caused me pain, because no good comes from no communication. It's about trying, in every way possible, to reduce harm, minimise my ego, work for the collective.

I may not always succeed in my ambitions to live by abolitionist, Islamic virtues. In fact, I can almost guarantee that I will not. Acknowledging that, in of itself, is a crucial part of this process. We will make mistakes because we are human, because we live in an individualised, carceral, punitive society where there is apparently a line between those who are good and worthy, and those who are bad and worthless. But anyone who is paying any attention can tell you that we are all so much more complex than that. It is in this complexity I find eternal hope. From the understanding of humanity described in the Quran, to the kindness of the security guard who broke the rules for a knowledge-hungry visitor from across the seas, hope comes from recognising possibility, the true potential for transformation in each and every one of us, and therefore, in society as a whole. If we can learn to embrace our fallible humanity, individually and collectively, we are one step closer to that just future so many of us dream of. Khair, inshallah.

Boris Johnson's 'brownwashing' is a return to Britain's imperial playbook

Originally published on 9 October 2020 in gal-dem, *a British new media publication committed to telling the stories of people of colour from marginalised genders. The piece was written with a view to pierce the myth of 'representation'; that even if the Conservative (Tory) government was said to be 'ethnically diverse', that did not automatically mean better outcomes for racialised communities in Britain.*

Lauded as one of the most ethnically diverse governments in history, Boris Johnson's 2019 'cabinet for modern Britain'[1] was received with much fanfare. It was positioned as a bold, nation-building exercise for the Brexiting state. A racially diverse cabinet, the story went, was an indicator that Boris's Britain had progressed from the days of Enoch Powell and 'No Irish, No Blacks, No Dogs' signs. But this was a myth, reliant on the misguided belief that any representation was a sign of progress.

Johnson's government is anything but progressive. For a start, Home Secretary Priti Patel continues to push through an immigration bill that wouldn't have allowed her own Gujarati parents

into the country from Uganda.[2] Patel is now reportedly consider-
ing sending asylum seekers to offshore detention centres modelled
on Australia's cruel, inhuman and degrading policies and has
been criticised by human rights groups after her comments at
the Conservative Party conference in which she said she would
'expedite the removal' of asylum seekers.[3]

Meanwhile, the government reviewer of the discriminatory
Prevent program, Lord Carlile, admitted he was 'biased towards'[4]
the policy. Prevent, the United Kingdom's counter-terrorism
strategy, is ostensibly aimed at 'preventing the radicalisation
of vulnerable people', but in practice has entrenched the surveillance of Muslim communities and further institutionalised
Islamophobia in Britain. Indeed, Muslims are forty times
more likely to be referred to Prevent than non-Muslims.[5] Key
elements of the strategy are based on 'flawed science',[6] according
to researchers, and it has widely been condemned by academics,
human rights lawyers and swathes of British Muslim communities for viewing the Muslim community through a securitised
lens.[7] The Muslim Council of Britain found the fundamental
approach of the program, part of the United Kingdom's long-
term strategy to counter terrorism, lacks an evidentiary basis,
lacks accountability and broadens the notion of what constitutes extremism to the point it discourages free speech.[8] Former
chairman of the UK Equality and Human Rights Commission
Trevor Phillips, suspended from the Labour Party in 2020 over
allegations of Islamophobia,[9] has been trusted to work across
an inquiry into the disproportionate impact of COVID-19 on
BAME (Black, Asian and minority ethnic) communities. Given
the first four doctors to die from the disease were Muslim, the

appointment is offensive at best, fatal for communities at worst. It is no wonder Black, Muslim and other marginalised communities feel unsafe[10] and unprotected by the state.[11] Boris's government is bad faith appointments and brownwashing as far as the eye can see.

How has this happened? A closer look at the reshuffled 2020 cabinet hints at a slightly different story to the one being told. Despite Black Britons representing 3 per cent of the population, British Indians 2.3 per cent and British Pakistanis 1.9 per cent,[12] the ethnic minorities in Johnson's cabinet are all British Indian. And even then, only a particular subset makes the cut. The four British Indians are either East African Asian, Hindu, or both. They are also almost all staunch Brexiteers. Britain's modern diversity, this is not.

Admittedly, the cabinet's ethnic minorities were previously drawn from a broader church, including British Pakistani Sajid Javid, but none of those members made it past the first reshuffle. Sajid's dismissal was rumoured to be connected to his demanding an investigation into Tory-party Islamophobia, but others were dismissed without explanation. Cambridge English professor Priyamvada Gopal observes in the *Independent* that coupled with the current make-up of the cabinet, Boris's choices only serve to perform 'inclusion without changing the exploitative and racist politics of the One Nation Conservatism'.[13] It was a bait and switch, focused on the performance of progress rather than what would create meaningful change for the communities this 'diversity' was meant to reflect.

In other words, a light sprinkling of brown faces doth not a progressive cabinet make.

In the wake of the brutal murder of George Floyd in Minnesota in May 2020, this hypothesis was put to the test. Black communities and their allies across the United Kingdom demanded justice and structural change, not just for Floyd but for many in the United Kingdom whose fate mirrored his. This was the moment for the cabinet to shine, to reflect the progressive values they were supposed to represent. Instead, their response exposed the fantasy at the heart of the fairytale – representation had never meant progress for the marginalised.

Boris Johnson immediately distanced the country from the protests, ignoring Britain's own record of police brutality and pivoting instead to the red herring of statues. Priti Patel declared the protests unlawful and threatened protesters with 'justice' for their 'thuggery' against the police, language deceivingly framing the #BlackLivesMatter movement as villainous and violent. The 2019 Foreign Secretary Dominic Raab claimed taking the knee came from *Game of Thrones*,[14] and then Health Secretary Matt Hancock named two South Asians when asked about Black cabinet ministers. This ignorance and insolence went unpunished. Johnson announced a commission into racial equality in mid-June 2020, then kneecapped the effort almost immediately by appointing his long-time confidante and head of the No. 10 policy unit, Munira Mirza, to lead it. Mirza believes institutional racism is a myth,[15] and soon after her appointment, British journalist and author of *Why I'm No Longer Talking to White People About Race* Reni Eddo-Lodge likened the move to 'asking Jack the Ripper to weigh in on feminism'.[16] The entire episode did little more than reveal the racist rot infesting Whitehall and remind us that staggering disregard for

Black people would continue to be a hallmark of Johnson's government.

Sadly, these decisions and declarations are unsurprising to anyone familiar with the failure of the politics of representation, which allows for the elevation of individuals from one minority group while pursuing discriminatory policies against others. It is a colonial sleight of hand as old as the Empire itself, harking back to practices of divide and rule that enabled imperial expansion. Today's political goal is Brexit, and imperial habits are hard to break.

The ethnic minorities finding parliamentary success today are largely descendant from one specific group with a particular imperial history: East African Asians descended from Indians, long employed by the British to oversee the East Africa Protectorate[17] on their behalf. They acted as sub-imperial agents, maintaining and reinforcing the colonial hierarchy until Kenyan independence in 1963. Africanisation policies and Idi Amin forced thousands of these now 'twice migrants' to the shores of Britain.[18] This was a cohort perfectly poised to benefit from Margaret Thatcher's 'enterprise' economy,[19] bringing with them wealth, strong English language skills[20] and 'family values', as well as lived experience of a colonial hierarchy that rewarded domination of Black Africans. Narindar Saroop, the first South Asian Tory parliamentary candidate, felt that these upwardly mobile Sikh and Hindu Indians were 'natural conservatives',[21] and so in 1976, the Anglo Asian Conservative Society was born.

Saroop was quite the character. An ardent Anglophile, he once described himself as the kind of man who 'sits on a tiger-skin rug, wearing a monocle, eating chicken tandoori and humming

"God Save the Queen'".[22] He was also a key player in attracting conservative South Asians to the Tory party, facilitating meetings with Thatcher herself, and helping them buy into her vision of a self-reliant and entrepreneurial Britain. Their businesses and investments grew, and soon British Indians would become Britain's wealthiest ethnic minority group, and a growing voter base for the Tories. In less than a decade, the British Indian Conservative vote almost tripled, from 9 per cent in 1979 to 24 per cent by 1987.[23] The strategy was so successful that David Cameron repeated it in 2010.

After failing to secure a majority with his Big Society vision,[24] Cameron called for a 'new special relationship' with India, ending the diplomatic boycott of Hindu-nationalist Narendra Modi in 2012* and facilitating a shift that was decidedly pro-Hindutva, and further right.[25] He was rewarded with Bollywood-style Hindi songs and Modiesque support, delivering a resounding majority for the Conservatives in 2015.[26] Although this victory would be the poisoned chalice heralding Cameron's political demise, for the party, it was a sign of things to come.

By 2017, the Conservative Party's share of the British Indian vote was up to 40 per cent, reflecting the growing Conservative Hindu and Sikh constituency. Although not all Conservative voters, British Indians were also the most pro-Brexit ethnic minority group, with 40 per cent voting Leave. So, when Boris won a landslide victory on the promise to 'Get Brexit Done', elevating loyal British Indians to visibly senior positions and brownwashing the cabinet was a no-brainer. But this was not the

---

* Before his party, the Bharatiya Janata Party, came to power in 2014.

anti-racist overture it was presented as – it was regression masquerading as progress. The party moved further right, pursuing anti-immigrant, xenophobic and Islamophobic policies, and used the identities of cabinet members as inoculation from any charges of racism.

As Gopal reminds us, 'A place at the majority table often comes at the price of silence or active complicity.'[27] Unless members of minority communities are using their positions of power to alleviate oppressions of other marginalised groups, representation is not genuine progress. In fact, the focus on a simple metric can often be a smokescreen for activism, and the current cabinet shows us as much. Remember, empire building was not only about taking advantage of divisions between communities but actively creating and exacerbating conflict for control. So while some might argue that having four British Indian members of the cabinet is at least some progress, it feels markedly closer to the indirect rule of the empire than any form of liberation.

Whether for imperial expansion or Brexit Nativism, as a Black woman, one thing is clear – being ruled by brown faces instead of white is simply a return to the imperial playbook, not progress at all.

The uprising in Sudan is more than just about bread prices

Published in UK paper the Independent *on 30 December 2018, this was an early piece in the literature about the 2018–19 Sudanese revolution that eventually ousted long-time dictator Omar al-Bashir. I was desperate to join my family and country-people on the ground in Sudan when the revolution kicked off, but my family would not countenance it. We do not have the ability to keep you safe, they said, and you have spoken against the government publicly for many years. I maintained that I wasn't high-profile enough in the Sudanese context to raise the ire of the government, but of course, what was I to know? If I was detained by the dictatorship, as many journalists, writers and activists had been, no one was coming to save me. In the end, I did not take the risk, and stayed in the diaspora, raising as much awareness as I could about what was happening on the ground in the English language media, collecting funds to support the revolutionaries, praying for success. I even featured the Sudanese Revolution in my novel for young teens,* Listen, Layla.

Although I did all I could from the diaspora, part of me still feels I should have gone, should have been part of the groundswell, should have faced the army side by side with my fellow Sudanese people, as my mother did in her youth. I wonder if I am weak, for choosing safety.

I wonder if choosing to not take the risk means I am less dedicated to the cause. After all, maybe it would have been fine, maybe I wouldn't have been hurt, or detained, or killed. Or maybe not. Allahu A3lam, Only God Knows. We can only live with the choices we've made . . .

2018. It's been almost thirty years since the largely bloodless coup that brought current Sudanese President Omar al-Bashir into power on 30 June 1989. But however peaceful his ascent, the same cannot be said for his reign, and the protests sweeping the nation this December are a testament to this.

It's eleven days since the start of the protests in the northern Sudanese town of Atbara – Amnesty International reported the death toll during the first five days to be thirty-seven.[1] While the unrest and anger show no signs of abating, the historical context is critical to understanding the difficulty in achieving the protestors' wishes for not only Bashir's removal, but a change in Sudan's fortunes.

Sudan's complex history – tribally, religiously and socially – makes it different to many of its Arab and north African counterparts. My family's story of fortune and diasporic displacement is in part a reflection of these dynamics, but our story is not unique, and can often be drawn back to a name many Sudanese are familiar with: Hassan al-Turabi.

Although Bashir led the military coup that brought him to power in 1989, the real godfather of the current system is Turabi, the head of the National Islamic Front (NIF) at the time. Turabi, the leader of Sudan's political arm of the Muslim Brotherhood (al-Akhwaan), had a deeply ideological mission to prosecute: the Arabisation and Islamisation of Sudan, at all costs.

It was this politicised approach to Islam and the lack of safety and future it portended that, less than two years later, would drive my parents and me out of our homeland.

My parents were city folk: part of the educated and professional class, my father an engineering lecturer with a PhD from London's Imperial College and my mother a successful city-based architect, both graduates of the University of Khartoum. They were part of an active and vibrant segment of society: products of a system that for a brief period of time, worked. It was this very segment of society that the NIF, once in power, immediately and systematically targeted and dismantled, understanding the threat that they posed to the dictatorship. The middle classes – the doctors, lawyers, accountants and engineers – were critical to the downfall of Sudan's previous military leader, General Jaafar Nimeiri, in 1985. While Nimeiri visited Washington, DC, for a medical check-up and talks with the US government, the opposition took the opportunity to organise widespread protests across Khartoum, including the professional associations and trade unionists. From doctors and lawyers to flight attendants and electricians, the general strike eventually led to the Commander in Chief of the Armed Forces, General Abdul Rahman Swar al-Dahab, taking control of Sudan as head of the Transitional Military Council, dismissing President Nimeiri and rapidly dismantling his regime.[2] Turabi and Bashir wouldn't let that happen again.

Leaders of unions, public service employees, academic staff – anyone who refused to dance to the NIF tune – were fired, threatened, disappeared, departed. The intellectual class was disastrously drained from the nation, leaving an enfeebled public service, health sector and education system.

This brain drain led to the diaspora that I am a part of – young people who grew up outside Sudan to parents who were brought up in a country that is unrecognisable to the one that we see today. Many of us are also the people you'll find on social media platforms like Instagram and Twitter, amplifying voices of activists and organisers on the ground as much as possible, relaying information to Twitter and mainstream media outlets from our family WhatsApp groups, hashtagging in all our mother tongues. For many of us – for myself at least – this is personal: the current regime has squandered Sudan's wealth and potential. It is responsible for the deaths of an unknowable number of its citizens and has ultimately destroyed the country we could have grown up safely in, and known as home.

But this story isn't about the diaspora. This is about the nation that many of us still do call home, no matter how tenuous the physical link. Although the trigger for the current spate of protests was bread prices, the underlying frustration that has fuelled people's anger is deeper, and much longer in the making. For many in Sudan, its current situation is virtually unliveable, with cash and fuel shortages galore, astronomical and unpredictable inflation, and basic services that sometimes do more harm than good. People don't chant 'We either live free or die like real men' and mean it, unless they're truly desperate.

But Bashir stepping down would not be the end to the woes of the Sudanese people. The oil revenue, a major source of funds for the government,[3] hasn't gone into social development but into national security, armed forces and weaponry. Bashir's regime – split from Turabi in the early 2000s – no longer has a particularly Islamist agenda. It seems largely interested in holding on to power alone, and has the firepower to have done so effectively for almost three decades.

The question is therefore, twofold.

Is it possible to topple Bashir? Possibly. Although the social infrastructure of previous successful popular uprisings, like the unions and professional classes, is no longer as active as in the 1980s, the grassroots movement is still powerful, especially when many feel like there is nowhere else to turn. With the movement buoyed by the diaspora's involvement and the freedom of communication through social media, Bashir's resignation is a definite possibility.

The second and more pertinent question, however, is much more difficult to answer. How do the Sudanese people dismantle the current infrastructure of what is ostensibly a police state, and what will it take to rebuild the nation into one that can enable it to truly realise its potential?

That will take more than one article to answer, unfortunately. But unless given deep and thoughtful consideration from across Sudan's diverse tribal, social and religious groups, the land of my birth will fall back into the same cycle it has seen since independence. Hopefully we can learn from our mistakes.

—

An update:

Less than four full months after the publication of this piece, on 11 April 2019, Omar al-Bashir was ousted from power by military forces. A Transitional Military Council (TMC) was created to rule, but protests continued unabated, demanding nothing less than a civilian government.

'7ureeya, salam wa 3adala, madaneeya 5iyar al-sha3b!'

'Freedom, peace and justice, civilian government is the choice of the people!'

As demonstrations continued to surge around the country, a sit-in pooled and swelled at the front of the army headquarters in Khartoum, a hub of music, joy and hope. Dignitaries visited, schools were set up, a medical quarter was created. It was seen as a microcosm of what Sudan could be, shouts of 'We are all Darfur' reverberating through crowds with regularity, a national solidarity previously unimaginable. But the bliss was short-lived.

On the day before Eid Al-Fitr, the last day of Ramadan, armed forces loyal to the TMC attacked the sit-in,[4] terrorising, raping and murdering the peaceful protestors. Instead of a day of celebration, Eid of 2019 was a day of mourning for Sudanese in the country and around the world. But despite the massacre, despite the internet being cut for weeks on end, despite the armed forces' interminable attempts to suppress the revolution, the people would not be dissuaded. On 30 June 2019, Sudan bore witness to the first 'million people protest', or the milyoneeya, hundreds of thousands of Sudanese from cities and towns around the country joining revolutionaries in Khartoum to call for civilian rule.

Eventually, in August 2019, an eleven-member Sovereignty Council was formed; five military and six civilians to rule for just over three years until elections were to be held in 2022. On 21 August 2019, civilian Dr Abdullah Hamdok was sworn in as civilian prime minister. The revolution had won its first battle.

It was not easy for Hamdok and his ministers. The work of uprooting deep tendrils of Bashir's military apparatus aside, Hamdok himself was the target of at least one assassination attempt,[5] and the civilian government distracted by attempted military coups.[6] The country, as of writing, remains in dire straits, basic commodities are in short supply (fuel, wheat, medicine, power[7]) and life for people on a day-to-day basis yet to improve. The path to freedom, peace and justice is far from easy. The complex history of Sudan, constant foreign interference, legacies of Arab, Ottoman and British imperialism and decades of dictatorship do not make for simple answers, clear-cut revolutions.

On 15 October 2021, Prime Minister Hamdok warned Sudan was facing the 'worst crisis' of its transition to civilian rule since the removal of al-Bashir.[8] 'The essence of this crisis ... is the inability to reach a consensus on a national project among the revolutionary and change forces,' Hamdok said.

Only ten days later, on 25 October 2021, the military seized power and control of the state. Internet and phone communication was cut off for weeks, peaceful protestors in the streets were teargassed, raped, killed. I built the sudancoup.com website, and worked with members of the Sudanese diaspora to try to do what we could from the outside, supporting and amplifying the calls from those on the ground: an end to military rule, freedom, peace and justice; no negotiation, no partnership, no compromise. The situation remains tense, fluid, uncertain. My family have yet again begged me to delay my planned visit, citing security concerns. The chaos and desperation they speak of on the streets is like nothing Sudan has seen in my lifetime that I can recall. But still, somehow, people continue to come out into the streets, protesting, striking, demanding a better future.

—

Sitting still, in the untethered realm of the diaspora, I wish, hope and pray that Sudan finds its way, inshallah; that the freedom, peace and justice that so many fought and died for, including my own cousin, are soon on their way.

An engineer's perspective

I wrote this piece initially for the New York Times, *but it was too 'in the weeds' for their audience, according to the editor I was working with. Not willing to pull it out of the shrubbery, I later pitched it and published it in* The Stick, *a wonderful but sadly short-lived quarterly magazine launched by former actor Samuel Johnson ('I just won the Gold Logie for my portrayal of Molly Meldrum,' he said to me in his intro email). The publication was pitched as a 'no-nonsense' and 'spin-free newspaper', with the entire cover price going towards cancer research through the charity Love Your Sister. The piece was filed in May 2017, and more recent information on the states' energy mixes is available in the footnotes.*

On 28 September 2016, South Australia was hit by a once-in-fifty-year storm. One of Australia's six states, and a world-leading pioneer in integrating intermittent renewable energy generation into a constrained electricity grid, the state's energy system was tested by the extreme weather event.

Over 40 per cent of South Australia's energy is generated by wind and solar power,[1] and there are no longer any coal-fired power stations operating in the state. The only back-up power comes from the neighbouring state of Victoria, heavily dependent on brown coal.[2] Unfortunately for South Australia, and the advocates of renewable energy, the storm caused the state to lose all power. The statewide blackout, which dragged on for days, was an unprecedented and catastrophic engineering failure. However, South Australia's failure should not be seen as the failure of the renewables transition. Instead, it is a prime opportunity to understand the delicate engineering challenge of integrating new, intermittent and asynchronous sources of power into ageing infrastructure reliant on conventional power generation. Understanding what happened in South Australia enables us to understand what is possible with today's current technologies, and what truly stands in the way of a complete transition to a carbon neutral future.

So what happened on that fateful Wednesday afternoon?

According to the Australian Energy Market Operator's (AEMO's) final report into the events, published in March 2017,[3] South Australia's series of woes began with two tornadoes with gale force winds of 260 kilometres per hour knocking out three major transmission lines. When a transmission line is damaged, it often short circuits. As a result of such a 'fault', the line almost immediately disconnects, protecting the rest of the system. Almost. For a fraction of a second, the voltage dips in the grid, and it was these voltage dips that led to the cascading failure of the system.

Typically, power generators – whether wind, gas or otherwise – are designed to 'ride-through' a voltage dip, allowing them to continue to operate through a fault. However, unbeknown to AEMO, responsible for operating energy markets and power systems, several wind farms in South Australia had been set up with a protection feature limiting their tolerance for disturbances. If the number of faults in a specified period of time exceeded a pre-set limit – for instance, two faults in two minutes – the safety mechanism activated and a wind turbine would either reduce its output, stop operating or disconnect from the network. Strangely, this critical protection feature had been left out of all simulation models submitted to AEMO, so the market operator had no idea that their wind turbines were vulnerable to disconnection due to voltage dips.

The damage wrought by the weather caused six voltage dips to occur over a two-minute period. Without warning, the nine wind farms activated their protection features and 456 megawatts, or almost a quarter of South Australia's energy demand, was lost from the system. The remainder of South Australia's generation was wind and 'slow responding thermal' (gas), and therefore unable to pick up the slack in time. Instead, Victoria, the neighbouring state, which was already providing 24 per cent of South Australia's electricity requirements at the time, began to compensate. During the seven seconds of power loss from the wind farms, the system began to draw significantly more electricity than the single interconnector between the two states could handle.

It was like trying to light a football field from a single power point, blowing the proverbial fuse. The interconnector tripped, and Australia's fourth largest state became an 'electrical island'. The entire population of 1.7 million was plunged into darkness. It was known as a Black System event, and it took thirteen days for the last of the remaining customers to have their power restored.

South Australia's Black System ushered in weeks of finger-pointing and blame-shifting among politicians, energy operators, pundits and consumers. Conservative politicians blamed renewable energy, renewable energy purists blamed the market operators and the majority of the state and nation simply wanted the problem to be solved.

What do we learn from an incident like this?

Part of why the South Australian example is so important is because it is tackling what is known within the industry as the 'energy trilemma'. This is the tension between energy security (reliability), equity (affordability and accessibility) and environmental sustainability. As we move importantly and inevitably towards sustainability, there can be no question that energy security and equity will be tested. How they balance out is being watched very closely.

From an engineer's perspective, the focus is often squarely on reliability. The challenge of integrating intermittent renewable power generation sources into a system that hasn't been designed for it means the energy supply is not always as resilient, and therefore, potentially less reliable. This poses a significant political risk for leaders and often the argument for baseload coal and gas generation is offered as a solution. However, in this case, AEMO found the operations of the gas generators had little to no material effect on the event, to the dismay of renewable energy opponents. Yet a quarter of the state's energy was coming from Victoria, largely powered by brown coal. So although South Australia may not have coal-fired power stations within its borders, it is still in some way dependent on their operation for baseload power. The answer for the perfect mix of power generation is certainly not clear-cut.

What is clearer are the broader consequences, and the potential loss if such an event is interpreted incorrectly. The lessons learnt from these massive engineering failures provide invaluable insight into how to 'design out' a system's weaknesses. Technical industries rely heavily on learning from major incidents; the oil and gas industry, for example, designed many safety systems from lessons learnt after the catastrophic explosion on the North Sea oil platform Piper Alpha in 1988 and the blow out and subsequent marine oil spill from the Macondo well in the Gulf of Mexico in 2010, the largest in history. The opportunity here to improve the system and avoid a similar incident in the future not only benefits South Australia, but can also have a global impact. By demonstrating how renewable sources of energy can be integrated into an ageing electricity grid, South Australia is providing a blueprint for the energy transition globally.

That is, if the interpretation of the event and the subsequent discussion remains true to the technical findings.

Unfortunately for engineers, the reality of the energy trilemma means that the technical solutions alone are not always enough, and run the risk of getting lost in posturing and agendas. The political and economic challenges are steep. Tackling these requires moving away from blatant dogmatic ideological approaches to a view that is committed to achieving the optimum balance of sustainability, affordability and reliability. For whether we like it or not, if we don't get sustainability right, there may not be a world for us to live in where affordability and reliability matter at all.

Notes

Words mean things

1 Wittgenstein, L. (transl. Anscombe, G. E. M., Hacker, P. M. S., Schulte, J.), *Philosophical Investigations*, Wiley-Blackwell, Malden, 2009, p. 43.

2 Beaumont-Thomas, B., 'Sam Fender: "Leftie is now a slur in working-class towns"', *Guardian*, 25 August 2021.

3 'What's taking the knee and why is it important?' *BBC News*, *Explainers*, 13 October 2021.

4 Associated Press, 'Trump says NFL should fire players who kneel during national anthem', *Los Angeles Times*, 22 September 2017.

5 Middleton, J., 'Tory MP continues boycott of England team over taking the knee – but "will cheer if they score"', *Independent*, 8 July 2021.

6 Walker, P., 'Dominic Raab criticised for comments on BLM protesters taking the knee', *Guardian*, 19 June 2020.

7 Sky News Australia, 'Australian cricket team "disgraced themselves" by taking the knee to BLM "cult"', YouTube, 22 July 2021; youtube.com/watch?v=gKmglpVdrsw (accessed 24 January 2022).

8 Anthony, A., 'Everything you wanted to know about the culture wars – but were afraid to ask', *Guardian*, 13 June 2021.

9 Anthony, 'Everything you wanted to know about the culture wars'.

10 The More in Common thinktank found that 12 per cent of voters accounted for 50 per cent of all social media users: Savage, M., '"Culture wars" are fought by tiny minority – UK study', *Guardian*, 25 October 2020.

11 Malik, N., 'The right is winning the culture war because its opponents don't know the rules', *Guardian*, 19 July 2021.

12 Media Education Foundation, 'Race, the floating signifier, featuring Stuart Hall', Transcript, 1997; mediaed.org/transcripts/Stuart-Hall-Race-the-Floating-Signifier-Transcript.pdf (accessed 24 January 2022).

13 Officially known as 'An Act for Better Ordering and Governing of Negroes': Dabiri, E., *What White People Can Do Next*, Penguin Books, London, Kindle edition, p. 51.

14 Handler, J. S., 'Custom and law: The status of enslaved Africans in seventeenth-century Barbados', *Slavery & Abolition*, 2016, vol. 37, no. 2, pp. 233–55; Rugemer, E. B., 'The development of mastery and race in the comprehensive slave codes of the greater Caribbean during the seventeenth century', *The William and Mary Quarterly*, 2013, vol. 70, no. 3, pp. 429–58.

15 Handler, J. S. and Reilly, M. C., 'Contesting "White Slavery" in the Caribbean', *New West Indian Guide*, 2017, vol. 91, pp. 30–55; Mullally, U., 'Emma Dabiri and Hazel Chu: "This is a real, important moment in Ireland"', *Irish Times*, 27 March 2021.

16 Media Education Foundation, 'Race, the floating signifier, featuring Stuart Hall'.

17 Mukhopadhyay, C. C., 'Getting rid of the word "Caucasian"' in Pollock, M. (ed.), *Everyday Antiracism: Getting real about race in school*, The New Press, New York, 2008.

18 'A new take on the 19th-century skull collection of Samuel Morton', Science Daily, 4 October 2018; sciencedaily.com/releases/2018/10/181004143943.htm (accessed 25 January 2022).

19 Even those who aren't Muslim but are seen as such are targeted: Basu, M., 'Fifteen years after 9/11, Sikhs still victims of anti-Muslim hate crimes', CNN, 15 September 2016.

20 Media Education Foundation, 'Race, the floating signifier, featuring Stuart Hall'.

In defence of hobbies

1 'The side hustle economy: A white paper from Henley Business School', Henley Business School, July 2018.

2 'Sense of us report', ING, 2021; campaigns.ing.com.au/assets/pdf/ING_Sense_of_Us_Report_A4_0321.pdf?v=15032021 (accessed 24 January 2022).

3 Griffith, E., 'Why are young people pretending to love work?', *New York Times*, 26 January 2019.

4 Pathak, S., 'Not working, side hustles and crying: How the workplace will change in 2020', Digiday, 10 January 2020;

digiday.com/marketing/not-working-side-hustles-crying-workplace-will-change-2020/ (accessed 24 January 2022).

5   Hill, K., 'I'm a Gen Zer who graduated during the pandemic. Here's why I think my generation's obsession with "hustle culture" has become unhealthy', *Business Insider*, 22 April 2021.

6   Griffith, 'Why are young people pretending to love work?'.

7   Quart, A., 'The con of the side hustle', *New York Times*, 6 April 2019.

8   Collinson, A., 'The toxic fantasy of the "side hustle"', *Prospect*, 19 August 2019.

9   Peetz, D., 'There's an obvious reason wages aren't growing, but you won't hear it from Treasury or the Reserve Bank', *The Conversation*, 9 September 2019.

10 Tily, G., 'Seventeen-year wage squeeze the worst in two hundred years', Trades Union Congress, 11 May 2018; tuc.org.uk/blogs/17-year-wage-squeeze-worst-two-hundred-years (accessed 24 January 2022).

11 MacQueen, R., 'What is happening with UK wages?' Economics Observatory, 20 January 2022; economicsobservatory.com/what-is-happening-with-UK-wages (accessed 19 March 2022).

Islam and social justice

1   Afsaruddin, A., 'What Sharia means: Five questions answered', *The Conversation*, 16 June 2017, referring to Auda, J., *Maqasid Al-Shariah: A beginner's guide*, International Institute of Islamic Thought, London, 2008.

2   Hallaq, W. B., *Sharī'a: Theory, practice, transformation*, Cambridge University Press, Cambridge, 2009, pp. 1–2.

3   Hallaq, *Sharī'a*, pp. 2–3.

4   In January 2017, US President Donald Trump signed an Executive Order that banned foreign nationals from seven predominantly Muslim countries from visiting the country for ninety days, suspended entry to the country of all Syrian refugees indefinitely, and prohibited any other refugees from coming into the country for 120 days: see 'Timeline of the Muslim ban', ACLU Washington; aclu-wa.org/pages/timeline-muslim-ban (accessed 24 January 2022).

5   Spivak, G., 'Can the subaltern speak? Speculations on widow sacrifice', first published in *Wedge*, vol. 7–8 (Winter–Spring 1985), pp. 120–30.

6   cooke, m., 'Gender and September 11: A roundtable: Saving brown women', *Signs: Journal of Women in Culture and Society*, 2002, vol. 28, no.1, pp. 468–70.

7   cooke, m., 'Gender and September 11', pp. 468–70.

8   Ahmed, L., *Women and Gender in Islam: Historical roots of a modern debate*, Yale University Press, New Haven, 1992, p. 151.

9   Viper, K., 'Feminism as imperialism', *Guardian*, 21 September 2002, citing Ahmed, *Women and Gender in Islam*.

10 Woodhull, W., *Transfigurations of the Maghreb: Feminism, decolonization, and literatures*, University of Minnesota Press, Minneapolis, 1993.

11 MacMaster, N., *Burning the Veil: The Algerian war and the 'emancipation' of Muslim women, 1954–62*, Manchester University Press, Manchester, 2009.

12 MacMaster, N., *Burning the Veil*. One woman was threatened with the torture of her brother if she did not participate.

13 Falecka, K., 'From colonial Algeria to modern day Europe, the Muslim veil remains an ideological background', *The Conversation*, 24 January 2017.

14 Faulkner, R. A., 'Assia Djebar, Frantz Fanon, women, veils, and land', *World Literature Today*, 1996, vol. 70, no. 4, pp. 847–55.

15 Kebsi, J., 'Unveil them to save them: France and the ongoing colonization of women's bodies', *Berkley Center for Religion, Peace & World Affairs*, 13 May 2021; berkleycenter.georgetown.edu/responses/ unveil-them-to-save-them-france-and-the-ongoing-colonization-of- muslim-women-s-bodies (accessed 24 January 2022).

16 '"Law against Islam": French vote in favour of hijab ban condemned', *Al Jazeera*, 9 April 2021.

17 'Text: Laura Bush on Taliban oppression of women', *Washington Post*, 17 November 2001.

18 The Associated Press tally of the dead includes more than 47,000 civilians, about 7500 foreign military personnel and contractors, 66,000 Afghan military and police personnel, 51,000 Taliban, hundreds of aid workers and dozens of journalists. See Knickmeyer, E., 'Costs of the Afghanistan war, in lives and dollars', *AP News*, 17 August 2021.

19 Johnson, E. A., Elbardicy, M., Rezvani, A., 'She is staying in Afghanistan to ensure women's gains aren't lost under Taliban rule', NPR, 17 August 2021; npr.org/2021/08/17/1028422817/afghanistan- women-taliban-afghan-womens-network-mahbooba-seraj (accessed 24 January 2022).

20 Carland, S., 'Yassmin Abdel-Magied and the Australian crucible', *Saturday Paper*, 25 February 2017.

21   Abdallah, S. L., 'Islamic feminism twenty years on: The economy of
      a debate and new fields of research', *Critique Internationale, Presses de
      sciences*, po, 2013; hal-sciencespo.archives-ouvertes.fr/hal-02320116/
      document (accessed 24 January 2022).
22   Rahemtulla, S., *Qur'an of the Oppressed: Liberation theology and gender
      justice in Islam*, Oxford University Press, Oxford, 2017, p. 24.
23   Rahemtulla, *Qur'an of the Oppressed*, pp. 47–8.
24   Rahemtulla, S., *Quran of the Oppressed*, p. 182.
25   Rahemtulla, *Quran of the Oppressed*, p. 41.
26   'Letters from Africa: "We're not cleaners" – sexism amid Sudan
      protests', *BBC News*, 1 April 2019.
27   Scahill, J., '1998 bombings of Sudan and Afghanistan', The Intercept,
      28 April 2021; theintercept.com/empire-politician/biden-bombings-
      sudan-al-shifa-afghanistan/ (accessed 24 January 2022).
28   Robinson, N. J., 'Bill Clinton's act of terrorism', *Jacobin*; jacobinmag.
      com/2016/10/bill-clinton-al-shifa-sudan-bombing-khartoum/ (accessed
      24 November 2021).
29   Koshy, Y., 'The last humanist: How Paul Gilroy became the most vital
      guide to our age of crisis', *Guardian, The long read*, 5 August 2021.
30   Mullen, L., 'Orwell's tattoos: Skin, guilt, and magic in "Shooting an
      Elephant"', *Humanities*, 2018, vol. 7, no. 4, p. 124.
31   Bowker, G., 'George Orwell: A paranoid rebel with tattoos on his
      knuckles', *Guardian*, 5 September 2007.
32   Koshy, 'The last humanist'.
33   Diani, H., 'Meet amina wadud, the rock star of Islamic feminism',
      Magdalene, 20 February 2020; magdalene.co/story/meet-amina-
      wadud-the-rock-star-of-islamic-feminist (accessed 24 January 2022).
34   Esack, F., *Qur'an, Liberation and Pluralism: An Islamic perspective of
      interreligious solidarity against oppression*, Oneworld Publications,
      Oxford, 1997, p. 23, footnote 55.
35   Rahemtulla, *Quran of the Oppressed*, p. 51.
36   Rahemtulla, *Quran of the Oppressed*, p. 24.

To all the cars I've loved before

  1   Seccombe, M., 'Why your current car may be the last fossil-fuel vehicle
      you own', *Saturday Paper*, 4 September 2021.

On the rigs

  1   Evershed, N., 'An unconventional gas boom: The rise of CSG in
      Australia', *Guardian*, 18 June 2018.

2 'Petroleum and energy industry outlook and statistics', Business Queensland, 3 August 2020; business.qld.gov.au/industries/mining-energy-water/resources/petroleum-energy/outlook-statistics/petroleum-gas (accessed 2 December 2021).
3 'In Australia, women made up only 13.3 percent of the oil, gas and mining workforces in 2009 but by 2015, the number had increased slightly to 14.3.': 'Promoting gender diversity and inclusion in the oil, gas and mining extractive industries – A women's human rights report', Advocates for Human Rights, January 2019; unece.org/fileadmin/DAM/energy/images/CMM/CMM_CE/AHR_gender_diversity_report_FINAL.pdf (accessed 24 January 2022).
4 Numbers are still difficult to come by, but a 2018 report showed 74 per cent of women in mining (including oil and gas extraction) having experienced workplace sexual harassment: Everyone's business: Fourth national survey on sexual harassment in Australian workplaces, Australian Human Rights Commission, 2018; humanrights.gov.au/sites/default/files/document/publication/AHRC_WORKPLACE_SH_2018.pdf (accessed 2 December 2021). A 2021 article showed action beginning to be taken, with BHP firing forty-eight staff since 2019 for sexual harassment: 'Sexual harassment rife in mining camps, Western Australian inquiry finds', *Reuters*, 20 August 2021.

As Lionel Shriver made light of identity, I had no choice but to walk out on her
1 'The right of reply', Brisbane Writers Festival, 10 September 2016; bwf.org.au/news/articles/the-right-of-reply (accessed 24 January 2022).
2 Nordland, R., 'Lionel Shriver's address on cultural appropriation roils a writers festival', *New York Times*, 12 September 2016.
3 Tolentino, J., 'Lionel Shriver puts on a sombrero', *New Yorker*, 14 September 2016.
4 Van Luyn, A., 'Lionel Shriver and the responsibilities of fiction writers', *The Conversation*, 16 September 2016.
5 Hopper, N., 'Lionel Shriver: "This entire hoo-ha illustrates my point"', *TIME*, 15 September 2016.
6 Shriver, L., 'Will the left survive the millenials?' *New York Times*, 23 September 2016.
7 Abdel-Magied, Y., 'A call for difficult conversations, not censorship', 'Letter', *New York Times*, 5 October 2016.
8 'Dangerous ideas', Yen-Rong Wong; inexorablist.com/dangerous-ideas/ (accessed 2 December 2021).

What are they so afraid of? I'm just speaking my mind.

1 90,000 words were written in the nine or so weeks after Anzac Day; by the time a year had passed, that number was over 200,000. Watkins, E., 'More than 200,000 words published about Yassmin Abdel-Magied since last Anzac Day', *Crikey*, 26 April 2018.

2 Delingpole, J., 'Read: The worst article written by anyone ever', *Breitbart*, 17 September 2016.

Life was easier before I was 'woke'

1 Hatmaker, D. M., 'Engineering identity: Gender and professional identity negotiation among women engineers', *Gender and Work Organization*, July 2013, vol. 20, no. 4, pp. 382–96.

2 Glass, J. L. et al., 'What's so special about STEM? A comparison of women's retention in STEM and professional occupations', *Social Forces*, 21 August 2013, vol. 92, no. 2, pp. 723–56.

Nostalgia, solastalgia

1 'Grace Grothaus', Cité Internationale des Arts; citedesartsparis.net/en/grace-grothaus (accessed 24 January 2022).

2 Marchant, N., 'Half of those surveyed are unaware of the link between climate change and diseases like COVID-19', Weforum; weforum.org/agenda/2021/01/climate-change-link-infectious-diseases-covid-19-study/ (accessed 25 January 2022).

3 Shrestha, N. et al., 'The impact of COVID-19 on globalization', *One Health*, December 2020, vol. 11, 100180.

Empowerment v Power

1 'Oppression', Merriam-Webster; merriam-webster.com/dictionary/oppression (accessed 18 November 2021).

2 'Muslim scholars reflecting on the larger objectives of Sharia have said that laws derived from it must always protect the following: life, intellect, family, property and the honor of human beings. These five objectives create what we may consider to be a premodern Islamic Bill of Rights, providing protection for civil liberties.' Afsaruddin, A., 'What Sharia means: 5 questions answered', *The Conversation*, 16 June 2017.

3 Bhandar, B., Ziadah, R. (eds), *Revolutionary Feminisms*, Verso, London, 2020, p. 63.

4 McCullough, M. F., 'A complexity theory of power', *Journal on Policy and Complex Systems*, 2018, vol. 4, no. 2, p. 34, referring to Capra, F.,

The Web of Life: A new scientific understanding of living systems, Anchor Books, New York, 1996, p. 190.

5   McCullough, 'A complexity theory of power', p. 31.
6   See Stein, J., 'Using the stages of team development', MIT Human Resources; hr.mit.edu/learning-topics/teams/articles/stages-development (accessed 18 November 2021). For Tuckman's original article, see Tuckman, B. W., 'Developmental sequence in small groups', first published in *Psychological Bulletin*, 1965, vol. 63, no. 6, pp. 384–99.
7   Where disagreements resolve, and a spirit of cooperation emerges.

What does my headscarf mean to you?
1   Goldin, C., Rouse, C., 'Orchestrating impartiality: The impact of "blind" auditions on female musicians.' *American Economic Review*, 2000, vol. 90, no. 4, pp. 715–41.
2   Goldin, C., 'Orchestrating impartiality'.
3   Moss-Racusin, C. A. et al., 'Faculty's subtle gender biases favor male students', *Proceedings of the National Academy of Sciences*, October 2012, vol. 109, no. 41, pp. 16,474–79.
4   Castilla E. J., Benard, S., 'The paradox of meritocracy in organizations', *Administrative Science Quarterly*, 2010, vol. 55, no. 4, pp. 543–676.
5   Booth, A. L. et al., 'Does ethnic discrimination vary across minority groups? Evidence for a field experiment', *Oxford Bulletin of Economics and Statistics*, vol. 74, no. 4, p. 558.
6   Weise, E., 'Google discloses its (lack of) diversity', *USA Today*, 28 May 2014.
7   'The Green Park Leadership 10,000: A review of diversity amongst the UK's most influential business leaders', Green Park, 2014; cupdf.com/document/2-green-park-leadership-10000-feb-14.html (accessed 2 December 2021). Update: In 2021, there were no Black leaders in C-suite roles at FTSE 100 companies: 'Green Park business leaders index 2021', Green Park, 10 August 2021; green-park.co.uk/insights/green-park-business-leaders-index-2021-ftse-100/s239697/ (accessed 2 December 2021).

To the moon
1   From the Edelman trust barometer: 2017 is labelled 'Trust in Crisis'. See 'Edelman Trust Barometer 2021', Edelman; edelman.com/sites/g/files/aatuss191/files/2021-03/2021%20Edelman%20Trust%20

Barometer.pdf. It is worth noting that trust is even lower in 2021 than it was in 2017.

2   'Bitcoin and me (Hal Finney)', Bitcoin Forum; bitcointalk.org/index. php?topic=155054.0, referred to in Greenberg, A., 'Bitcoin's earliest adopter is cryonically freezing his body to see the future', *Wired*, 28 August 2014.

3   As of October 2021, 18.8 million have been mined. 'Total Circulating Bitcoin', Blockchain; blockchain.com/charts/total-bitcoins.

4   This time varies a lot, and can range from five to twenty-five minutes, depending on the month. 'Median confirmation time', Blockchain; blockchain.com/charts/median-confirmation-time.

5   In October 2021, 0.1 BTC was valued at $5900 USD. 'Blockchain Charts', Blockchain; blockchain.com/charts#currency.

Whose borders are they anyway?

1   Based on ability to travel without a visa: 'The Henley Passport Index'; henleypassportindex.com (accessed 25 November 2021). Australia is routinely in the top ten. The Heritage Foundation Index in 2021 also puts Sudan 175th in the world for economic freedom, last save for Cuba, Venezuela and North Korea: '2021 Index of Economic Freedom', Heritage Foundation Index; heritage.org/index/ranking (accessed 25 November 2021).

2   Moreton-Robinson, A., '"Our story is in the land": Why the Indigenous sense of belonging unsettles white Australia', *ABC Religion and Ethics*, 9 November 2020.

3   Heater, D., *A Brief History of Citizenship*, Edinburgh University Press, Edinburgh, 2004.

4   Although 'nation' and 'state' are often used interchangeably as terms, these terms are not straightforward synonyms, nor are they necessarily fixed. As English writer Hugh Seton-Watson observes: 'I am driven to the conclusion that no "scientific definition" of the nation can be devised; yet the phenomenon has existed and exists.': Seton-Watson, H., *Nations and States*, Routledge, 2020, p.5.

5   Anderson, B., *Imagined Communities*, Verso, 2016, p. 6.

6   Anderson, *Imagined Communities*, p. 7.

7   'The civic identity is enshrined in the rights conveyed by the state and the duties performed by the individual citizens, who are all autonomous persons, equal in status. Good citizens are those who feel an allegiance to the state and have a sense of responsibility in discharging their duties.': Heater, *A Brief History of Citizenship*, p. 2.

8 'Australian citizenship pledge', Department of Home Affairs; immi.
   homeaffairs.gov.au/citizenship/ceremony/what-is-the-pledge (accessed
   25 November 2021).

9 'The most common way you become an Australian citizen under this
   Division [of the *Australian Citizenship Act 2007*] is by being born in
   Australia and by having a parent who is an Australian citizen or a
   permanent resident at the time of your birth.': s. 11A of the *Australian
   Citizenship Act 2007*.

10 The Northern Territory Emergency Response, or 'The Intervention',
    was a controversial pack of measures targeting First Nations people
    in the Northern Territory. Passed by John Howard's government
    in 2007 with bipartisan support, the measures included changes
    to the delivery of education, employment, health services, welfare
    support, acquisition of land and more. They deployed the defence
    force into remote communities, removed the permit system for access
    to Aboriginal land, quarantined 50 per cent of welfare payments
    and abolished government-funded Community Development
    Employment Projects (CDEP). The act suspended the application
    of the *Racial Discrimination Act 1975*, so it is no surprise a United
    Nations Special Rapporteur found the Emergency Response to be
    racially discriminating and infringing on the human rights of First
    Nations people in the Northern Territory. It is important to note the
    Intervention was justified by an inquiry into alleged sexual abuse in the
    Territory, a report that has been heavily critiqued by the Indigenous
    communities in question.

11 The first instances of citizenship can be found in Ancient Greece
    city-states known as *poleis*, each *polis* being ruled by its citizens in a
    form of direct democracy. The origin of the word 'citizen' itself traces
    back to the Latin term *civitas*, used during the Roman Republic.
    The *civitas* was the social body of *cives*, or citizens, united by law
    ('*concilium coetusque hominum jure sociati*'), with accordant rights and
    responsibilities. Citizenship in Ancient Greece was a small, jealously
    guarded class, citizens directly controlling the political power and
    wealth of their polis in return for army service and voting duties. Only
    after the Treaty of Westphalia, signed in 1648 to end the Thirty Years'
    War, did the concept of the sovereign 'nation-state' emerge.

12 He qualifies, a civilised being, 'according to the standings prevailing
    in the society': Marshall, T. H., *Citizenship and Social Class: And other
    essays*, Cambridge University Press, Cambridge, 1950.

13 DeGoover, S. et al., *The Right to Have Rights*, Verso, London, 2018.

14 Pandey, S., 'Are the concepts of human rights western-centric (euro-centric) or "universalizable"?', 2016; doi: 10.13140/RG.2.2.33442.63687.

15 Fictional character from the *Harry Potter* series by J. K. Rowling, stationed at the Hogwarts school by the Ministry of Magic as 'High Inquisitor' in an attempt to control the school and dissenting students.

16 University of California Television, 'Gayatri Spivak: The trajectory of the subaltern in my work', YouTube, 8 February 2008; youtube.com/watch?v=2ZHH4ALRFHw (accessed 25 November 2021).

17 Gorham, E., 'Social citizenship and its fetters', *Polity*, 1995, vol. 28, no. 1, pp. 25–47.

18 Chebli, A., 'I refused to become an FBI informant, and the government put me on the No Fly List', American Civil Liberties Union, News & Commentary; aclu.org/news/national-security/i-refused-to-become-an-fbi-informant-and-the-government-put-me-on-the-no-fly-list/ (accessed 25 November 2021). Chebli and the American Civil Liberties Union filed a lawsuit and Chebli was later removed from the list; however, it is impossible to know how many other Muslims this behaviour has affected.

19 Soutphommasane, T., Stears, M., 'Government responses to COVID-19 are undermining our democratic commitments – why have progressives remained silent?', *ABC News*, 8 September 2021.

20 Wahlquist, C., Simons, M., 'Melbourne's "hard lockdown" orders residents of nine public housing towers to stay at home as coronavirus cases surge', *Guardian*, 4 July 2020; Rachwani, M., Allam, L., 'Troops enforcing western Sydney lockdown will alienate community, advocates warn', *Guardian*, 30 July 2021.

21 Rodell, B., Simons, C., 'A police swarm. Frantic calls. Then 3000 people locked inside.', *New York Times*, 12 November 2020.

22 'When you look at the response to outbreaks in the northern beaches or eastern suburbs, those communities were approached like they were reasonable and civil . . . but when it comes to us, we're treated like uneducated, barbaric western suburbs heathens, that need to feel the full brute strength of the law,' said one resident: Rachwani, M., 'Troops enforcing western Sydney lockdown will alienate community, advocates warn', *Guardian*.

23 Zhou, N., 'Australians who live overseas may be unable to leave country if they return for visit', *Guardian*, 7 August 2021.

24 Former FBI agent and whistleblower Terry Albury told the *New York Times*, 'We've built this entire apparatus and convinced the world that there is a terrorist in every mosque, and that every

newly arrived Muslim immigrant is secretly anti-American, and because we have promoted that false notion, we have to validate it.' 'I'm part of something that's really evil', *The Daily* podcast; nytimes.com/2021/09/09/podcasts/the-daily/counterterrorism-fbi-september-11-terry-albury.html (accessed 25 November 2021).

25 Pilkington, E., '"Panic made us vulnerable": How 9/11 made the US surveillance state – and the Americans who fought back', *Guardian*, 4 September 2021.

26 'Shamima Begum will not be allowed here, Bangladesh says', *BBC News*, 21 February 2019.

27 McKinney, C. J., 'Shamima Begum case to take at least another year', Free Movement; freemovement.org.uk/shamima-begum-case-to-take-at-least-another-year/ (accessed 14 January 2022).

28 Ansari, F., 'The Home Secretary can legally deprive Shamima Begum of her citizenship – but he shouldn't', Free Movement; freemovement.org.uk/home-office-shamima-begum/ (accessed 14 January 2022).

29 Siddique, H., 'New bill quietly gives powers to remove British citizenship without notice', *Guardian*, 18 November 2021.

30 Masters, M., Regilme, S. S. F. Jr., 'Human rights and British citizenship: The case of Shamima Begum as citizen to *Homo Sacer*', *Journal of Human Rights Practice*, 2020, vol. 12, issue 2, pp. 341–63.

31 Balibar, E., 'Europe as Borderland', *Environment and Planning D: Society and Space*, 2009, vol. 27, no. 2, pp. 190–215 (p. 211).

32 This makes sense, given people 'generally build organisations by reshaping and piecing together chunks of existing social structure rather than inventing new forms': Tilly, C., 'Citizenship, identity and social history', *International Review of Social History*, 1995, vol. 40, supp. 3, pp. 1–17. In western Europe, gender acted as this organisational building block for a long time. Descent (*jus sanguinis*) and residence (*jus solis*) have also been used.

33 Wurgaft, B. A., 'The state that I am in: Hannah Arendt in America', *Los Angeles Review of Books*, 28 February 2016.

34 Spivak, G. C., 'Nationalism and the imagination', *Lectora*, 2009, vol. 15, pp. 75–98.

35 Weber, E. I., 'Australian others: Penal logic and the pandemic', *Meanjin*, 8 September 2021; meanjin.com.au/blog/australian-others-penal-logic-and-the-pandemic/ (accessed 25 November 2021).

36 Hall, S., 'Cultural identity and diaspora', first published as 'Cultural identity and cinematic representation' in *Framework: The Journal of Cinema and Media*, 1989, no. 36, pp. 68–81.

Tyranny and free speech

1 Mill, J. S., *On Liberty*, 1859, Ch 2.
2 'Free speech', Human Rights Watch; hrw.org/topic/free-speech (accessed 2 December 2021).
3 Albrechtsen, J., 'Left speaking upside down', *Australian*, 29 April 2015.
4 Mill, *On Liberty*, p. 9.
5 Kampmark, B., 'The long crucifixion of Gillian Triggs', Independent Australia; independentaustralia.net/life/life-display/gillian-triggs-human-rights-and-ideology,10573 (accessed 2 December 2021).
6 Full quote: 'Practically no one, no matter how strong, can go through being on the front page, day after day, as a hate figure, and come through unscathed. We are social creatures, the nation is an ersatz community, and so the front page is like being shamed in the village. Doesn't matter how spurious what you're accused of is, you feel the concentrated fury, and that is what is intended.' Rundle, G., 'Abdel-Magied Anzac furore indicates a dark turn in the culture wars', *Crikey*, 3 May 2017.

Why the protests in the US are an awakening for non-Black people around the world

1 Travis, A., 'Young Black people nine times more likely to be jailed than young white people – report', *Guardian*, 1 September 2017.
2 'Aboriginal and Torres Strait Islander prisoner characteristics', Australian Bureau of Statistics, 30 June 2018; abs.gov.au/ausstats/abs@.nsf/Lookup/by%20Subject/4517.0~2018~Main%20Features~Aboriginal%20and%20Torres%20Strait%20Islander%20prisoner%20characteristics%20~13 (accessed 2 December 2021).
3 'Profile of Indigenous Australians', Australian Institute of Health and Welfare, 16 September 2021; aihw.gov.au/reports/australias-welfare/profile-of-indigenous-australians (accessed 2 December 2021).
4 'Quoting a meme, Scott Morrison says US violence will not bring about change', *SBS News*, 1 June 2020.
5 Shand-Baptiste, K., 'UK schools have targeted Black children for generations – the education system is overdue for a reckoning', *Independent*, 12 January 2020.
6 Bassam, T., 'Sharp rise in football racism as incidents go up by more than 50% in one year', *Guardian*, 31 January 2020.
7 Adegoke, Y., 'The leaked Labour report reveals a shocking level of racism and sexism towards its Black MPs', *inews.co.uk*, 19 April 2020.

On abolition

1 Lefrak, M., 'Why the African American Museum won't get rid of timed entry tickets yet', WAMU 88.5, 2 October 2018; wamu.org/story/18/10/02/african-american-museum-wont-get-rid-timed-entry-tickets-yet/ (accessed 25 January 2022).
2 Davis, A., *Women, Race and Class*, Vintage Books, New York, 1981.
3 Kaba, M., 'Yes, we mean literally abolish the police', *New York Times*, 12 June 2020.
4 McEvoy, J., 'Books about racism dominate best-seller lists amid protests', *Forbes*, 11 June 2020.
5 Flood, A., 'Reni Eddo-Lodge becomes first Black British author to top UK book charts', *Guardian*, 17 June 2020.
6 Morgan, K., 'About that wave of anti-racist bestsellers over the summer', *Literary Hub*, 25 November 2020.
7 Haddad, M., 'How many people have been killed by US police since George Floyd?', *Al Jazeera*, 25 May 2021.
8 Allam, L. et al., 'The 474 deaths inside: Tragic toll of Indigenous deaths in custody revealed', *Guardian*, 9 April 2021.
9 'French police sue sister of Adama Traoré, Black man who died in custody', *RFI*, 6 May 2021; rfi.fr/en/france/20210506-gendarmes-sue-sister-of-adama-traoré-french-black-man-who-died-in-custody-defamation-assa-traoré-paris (accessed 25 January 2022).
10 Knight, S., 'Britain's idyllic country houses reveal a darker history', *New Yorker*, 16 August 2021.
11 'The Overton window', Conceptually; conceptually.org/concepts/overton-window (accessed 25 January 2022). For further information on the Overton window, named after American policy analyst Joseph P. Overton, see 'The Overton window', Mackinac Center for Public Policy, mackinac.org/OvertonWindow (accessed 18 January 2022).
12 'Ruth Wilson Gilmore on COVID-19, decarceration, and abolition'; Haymarket Books, 17 April 2020; haymarketbooks.org/blogs/128-ruth-wilson-gilmore-on-covid-19-decarceration-and-abolition (accessed 25 January 2022).
13 Lamble, S., 'Practising everyday abolition', *Abolitionist Futures*, August 2019; abolitionistfutures.com/latest-news/practising-everyday-abolition (accessed 25 January 2022).
14 Burton, N., 'Cancel culture is real, but adrienne maree brown says we should be careful about throwing people away', Shondaland, 9 February 2021; shondaland.com/inspire/books/a35452132/adrienne-maree-brown-we-will-not-cancel-us/ (accessed 25 January 2022).

15   Gossett, R., Spade, D., and Dector, H., 'No one is disposable: Everyday
     practices of prison abolition', Bernard Center for Research on Women,
     2014; bcrw.barnard.edu/no-one-is-disposable/ (accessed 25 January
     2022).
16   Lynch, T. J., 'Republicans have used a "law and order" message to
     win elections before. This is why Trump could do it again', *The
     Conversation*, 1 September 2020.
17   Stemen, D., 'The prison paradox: More incarceration will not make
     us safer', Vera Institute of Justice, July 2017; vera.org/downloads/
     publications/for-the-record-prison-paradox_02.pdf (accessed
     25 January 2022).
18   'Trust in institutions', Essential Report, 12 October 2021;
     essentialvision.com.au/?s=trust+in+institutions&searchbutton=Search
     (accessed 25 January 2022).
19   Hess, A., 'The protests come for "Paw Patrol"', *New York Times*,
     10 June 2020.
20   The show stated that the characters will 'examine their roles in the
     world' in the new season as a response to the movement's resurgence
     in 2020: Cremona, P., 'Brooklyn Nine-Nine's Andy Samberg on
     how show will handle issues which inspired Black Lives Matter
     movement', RadioTimes, 30 November 2020; radiotimes.com/tv/
     comedy/brooklyn-nine-nine-andy-samberg-police-black-lives-matter/
     (accessed 25 January 2022).
21   Hess, 'The protests come for "Paw Patrol"'.
22   Lamble, S., 'Practising everyday abolition'.

Boris Johnson's 'brownwashing' is a return to Britain's imperial playbook

 1   Craig, J., 'Boris Johnson to reveal "cabinet for modern Britain" – but
     Jeremy Hunt is not happy', *Sky News*, 24 July 2019.
 2   Woodcock, A., 'Home Secretary Priti Patel admits own parents might
     not have been allowed into UK under her new immigration laws',
     Independent, 19 February 2020.
 3   Elgot, J., McDonald, H., 'Priti Patel says Tories will bring in new
     laws for "broken" UK asylum system', *Guardian*, 5 October 2020.
     See also 'Here's why you should care about Priti Patel's catastrophic
     plan for our asylum system', Freedom From Torture, 16 April 2021;
     freedomfromtorture.org/news/everything-you-need-to-know-about-
     priti-patels-anti-refugee-bill (accessed 25 January 2022).
 4   Townsend, M., Raja, A., 'Appointment of "biased" Carlile to Prevent
     review "shatters its credibility"', *Guardian*, 18 August 2019.

5   Versi, M., 'The latest Prevent figures show why the strategy needs an independent review', *Guardian*, 10 November 2017.

6   Ross, A., 'Academics criticise anti-radicalisation strategy in open letter', *Guardian*, 29 September 2016.

7   Warrell, H., 'Inside Prevent, the UK's controversial anti-terrorism programme', *Financial Times Magazine*, 24 January 2019.

8   'The impact of Prevent on Muslim communities', Muslim Council of Britain, February 2016; archive.mcb.org.uk/wp-content/uploads/2016/12/MCB-CT-Briefing2.pdf (accessed 13 January 2022).

9   'Trevor Phillips suspended from Labour over Islamophobia allegations', *BBC News*, 9 March 2020.

10 Manzoor-Khan, S., 'Under Boris Johnson, Islamophobia will reach a sinister new level', *Guardian*, 5 January 2020.

11 Goodfellow, M., 'Boris Johnson and his regressive cabinet mean disaster for Britain', *Washington Post*, 26 July 2019.

12 'Ethnicity facts and figures', GOV.UK, 'Population of England and Wales', last updated 7 August 2020; ethnicity-facts-figures.service.gov.uk/uk-population-by-ethnicity/national-and-regional-populations/population-of-england-and-wales/latest (accessed 25 January 2022).

13 Gopal, P., 'Boris Johnson's slightly less white cabinet isn't progress – it's a PR stunt designed to excuse racism', *Independent*, 2 October 2019.

14 'Dominic Raab: Taking a knee 'seems to be from Game of Thrones', Guardian News, YouTube, 18 June 2020; youtube.com/watch?v=Vwti7AMWDQo (accessed 25 January 2022).

15 Mirza, M., 'Lammy review: The myth of institutional racism', Spiked, 11 September 2017; spiked-online.com/2017/09/11/lammy-review-the-myth-of-institutional-racism/ (accessed 25 January 2022).

16 Iqbal, N., 'Reni Eddo-Lodge: "The debate on racism is a game to some and I don't want to play"', *Guardian*, 21 June 2020.

17 'The East Africa Protectorate', Britannica; britannica.com/place/Kenya/The-East-Africa-Protectorate (accessed 1 December 2021).

18 '1968: More Kenyan Asians flee to Britain', On This Day, *BBC News*; news.bbc.co.uk/onthisday/hi/dates/stories/february/4/newsid_2738000/2738629.stm

19 'Speech at the Diwali banquet', Margaret Thatcher, 24 October 1988; margaretthatcher.org/document/107356 (accessed 25 January 2022). See also Shah, N., 'How did British Indians become so prominent in the Conservative Party?', *Guardian*, 27 February 2020.

20 Harris, P., 'They fled with nothing but built a new empire', *Guardian*, 11 August 2002.

21 Francis, M., 'Mrs Thatcher's peacock blue sari: Ethnic minorities, electoral politics and the Conservative Party, c. 1974–86', *Contemporary British History*, 2017, vol. 31, no. 2, pp. 274–93 (p. 279).

22 Roy, A., 'Saroop, the last Indian', Eye on England, *Telegraph* (Calcutta), 26 March 2006.

23 'The Conservative Party and British Indians, 1975–1990', The History of Parliament; thehistoryofparliament.wordpress.com/2018/04/19/the-conservative-party-and-british-indians-1975-1990/ (accessed 1 December 2021).

24 Packman, C., 'David Cameron and the Conservative identity crisis', Open Democracy UK; opendemocracy.net/en/opendemocracyuk/david-camerons-failed-project/ (accessed 13 January 2022).

25 Nelson, D., 'Ministers to build a new "special relationship" with India', *Telegraph*, 7 July 2010. See also Burke, J., 'UK government ends boycott of Narendra Modi', *Guardian*, 23 October 2012.

26 'British PM David Cameron's party woos Indian-origin voters with Hindi song', Indians Abroad, NDTV, 24 April 2015. The songs were specifically designed for the campaign, as the piece reports: 'Prime Minister David Cameron led party, which heads the current coalition government in the country, launched "Neela Hai Aasma (Blue Sky)" in reference to the symbolic blue colour of the party. The catchy tune set to Indian beats encourages the British Indian community to join hands with the British PM in taking the United Kingdom forward with a chorus repeating the name "David Cameron".' For the video, see 'Conservative Friends of India – "Neela hai Aasma" (Blue Sky)', Conservative Friends of India, YouTube, 24 April 2015; youtube.com/watch?v=9Ep36luEld8&t=9s (accessed 25 January 2022). See also '"You don't have to be white to vote right": Why young Asians are rebelling by turning Tory', *Telegraph*, 27 May 2015.

27 Gopal, P., 'Boris Johnson's slightly less white cabinet isn't progress', *Independent*, 2 October 2019.

The uprising in Sudan is more than just about bread prices

1 'Sudan: 37 protesters dead in government crackdown on demonstrations', Press Release, Amnesty International, 24 December 2018; amnesty.org/en/latest/press-release/2018/12/sudan-protesters-dead-in-government-crackdown-on-protests/ (accessed 2 December 2021).

2 Salih, K. O., 'The Sudan, 1985–9: The fading democracy', *Journal of Modern African Studies*, June 1990, vol. 28, pp. 199–224.

3   Oil revenue in 2011 accounted for half of Khartoum's revenue and
    nearly 98 per cent of the southern government's revenue: 'Background:
    Sudan's oil industry', *Al Jazeera*, 2 July 2011.
4   'Protesters shot as Sudan military tries to clear Khartoum sit-in',
    Al Jazeera, 3 June 2019.
5   'Sudan PM Abdalla Hamdok survives assassination attempt', *BBC
    News*, 9 March 2020.
6   'Sudan transitional government says coup attempt has failed',
    Al Jazeera, 21 September 2021.
7   'Sudan warns medicine, fuel, wheat running out amid port blockade',
    Al Jazeera, 4 October 2021.
8   'Sudan PM says "serious crisis" a threat to transition and country',
    MSN News, 16 October 2021.

An engineer's perspective

1   This was the 2016 number; in 2021, South Australia has reached
    an impressive and world leading 60 per cent: Parkinson, S., 'South
    Australia achieves world-leading 60pct wind and solar share over
    last year', Renew Economy, 8 February 2021; reneweconomy.com.au/
    south-australia-achieves-world-leading-60pct-wind-and-solar-share-
    over-last-year/ (accessed 2 December 2021).
2   This was true in 2016, but in 2021 things had changed significantly
    following state government energy targets. In March 2021, Victoria
    recorded its grid running on 50 per cent renewables for the first time:
    Towell, N., 'Victoria's grid runs on 50 per cent renewable energy
    for first time', *Sydney Morning Herald*, 28 March 2021; smh.com.au/
    environment/climate-change/victoria-s-grid-runs-on-50-per-cent-
    renewable-energy-for-first-time-20210326-p57ee5.html (accessed
    2 December 2021).
3   'Black System South Australia 28 September 2016', Australian Energy
    Market Operator, March 2017; aemo.com.au//media/Files/Electricity/
    NEM/Market_Notices_and_Events/Power_System_Incident_
    Reports/2017/Integrated-Final-Report-SA-Black-System-28-
    September-2016.pdf (accessed 2 December 2021).

Bibliography

'1968: More Kenyan Asians flee to Britain', On This Day, *BBC News*; news. bbc.co.uk/onthisday/hi/dates/stories/february/4/newsid_2738000/ 2738629.stm

'2021 Index of Economic Freedom', Heritage Foundation Index; heritage. org/index/ranking (accessed 25 November 2021).

'A new take on the 19th-century skull collection of Samuel Morton', Science Daily, 4 October 2018; sciencedaily.com/releases/2018/10/181004143943. htm (accessed 25 January 2022).

Abdallah, S. L., 'Islamic feminism twenty years on: The economy of a debate and new fields of research', *Critique Internationale, Presses de sciences*, po, 2013; hal-sciencespo.archives-ouvertes.fr/hal-02320116/ document (accessed 24 January 2022).

Abdel-Magied, Y., 'A call for difficult conversations, not censorship', 'Letter', *New York Times*, 5 October 2016.

Aboriginal and Torres Strait Islander prisoner characteristics', Australian Bureau of Statistics, 30 June 2018; abs.gov.au/ausstats/ abs@.nsf/Lookup/by%20Subject/4517.0~2018~Main%20 Features~Aboriginal%20and%20Torres%20Strait%20Islander%20 prisoner%20characteristics%20~13 (accessed 2 December 2021).

Adegoke, Y., 'The leaked Labour report reveals a shocking level of racism and sexism towards its Black MPs', *inews.co.uk*, 19 April 2020.

Afsaruddin, A., 'What Sharia means: 5 questions answered', *The Conversation*, 16 June 2017.

Ahmed, L., *Women and Gender in Islam: Historical roots of a modern debate*, Yale University Press, New Haven, 1992, p. 151.

Albrechtsen, J., 'Left speaking upside down', *Australian*, 29 April 2015.

Allam, L. et al., 'The 474 deaths inside: Tragic toll of Indigenous deaths in custody revealed', *Guardian*, 9 April 2021.

Anderson, B., *Imagined Communities*, Verso, London, 2016.

Ansari, F., 'The Home Secretary can legally deprive Shamima Begum of her citizenship – but he shouldn't', Free Movement; freemovement. org.uk/home-office-shamima-begum/ (accessed 14 January 2022).

Anthony, A., 'Everything you wanted to know about the culture wars – but were afraid to ask', *Guardian*, 13 June 2021.

Associated Press, 'Trump says NFL should fire players who kneel during national anthem', *Los Angeles Times*, 22 September 2017.

'Australian citizenship pledge', Department of Home Affairs; immi. homeaffairs.gov.au/citizenship/ceremony/what-is-the-pledge (accessed 25 November 2021).

'Background: Sudan's oil industry', *Al Jazeera*, 2 July 2011.

Balibar, E., 'Europe as Borderland', *Environment and Planning D: Society and Space*, 2009, vol. 27, no. 2, pp. 190–215.

Bassam, T., 'Sharp rise in football racism as incidents go up by more than 50% in one year', *Guardian*, 31 January 2020.

Basu, M., 'Fifteen years after 9/11, Sikhs still victims of anti-Muslim hate crimes', CNN, 15 September 2016.

Beaumont-Thomas, B., 'Sam Fender: "Leftie is now a slur in working-class towns"', *Guardian*, 25 August 2021.

Bhandar, B., Ziadah, R. (eds), *Revolutionary Feminisms*, Verso, London, 2020, p. 63.

'Bitcoin and me (Hal Finney)', Bitcoin Forum; bitcointalk.org/index. php?topic=155054.0

'Black System South Australia 28 September 2016', Australian Energy Market Operator, March 2017; aemo.com.au//media/Files/ Electricity/NEM/Market_Notices_and_Events/Power_System_ Incident_Reports/2017/Integrated-Final-Report-SA-Black-System-28-September-2016.pdf (accessed 2 December 2021).

'Blockchain charts', Blockchain; blockchain.com/charts#currency.

Booth, A. L. et al., 'Does ethnic discrimination vary across minority groups? Evidence for a field experiment', *Oxford Bulletin of Economics and Statistics*, vol. 74, no. 4.

Bowker, G., 'George Orwell: A paranoid rebel with tattoos on his knuckles', *Guardian*, 5 September 2007.

'British PM David Cameron's party woos Indian-origin voters with Hindi song', Indians Abroad, NDTV, 24 April 2015.

Burke, J., 'UK government ends boycott of Narendra Modi', *Guardian*, 23 October 2012.

Burton, N., 'Cancel culture is real, but adrienne maree brown says we should be careful about throwing people away', Shondaland,

9 February 2021; shondaland.com/inspire/books/a35452132/
adrienne-maree-brown-we-will-not-cancel-us/ (accessed 25 January
2022).

Capra, F., *The Web of Life: A new scientific understanding of living systems*,
Anchor Books, New York, 1996.

Carland, S., 'Yassmin Abdel-Magied and the Australian crucible', *Saturday
Paper*, 25 February 2017.

Castilla E. J., Benard, S., 'The paradox of meritocracy in organizations',
Administrative Science Quarterly, 2010, vol. 55, no. 4, pp. 543–676.

Chebli, A., 'I refused to become an FBI informant, and the government
put me on the No Fly List', American Civil Liberties Union, News &
Commentary; aclu.org/news/national-security/i-refused-to-become-
an-fbi-informant-and-the-government-put-me-on-the-no-fly-list/
(accessed 25 November 2021).

Collinson, A., 'The toxic fantasy of the "side hustle"', *Prospect*, 19 August
2019.

'Conservative Friends of India – Neela hai Aasma' (Blue Sky'),
Conservative Friends of India, YouTube, 24 April 2015; youtube.com/
watch?v=9Ep36luEld8&t=9s (accessed 25 January 2022).

cooke, m., 'Gender and September 11: A roundtable: Saving brown
women', *Signs: Journal of Women in Culture and Society*, 2002, vol. 28,
no.1, pp. 468–70.

Craig, J., 'Boris Johnson to reveal "cabinet for modern Britain" – but
Jeremy Hunt is not happy', *Sky News*, 24 July 2019.

Cremona, P., 'Brooklyn Nine-Nine's Andy Samberg on how show
will handle issues which inspired Black Lives Matter movement',
RadioTimes, 30 November 2020; radiotimes.com/tv/comedy/
brooklyn-nine-nine-andy-samberg-police-black-lives-matter/
(accessed 25 January 2022).

Dabiri, E., *What White People Can Do Next*, Penguin Books, London,
Kindle edition.

'Dangerous ideas', Yen-Rong Wong; inexorablist.com/dangerous-ideas/
(accessed 2 December 2021).

Davis, A., *Women, Race and Class*, Vintage Books, New York, 1981.

DeGoover, S. et al., *The Right to Have Rights*, Verso, London, 2018.

Delingpole, J., 'Read: The worst article written by anyone ever', *Breitbart*,
17 September 2016.

Diani, H., 'Meet amina wadud, the rock star of Islamic feminism',
Magdalene, 20 February 2020; magdalene.co/story/meet-amina-
wadud-the-rock-star-of-islamic-feminist (accessed 24 January 2022).

'Dominic Raab: Taking a knee 'seems to be from Game of Thrones'', Guardian News, YouTube, 18 June 2020; youtube.com/watch?v=Vwti7AMWDQo (accessed 25 January 2022).

'Edelman Trust Barometer 2021', Edelman; edelman.com/sites/g/files/aatuss191/files/2021-03/2021%20Edelman%20Trust%20Barometer.pdf.

Elgot, J., McDonald, H., 'Priti Patel says Tories will bring in new laws for "broken" UK asylum system', Guardian, 5 October 2020 (accessed 25 January 2022).

Esack, F., *Qur'an, Liberation and Pluralism: An Islamic perspective of interreligious solidarity against oppression*, Oneworld Publications, Oxford, 1997.

'Ethnicity facts and figures', GOV.UK, 'Population of England and Wales', last updated 7 August 2020; ethnicity-facts-figures.service.gov.uk/uk-population-by-ethnicity/national-and-regional-populations/population-of-england-and-wales/latest (accessed 25 January 2022).

Evershed, N., 'An unconventional gas boom: The rise of CSG in Australia', *Guardian*, 18 June 2018.

'Everyone's business: Fourth national survey on sexual harassment in Australian workplaces', Australian Human Rights Commission, 2018; humanrights.gov.au/sites/default/files/document/publication/AHRC_WORKPLACE_SH_2018.pdf (accessed 2 December 2021).

Falecka, K., 'From colonial Algeria to modern day Europe, the Muslim veil remains an ideological background', *The Conversation*, 24 January 2017.

Faulkner, R. A., 'Assia Djebar, Frantz Fanon, women, veils, and land', *World Literature Today*, 1996, vol. 70, no. 4, pp. 847–55.

Flood, A., 'Reni Eddo-Lodge becomes first Black British author to top UK book charts', *Guardian*, 17 June 2020.

Francis, M., 'Mrs Thatcher's peacock blue sari: Ethnic minorities, electoral politics and the Conservative Party, c. 1974–86', *Contemporary British History*, 2017, vol. 31, no. 2, pp. 274–93.

'Free speech', Human Rights Watch; hrw.org/topic/free-speech (accessed 2 December 2021).

'French police sue sister of Adama Traoré, Black man who died in custody', *RFI*, 6 May 2021; rfi.fr/en/france/20210506-gendarmes-sue-sister-of-adama-traoré-french-black-man-who-died-in-custody-defamation-assa-traoré-paris (accessed 25 January 2022).

Glass, J. L. et al., 'What's so special about STEM? A comparison of women's retention in STEM and professional occupations', *Social Forces*, 21 August 2013, vol. 92, no. 2, pp. 723–56.

Goldin, C., Rouse, C., 'Orchestrating impartiality: The impact of "blind" auditions on female musicians', *American Economic Review*, 2000, vol. 90, no. 4, pp. 715–41.

Goodfellow, M., 'Boris Johnson and his regressive cabinet mean disaster for Britain', *Washington Post*, 26 July 2019.

Gopal, P., 'Boris Johnson's slightly less white cabinet isn't progress – it's a PR stunt designed to excuse racism', *Independent*, 2 October 2019.

Gorham, E., 'Social citizenship and its fetters', *Polity*, 1995, vol. 28, no. 1, pp. 25–47.

Gossett, R., Spade, D., Dector, H., 'No one is disposable: Everyday practices of prison abolition', Bernard Center for Research on Women, 2014; bcrw.barnard.edu/no-one-is-disposable/ (accessed 25 January 2022).

'Grace Grothaus', Cité Internationale des Arts; citedesartsparis.net/en/grace-grothaus (accessed 24 January 2022).

Greenberg, A., 'Bitcoin's earliest adopter is cryonically freezing his body to see the future', *Wired*, 28 August 2014.

'Green Park business leaders index 2021', Green Park, 10 August 2021; green-park.co.uk/insights/green-park-business-leaders-index-2021-ftse-100/s239697/ (accessed 2 December 2021).

Griffith, E., 'Why are young people pretending to love work?', *New York Times*, 26 January 2019.

Haddad, M., 'How many people have been killed by US police since George Floyd?', *Al Jazeera*, 25 May 2021.

Hall, S., 'Cultural identity and diaspora', first published as 'Cultural identity and cinematic representation' in *Framework: The Journal of Cinema and Media*, 1989, no. 36, pp. 68–81.

Hallaq, W. B., *Sharī'a: Theory, practice, transformations*, Cambridge University Press, Cambridge, 2009.

Handler, J. S., 'Custom and law: The status of enslaved Africans in seventeenth-century Barbados', *Slavery & Abolition*, 2016, vol. 37, no. 2, pp. 233–55.

——, Reilly, M. C., 'Contesting "White Slavery" in the Caribbean', *New West Indian Guide*, 2017, vol. 91, pp. 30–55.

Harris, P., 'They fled with nothing but built a new empire', *Guardian*, 11 August 2002.

Hatmaker, D. M., 'Engineering identity: Gender and professional identity negotiation among women engineers', *Gender and Work Organization*, July 2013, vol. 20, no. 4, pp. 382–96.

Heater, D., *A Brief History of Citizenship*, Edinburgh University Press, Edinburgh, 2004.

'Here's why you should care about Priti Patel's catastrophic plan for
our asylum system', Freedom From Torture, 16 April 2021;
freedomfromtorture.org/news/everything-you-need-to-know-about-
priti-patels-anti-refugee-bill (accessed 25 January 2022).

Hess, A., 'The protests come for "Paw Patrol"', New York Times, 10 June
2020.

Hill, K., 'I'm a Gen Zer who graduated during the pandemic. Here's why
I think my generation's obsession with "hustle culture" has become
unhealthy', Business Insider, 22 April 2021.

Hopper, N., 'Lionel Shriver: "This entire hoo-ha illustrates my point"',
TIME, 15 September 2016.

'I'm part of something that's really evil', The Daily podcast; nytimes.
com/2021/09/09/podcasts/the-daily/counterterrorism-fbi-september-11-
terry-albury.html (accessed 25 November 2021).

Iqbal, N., 'Reni Eddo-Lodge: "The debate on racism is a game to some and
I don't want to play"', Guardian, 21 June 2020.

Johnson, E. A., Elbardicy, M., Rezvani, A., 'She is staying in Afghanistan
to ensure women's gains aren't lost under Taliban rule', NPR,
17 August 2021; npr.org/2021/08/17/1028422817/afghanistan-
women-taliban-afghan-womens-network-mahbooba-seraj (accessed
24 January 2022).

Kaba, M., 'Yes, we mean literally abolish the police', New York Times,
12 June 2020.

Kampmark, B., 'The long crucifixion of Gillian Triggs', Independent
Australia; independentaustralia.net/life/life-display/gillian-triggs-
human-rights-and-ideology,10573 (accessed 2 December 2021).

Kebsi, J., 'Unveil them to save them: France and the ongoing colonization
of women's bodies', Berkley Center for Religion, Peace & World
Affairs, 13 May 2021; berkleycenter.georgetown.edu/responses/
unveil-them-to-save-them-france-and-the-ongoing-colonization-of-
muslim-women-s-bodies (accessed 24 January 2022).

Knickmeyer, E., 'Costs of the Afghanistan war, in lives and dollars',
AP News, 17 August 2021.

Knight, S., 'Britain's idyllic country houses reveal a darker history', New
Yorker, 16 August 2021.

Koshy, Y., 'The last humanist: How Paul Gilroy became the most vital
guide to our age of crisis', Guardian, The long read, 5 August 2021.

Lamble, S., 'Practising everyday abolition', Abolitionist Futures, August
2019; abolitionistfutures.com/latest-news/practising-everyday-abolition
(accessed 25 January 2022).

'"Law against Islam": French vote in favour of hijab ban condemned', *Al Jazeera*, 9 April 2021.

Lefrak, M., 'Why the African American Museum won't get rid of timed entry tickets yet', WAMU 88.5, 2 October 2018; wamu.org/story/18/10/02/african-american-museum-wont-get-rid-timed-entry-tickets-yet/ (accessed 25 January 2022).

'Letters from Africa: "We're not cleaners" – sexism amid Sudan protests', *BBC News*, 1 April 2019.

Lynch, T. J., 'Republicans have used a "law and order" message to win elections before. This is why Trump could do it again', *The Conversation*, 1 September 2020.

MacMaster, N., *Burning the Veil: The Algerian war and the 'emancipation' of Muslim women, 1954–62*, Manchester University Press, Manchester, 2009.

Malik, N., 'The right is winning the culture war because its opponents don't know the rules', *Guardian*, 19 July 2021.

Manzoor-Khan, S., 'Under Boris Johnson, Islamophobia will reach a sinister new level', *Guardian*, 5 January 2020.

Marchant, N., 'Half of those surveyed are unaware of the link between climate change and diseases like COVID-19', Weforum; weforum.org/agenda/2021/01/climate-change-link-infectious-diseases-covid-19-study/ (accessed 25 January 2022).

Marshall, T. H., *Citizenship and Social Class: And other essays*, Cambridge University Press, Cambridge, 1950.

Masters, M., Regilme, S. S. F. Jr., 'Human rights and British citizenship: The case of Shamima Begum as citizen to *Homo Sacer*', *Journal of Human Rights Practice*, 2020, vol. 12, issue 2, pp. 341–63.

McCullough, M. F., 'A complexity theory of power', *Journal on Policy and Complex Systems*, 2018, vol. 4, no. 2.

McEvoy, J., 'Books about racism dominate best-seller lists amid protests', *Forbes*, 11 June 2020.

McKinney, C. J., 'Shamima Begum case to take at least another year', Free Movement; freemovement.org.uk/shamima-begum-case-to-take-at-least-another-year/ (accessed 14 January 2022).

Media Education Foundation, 'Race, the floating signifier, featuring Stuart Hall', Transcript, 1997; mediaed.org/transcripts/Stuart-Hall-Race-the-Floating-Signifier-Transcript.pdf (accessed 24 January 2022).

'Median confirmation time', Blockchain; blockchain.com/charts/median-confirmation-time.

Middleton, J., 'Tory MP continues boycott of England team over taking the knee – but "will cheer if they score"', *Independent*, 8 July 2021.

Mirza, M., 'Lammy review: The myth of institutional racism', Spiked, 11 September 2017; spiked-online.com/2017/09/11/lammy-review-the-myth-of-institutional-racism/ (accessed 25 January 2022).

Moreton-Robinson, A., '"Our story is in the land": Why the Indigenous sense of belonging unsettles white Australia', *ABC Religion and Ethics*, 9 November 2020.

Morgan, K., 'About that wave of anti-racist bestsellers over the summer', *Literary Hub*, 25 November 2020.

Moss-Racusin, C. A. et al., 'Faculty's subtle gender biases favor male students', *Proceedings of the National Academy of Sciences*, October 2012, vol. 109, no. 41, pp. 16,474–79.

Mukhopadhyay, C. C., 'Getting rid of the word "Caucasian"' in Pollock, M. (ed.) *Everyday Antiracism: Getting real about race in school*, The New Press, New York, 2008.

Mullally, U., 'Emma Dabiri and Hazel Chu: "This is a real, important moment in Ireland"', *Irish Times*, 27 March 2021.

Mullen, L., 'Orwell's tattoos: Skin, guilt, and magic in "Shooting an Elephant"', *Humanities*, 2018, vol. 7, no. 4, p. 124.

Nelson, D., 'Ministers to build a new "special relationship" with India', *Telegraph*, 7 July 2010.

Nordland, R., 'Lionel Shriver's address on cultural appropriation roils a writers festival', *New York Times*, 12 September 2016.

Packman, C., 'David Cameron and the Conservative identity crisis', Open Democracy UK; opendemocracy.net/en/opendemocracyuk/david-camerons-failed-project/ (accessed 13 January 2022).

Pandey, S., 'Are the concepts of human rights western-centric (euro-centric) or "universalizable"?', 2016; doi: 10.13140/RG.2.2.33442.63687.

Parkinson, S., 'South Australia achieves world-leading 60pct wind and solar share over last year', Renew Economy, 8 February 2021; reneweconomy.com.au/south-australia-achieves-world-leading-60pct-wind-and-solar-share-over-last-year/ (accessed 2 December 2021).

Pathak, S., 'Not working, side hustles and crying: How the workplace will change in 2020', Digiday, 10 January 2020; digiday.com/marketing/not-working-side-hustles-crying-workplace-will-change-2020/ (accessed 24 January 2022).

Peetz, D., 'There's an obvious reason wages aren't growing, but you won't hear it from Treasury or the Reserve Bank', *The Conversation*, 9 September 2019.

'Petroleum and energy industry outlook and statistics', Business Queensland, 3 August 2020; business.qld.gov.au/industries/

mining-energy-water/resources/petroleum-energy/outlook-statistics/
petroleum-gas (accessed 2 December 2021).

Pilkington, E., '"Panic made us vulnerable": How 9/11 made the US
surveillance state – and the Americans who fought back', *Guardian*,
4 September 2021.

'Profile of Indigenous Australians', Australian Institute of Health and
Welfare, 16 September 2021; aihw.gov.au/reports/australias-welfare/
profile-of-indigenous-australians (accessed 2 December 2021).

'Promoting gender diversity and inclusion in the oil, gas and mining
extractive industries – A Women's Human Rights Report', Advocates
for Human Rights, January 2019; unece.org/fileadmin/DAM/energy/
images/CMM/CMM_CE/AHR_gender_diversity_report_FINAL.pdf
(accessed 24 January 2022).

'Protesters shot as Sudan military tries to clear Khartoum sit-in', *Al Jazeera*,
3 June 2019.

Quart, A., 'The con of the side hustle', *New York Times*, 6 April 2019.

'Quoting a meme, Scott Morrison says US violence will not bring about
change', *SBS News*, 1 June 2020.

Rachwani, M., Allam, L., 'Troops enforcing western Sydney lockdown will
alienate community, advocates warn', *Guardian*, 30 July 2021.

Rahemtulla, S., *Qur'an of the Oppressed: Liberation theology and gender justice
in Islam*, Oxford University Press, Oxford, 2017, p. 24.

Robinson, N. J., 'Bill Clinton's act of terrorism', *Jacobin*; jacobinmag.
com/2016/10/bill-clinton-al-shifa-sudan-bombing-khartoum/ (accessed
24 November 2021).

Rodell, B., Simons, C., 'A police swarm. Frantic calls. Then 3000 people
locked inside.', *New York Times*, 12 November 2020.

Ross, A., 'Academics criticise anti-radicalisation strategy in open letter',
Guardian, 29 September 2016.

Roy, A., 'Saroop, the last Indian', Eye on England, *Telegraph* (Calcutta),
26 March 2006.

Rugemer, E. B., 'The development of mastery and race in the comprehensive
slave codes of the greater Caribbean during the seventeenth century',
The William and Mary Quarterly, 2013, vol. 70, no. 3, pp. 429–58.

Rundle, G., 'Abdel-Magied Anzac furore indicates a dark turn in the
culture wars', *Crikey*, 3 May 2017.

'Ruth Wilson Gilmore on COVID-19, decarceration, and abolition',
Haymarket Books, 17 April 2020; haymarketbooks.org/blogs/128-ruth-
wilson-gilmore-on-covid-19-decarceration-and-abolition (accessed
25 January 2022).

Salih, K. O., 'The Sudan, 1985–9: The fading democracy', *Journal of Modern African Studies*, June 1990, vol. 28, pp. 199–224.

Savage, M., '"Culture wars" are fought by tiny minority – UK study', *Guardian*, 25 October 2020.

Scahill, J., '1998 bombings of Sudan and Afghanistan', The Intercept, 28 April 2021; theintercept.com/empire-politician/biden-bombings-sudan-al-shifa-afghanistan/ (accessed 24 January 2022).

Seccombe, M., 'Why your current car may be the last fossil-fuel vehicle you own', *Saturday Paper*, 4 September 2021.

'Sense of us report', ING, 2021; campaigns.ing.com.au/assets/pdf/ING_Sense_of_Us_Report_A4_0321.pdf?v=15032021 (accessed 24 January 2022).

Seton-Watson, H., *Nations and States*, Routledge, 2020.

'Sexual harassment rife in mining camps, Western Australian inquiry finds', *Reuters*, 20 August 2021.

Shah, N., 'How did British Indians become so prominent in the Conservative Party?', *Guardian*, 27 February 2020 (accessed 25 January 2022).

'Shamima Begum will not be allowed here, Bangladesh says', *BBC News*, 21 February 2019.

Shand-Baptiste, K., 'UK schools have targeted Black children for generations – the education system is overdue for a reckoning', *Independent*, 12 January 2020.

Shrestha, N. et al., 'The impact of COVID-19 on globalization', *One Health*, December 2020, vol. 11, 100180.

Shriver, L., 'Will the left survive the millenials?', *New York Times*, 23 September 2016.

Siddique, H., 'New bill quietly gives powers to remove British citizenship without notice', *Guardian*, 18 November 2021.

Sky News Australia, 'Australian cricket team "disgraced themselves" by taking the knee to BLM "cult"', YouTube, 22 July 2021; youtube.com/watch?v=gKmglpVdrsw (accessed 24 January 2022).

Soutphommasane, T., Stears, M., 'Government responses to COVID-19 are undermining our democratic commitments – why have progressives remained silent?', *ABC News*, 8 September 2021.

'Speech at the Diwali banquet', Margaret Thatcher, 24 October 1988; margaretthatcher.org/document/107356 (accessed 25 January 2022).

Spivak, G., 'Can the subaltern speak? Speculations on widow sacrifice', first published in *Wedge*, vol. 7–8 (Winter–Spring 1985), pp. 120–30.

——, 'Nationalism and the imagination', *Lectora*, 2009, vol. 15, pp. 75–98.

Stein, J., 'Using the stages of team development', MIT Human Resources; hr.mit.edu/learning-topics/teams/articles/stages-development (accessed 18 November 2021).

Stemen, D., 'The prison paradox: More incarceration will not make us safer', Vera Institute of Justice, July 2017; vera.org/downloads/ publications/for-the-record-prison-paradox_02.pdf (accessed 25 January 2022).

'Sudan: 37 protesters dead in government crackdown on demonstrations', Press Release, Amnesty International, 24 December 2018; amnesty.org/ en/latest/press-release/2018/12/sudan-protesters-dead-in-government-crackdown-on-protests/ (accessed 2 December 2021).

'Sudan PM Abdalla Hamdok survives assassination attempt', *BBC News*, 9 March 2020.

'Sudan PM says "serious crisis" a threat to transition and country', MSN News, 16 October 2021.

'Sudan transitional government says coup attempt has failed', *Al Jazeera*, 21 September 2021.

'Sudan warns medicine, fuel, wheat running out amid port blockade', *Al Jazeera*, 4 October 2021.

'Text: Laura Bush on Taliban oppression of women', *Washington Post*, 17 November 2001.

'The Conservative Party and British Indians, 1975–1990', The History of Parliament; thehistoryofparliament.wordpress.com/2018/04/19/ the-conservative-party-and-british-indians-1975-1990/ (accessed 1 December 2021).

'The East Africa Protectorate', Britannica; britannica.com/place/Kenya/ The-East-Africa-Protectorate (accessed 1 December 2021).

'The Green Park Leadership 10,000: A review of diversity amongst the UK's most influential business leaders' Green Park, 2014; cupdf. com/document/2-green-park-leadership-10000-feb-14.html (accessed 2 December 2021).

'The Henley Passport Index'; henleypassportindex.com (accessed 25 November 2021).

'The impact of Prevent on Muslim communities', Muslim Council of Britain, February 2016; archive.mcb.org.uk/wp-content/ uploads/2016/12/MCB-CT-Briefing2.pdf (accessed 13 January 2022).

'The Overton window', Conceptually; conceptually.org/concepts/overton-window (accessed 25 January 2022).

'The Overton window', Mackinac Center for Public Policy, mackinac.org/ OvertonWindow (accessed 18 January 2022).

'The right of reply', Brisbane Writers Festival, 10 September 2016; bwf.org.au/news/articles/the-right-of-reply (accessed 24 January 2022).

'The side hustle economy: A white paper from Henley Business School', Henley Business School, July 2018.

Tilly, C., 'Citizenship, identity and social history', *International Review of Social History*, 1995, vol. 40, supp. 3, pp. 1–17.

Tily, G., 'Seventeen-year wage squeeze the worst in two hundred years', Trades Union Congress, 11 May 2018; tuc.org.uk/blogs/17-year-wage-squeeze-worst-two-hundred-years (accessed 24 January 2022).

'Timeline of the Muslim ban', ACLU Washington; aclu-wa.org/pages/timeline-muslim-ban (accessed 24 January 2022).

Tolentino, J., 'Lionel Shriver puts on a sombrero', *New Yorker*, 14 September 2016.

'Total Circulating Bitcoin', Blockchain; blockchain.com/charts/total-bitcoins.

Towell, N., 'Victoria's grid runs on 50 per cent renewable energy for first time', *Sydney Morning Herald*, 28 March 2021.

Townsend, M., Raja, A., 'Appointment of "biased" Carlile to Prevent review "shatters its credibility"', *Guardian*, 18 August 2019.

Travis, A., 'Young Black people nine times more likely to be jailed than young white people – report', *Guardian*, 1 September 2017.

'Trevor Phillips suspended from Labour over Islamophobia allegations', *BBC News*, 9 March 2020.

'Trust in institutions', Essential Report, 12 October 2021; essentialvision.com.au/?s=trust+in+institutions&searchbutton=Search (accessed 25 January 2022).

Tuckman, B. W., 'Developmental sequence in small groups', first published in *Psychological Bulletin*, 1965, vol. 63, no. 6, pp. 384–99.

University of California Television, 'Gayatri Spivak: The trajectory of the subaltern in my work', YouTube, 8 February 2008; youtube.com/watch?v=2ZHH4ALRFHw (accessed 25 November 2021).

Van Luyn, A., 'Lionel Shriver and the responsibilities of fiction writers', *The Conversation*, 16 September 2016.

Versi, M., 'The latest Prevent figures show why the strategy needs an independent review', *Guardian*, 10 November 2017.

Viper, K., 'Feminism as imperialism', *Guardian*, 21 September 2002.

Wahlquist, C., Simons, M., 'Melbourne's "hard lockdown" orders residents of nine public housing towers to stay at home as coronavirus cases surge', *Guardian*, 4 July 2020;

Walker, P., 'Dominic Raab criticised for comments on BLM protesters taking the knee', *Guardian*, 19 June 2020.

Warrell, H., 'Inside Prevent, the UK's controversial anti-terrorism programme', *Financial Times Magazine*, 24 January 2019.

Watkins, E., 'More than 200,000 words published about Yassmin Abdel-Magied since last Anzac Day', *Crikey*, 26 April 2018.

Weber, E. I., 'Australian others: Penal logic and the pandemic', *Meanjin*, 8 September 2021; meanjin.com.au/blog/australian-others-penal-logic-and-the-pandemic/ (accessed 25 November 2021).

Weise, E., 'Google discloses its (lack of) diversity', *USA Today*, 28 May 2014.

'What's taking the knee and why is it important?' *BBC News*, *Explainers*, 13 October 2021.

Wittgenstein, L. (transl. Anscombe, G. E. M., Hacker, P. M. S., Schulte, J.), *Philosophical Investigations*, Wiley-Blackwell, Malden, 2009, p. 43.

Woodcock, A., 'Home Secretary Priti Patel admits own parents might not have been allowed into UK under her new immigration laws', *Independent*, 19 February 2020.

Woodhull, W., *Transfigurations of the Maghreb: Feminism, decolonization, and literatures*, University of Minnesota Press, Minneapolis, 1993.

Wurgaft, B. A., 'The state that I am in: Hannah Arendt in America', *Los Angeles Review of Books*, 28 February 2016.

'"You don't have to be white to vote right": Why young Asians are rebelling by turning Tory', *Telegraph*, 27 May 2015.

Zhou, N., 'Australians who live overseas may be unable to leave country if they return for visit', *Guardian*, 7 August 2021.

Acknowledgements

This book has been almost a decade in the making. Thank you to those who believed in me before I believed in my (writerly) self: Clare Forster, Meredith Curnow, Julianne Schultz. Thank you to all the editors who have supported and published my work over the years: Erik Jensen, Gabrielle Jackson, Jerath Head, Jonathan Green (among others!). Thank you to all the early readers of this collection, patiently reading and rereading pieces as I put my thoughts down on paper before I'd even properly collected them: Ellen Lapper, Samira Saidi, Dhakshayini Sooriyakumaran, the Monday Morning Writers Group. Kalhari Jayaweera, thank you for your brilliant editing. Thank you, Tim James Matthews and Eleanor Ivory Weber, for your insights on citizenship. Thank you, Sasha Ockenden, for thoughtful feedback, Dylin Hardcastle for consistent encouragement, and Tara June Winch for your sprinkle of literary magic, showing me how I could write, but *with flair*.

I must also acknowledge the Australia Council and thank the judges for selecting me as a recipient of the international development residency at the Cité Internationale des Arts in Paris. I would not be the writer I am today without the time, space and intentionality those months at the Keesing Studio provided.

For anyone reading this thinking, 'I could never be good enough to get a residency like that', I thought so too, but I was wrong. Apply, because it could change your life. It changed mine.

Nafisa Bakkar, thank you for being my ever-present work (and writer!) wife. The Portal Collective, for being the best revolutionary group chat one could ask for. And of course, *mon* khawajah, this list would not be complete without you. The keystone to my acknowledgement arch, thank you for graciously accepting a life where you will read every single piece I ever write at least ten different times, without complaint. There are many ways to support a partner who is a writer, but this, for me, might be the most important one. *Je t'aime, beaucoup!*

About the author

Yassmin Abdel-Magied is a Sudanese Australian writer, recovering mechanical engineer and award-winning social advocate who writes and speaks on politics, society, culture and technology. She has published three books with Penguin Random House, including two middle grade novels (*You Must Be Layla* and the award-winning *Listen, Layla*), which she is now adapting for screen. Yassmin is also developing a slate of projects for the stage and screen.

A globally sought-after adviser on issues at the intersections of race, gender and faith, Yassmin has spoken in over twenty-five countries on social justice and inclusive leadership. She founded her first organisation, Youth Without Borders, at the age of sixteen, leading it for nine years before co-founding two other organisations focused on serving women of colour. Her TED talk 'What does my headscarf mean to you?' has been viewed over 2.5 million times and was selected as one of TED's top 10 ideas.

In all her work, Yassmin is an advocate for transformative justice and a fairer, safer world for all.

Discover a
new favourite

Visit **penguin.com.au/readmore**